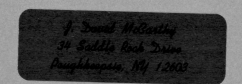
P9-CLD-511

THE STORY OF
ENGLISH

in North
English
an Asiatic
now grown
(b) its nut.
Eng'lish, *n.*
2. the lang
in the Unite
British Empi
3. the Engli
or place;
Middle English

THE STORY OF ENGLISH

HOW THE ENGLISH LANGUAGE CONQUERED THE WORLD

PHILIP GOODEN

Quercus

CONTENTS

Left: *Geoffrey Chaucer, an illustration from the Ellesmere manuscript of the* Canterbury Tales.

Left: A Victorian engraving of Caliban, Prospero and Miranda from Shakespeare's play The Tempest *(1610–11).*

Above: Text messaging has given rise to a new, clipped mode of communication in English composed of contractions and acronyms.

Myths and rumours of a universal language go back to the earliest days of mankind, and seem to reflect some fundamental human aspiration. Research, beginning in the 18th century, indicates that there was once a proto-language called Indo-European, from which sprang the great diversity of tongues that spread across the northern hemisphere. Artificial attempts to create a new universal language were in fashion towards the end of the 19th century, although the speakers of even the most successful – Esperanto – amount to only a tiny fraction of those who speak the two most widely used languages in the world, Mandarin (the official language of China) and English. But the myth or ideal of a universal tongue persists.

A UNIVERSAL LANGUAGE?

Early in the Book of Genesis the descendants of Noah set about building a tower in Mesopotamia, an area between the Tigris and Euphrates rivers in what is now Iraq. It was a time, we are told, when 'the whole Earth was of one language and of one speech'. The motive of the tower-builders seems to have been the Donald Trump-like one of spreading their fame by building higher and bigger than anyone else. But the attempt to create an edifice whose top would reach up to heaven served only to bring down on their heads the wrath of God. In punishment, God 'confound[ed] their language' and the descendants of Noah were scattered 'abroad upon the face of the Earth'. After speaking one language they found themselves talking in many tongues. People could no longer plan or work together, as they were unable to understand each other. Everything was confusion or 'Babel', the name given to the abandoned tower.

Whether treated as an outright fable or as having some grounding in reality, the story of the Tower of Babel is usually interpreted as a warning against what the ancient Greeks would later call *hubris*, overweening arrogance. But a less noticed

A detail from The Tower of Babel *(1563) by Pieter Brueghel (1525–1569). The term 'babel' is now used figuratively to describe a scene of noise and confusion.*

feature of the tale is that it refers to a period in human history – or prehistory – when humankind used 'one language'. It was a period when a multiplicity of tongues was regarded as a curse, resulting in confusion and dispersal. In other words, the monolingual era was one of simplicity, even innocence. You could understand not only the woman next door but the stranger at your gate. Nothing would get lost in translation, for the simple reason that there was nothing that needed translating.

Could such an era have any basis in history? Was there a time when the world's inhabitants used the same tongue? The answer to that will probably never be known. But if we narrow the question so that it applies to a great swathe of the northern hemisphere there is a better chance of an answer. For there was most likely a single source for the majority of languages which took root across western Asia, the Middle East, the Indian subcontinent and Europe in a process that began several thousand years ago. The majority of these languages have died out while all of those that survived have been transformed almost out of recognition from their starting-points. The survivors are still being transformed, since no living language is fixed and constant. And, of all the languages which had their probable origins in 'one language … one speech' many millennia ago, the most successful and the most widely spoken – up to the present day – is English.

> *I am not like a lady at the court of Versailles, who said: 'What a dreadful pity that the bother at the tower of Babel should have got language all mixed up; but for that, everyone would always have spoken French'.*
>
> VOLTAIRE, LETTER TO EMPRESS CATHERINE THE GREAT OF RUSSIA (1767)

THE ASIATICK SOCIETY

The discovery of this early or proto-language really begins with the researches of Sir William Jones (1746–94). Jones was appointed a judge in Calcutta's supreme court during the early days of British rule in India. Before taking up the law he had been an enthusiastic scholar of languages, with a particular interest in the East, whose civilizations he regarded as superior to the traditional cultures of Greece and Rome. Towards the end of his life Jones brought together these two academic disciplines by publishing books on both Mohammedan and Hindu law.

Once established in Calcutta at the age of 37, Jones set himself to learn Sanskrit, an Indian language surviving only in ancient texts. His attention was caught by the way in which certain Sanskrit words were echoed in later languages, both living and dead. For example, the Sanskrit for 'three' is *trayas* while the equivalent Latin word is *tres* and the Greek *trias*. These similarities occur with other numbers between one and ten. When it comes to family members – always a marker for linguistic connection – we find that the Sanskrit for 'brother' is *bhrata* (compare with German *Bruder*) while the word for 'father' is *pitar* (compare with Latin *pater* and German *Vater*).

Although not the first scholar to notice similarities between words in Sanskrit and terms in Greek and Latin and elsewhere, Sir William Jones was the first to make an extended study of these linguistic echoes. Only six months after he had started to learn Sanskrit he confidently announced his conclusions at a meeting of the Asiatick Society in Calcutta:

> *The Sanscrit language, whatever be its antiquity, is of a wonderful structure; more perfect than the Greek, more copious than the Latin, and more exquisitely refined than either, yet bearing to both of them a stronger affinity, both in the roots of verbs and in the forms of grammar, than could possibly have been produced by accident; so strong indeed that no philologer could examine them all three, without believing them to have sprung from some common source, which perhaps no longer exists.*

2 February 1786, the date of Sir William Jones's speech to the learned society of which he was the founding president, is a red-letter day in the history of language studies. His extraordinary perception that peoples, cultures and civilizations separated both in time and space have a common linguistic root has been supported by all subsequent research. The language spoken by Julius Caesar is related not only to modern Italian but to the language once used on the banks of the Ganges. Or, as Jones put it, 'Pythagoras and Plato derived their sublime theories from the same fountain with the sages of India'.

Sanskrit, now extinct in its spoken form, is the language in which all the major Hindu religious texts (e.g., the Rigveda *and the* Upanishads) *are written, along with the ancient sacred epics, the* Ramayana *and the* Mahabharata.

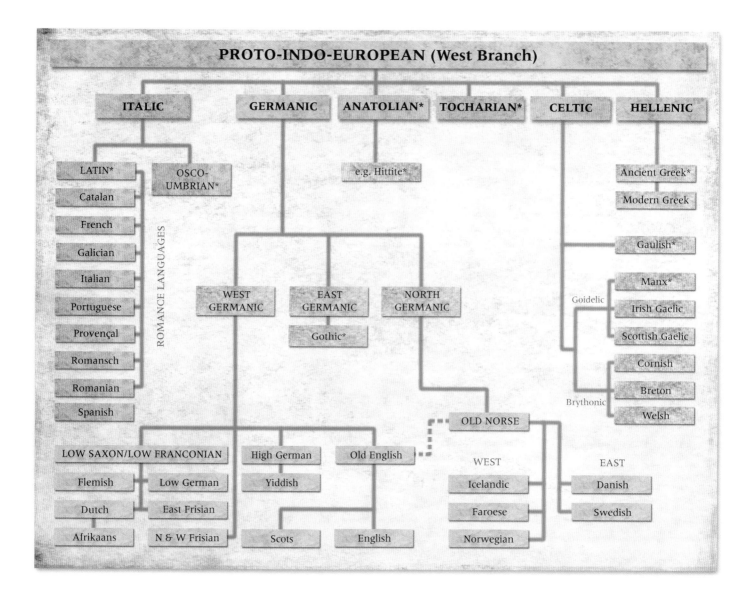

PROTO-INDO-EUROPEAN (West Branch)

ITALIC | GERMANIC | ANATOLIAN* | TOCHARIAN* | CELTIC | HELLENIC

LATIN*
OSCO-UMBRIAN*
Catalan
French
Galician
Italian
Portuguese
Provençal
Romansch
Romanian
Spanish

ROMANCE LANGUAGES

e.g. Hittite*

Ancient Greek*
Modern Greek
Gaulish*

WEST GERMANIC
EAST GERMANIC
NORTH GERMANIC
Gothic*

Goidelic
Manx*
Irish Gaelic
Scottish Gaelic
Cornish
Breton
Brythonic
Welsh

LOW SAXON/LOW FRANCONIAN
High German
Old English
OLD NORSE

Flemish
Low German
Yiddish
Dutch
East Frisian
Afrikaans
N & W Frisian
Scots
English

WEST
Icelandic
Faroese
Norwegian

EAST
Danish
Swedish

A simplified family tree showing the West Branch of the Indo-European languages. Asterisks (*) denote languages that are now extinct. In addition to the limb of the tree shown here, there is also an East Branch, comprising, among others, the Balto-Slavonic (e.g., Latvian, Russian and Czech) and Indo-Iranian (e.g., Sanskrit [dead as a spoken language], Urdu and Farsi) groups.

This original language, called Indo-European, no longer exists. It is buried under thousands of years and the dispersed lives of millions of speakers. There is, of course, nothing written down in Indo-European. But language historians have been able to reconstruct the probable forms of words in Indo-European by working backwards from languages that have left written traces. By examining the shared elements in words of similar sound or meaning, and applying the rules of word change and formation, it has been possible to build – or rebuild – sounds and meanings from thousands of years ago. A couple of examples: in almost all the languages of Europe and western Asia the word for 'mother' begins with an 'm-' sound, which tells us that in the original language it would have started with the same sound. In modern German 'water' is *Wasser* while in French it is *eau* and in 2000-year-old Latin it was *aqua*. The words look different enough on the page but they have a similarity of sound that indicates a common linguistic source.

Indeed, research at the University of Reading using supercomputers has pushed back the boundaries beyond Indo-European to an even older tongue that might have been used in the Neolithic period more than 10,000 years ago. People in the Stone Age may have pronounced basic terms like pronouns (*I, who, we*) and numbers (*two, three, five*) in ways that have not changed greatly over subsequent millennia. This is because such words, being in constant use and having a precise meaning, have evolved more slowly than terms that are rarely found. The personal pronouns that enable us to connect to each other and the numbers that we can count off on our fingers are, literally, too important to be permitted the luxury of much change.

Reconstructing the probable sound and shape of very old words is like recreating what someone would have looked like on the evidence of a skull or, given the delicate nature of the linguistic evidence, tiny fragments of a skull. The process may sound tentative but it is also highly persuasive in its findings. When we discover that there are similarities in, say, the words for 'plough' in old Norse and Middle English, in Latin and Armenian, it suggests that those who tilled the land many centuries ago were themselves descended from speakers of a single tongue many thousands of years before that. Also, by looking at the range of vocabulary in this proto-language it is possible to come to conclusions about the kind of society our linguistic ancestors inhabited. Terms for domestic animals or ways of making fabric for clothes, references to 'house' or 'door', to say nothing of that original 'plough', indicate a relatively settled society of farmers and animal-keepers.

Examination of their re-created vocabulary also tells researchers that these early speakers were unfamiliar both with the tropical areas of the world (no words for 'lion' or 'camel') and the far north, which would in any case have been an unlikely place for extensive settlements. The origins of the speakers of Indo-European have been placed at various sites in what is now central Europe or western Asia. The most plausible area lies north of the Black Sea, a steppe region once inhabited by the Yamnaya culture. At some point, or rather at several points about 4500 or more years ago, the occupants of this area began to spread out in all directions, presumably in search of new territory for hunting and farming. They and their descendants took their luggage of words with them, westwards into the heart of Europe and south towards the Mediterranean. Some must have moved into Asia towards the Indian subcontinent and a few even reached as far as China.

It may be a cliché to describe the spread of language(s) as being like the growth of a tree but the image is a vivid one and mostly right. As

A shprakh iz a diyalekt mit an armey un a flot.
['A language is a dialect with an army and a navy.']

Jewish Linguist Max Weinreich (1945)

Map showing the early distribution of the major Indo-European language groups.

early distribution of Indo-European languages

Yamnaya culture, 3500–2500 BC

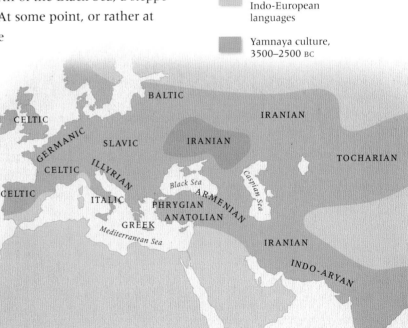

languages develop on the spot or are carried from place to place they sprout fresh limbs and branches, and those branches in turn put out new growths. In the end, the tip of one twig will be many yards distant from the tip of another twig on the opposite side of the tree. Yet they grew originally from the same trunk.

The Indo-European trunk, from which came ancestral languages as various and forgotten as Hittite, Tocharian and Gothic, is also the ultimate source of modern Spanish and German and English. The tree analogy falls down only in one respect: languages, unlike the branches of trees, can survive the death of the trunk or limb from which they grew. In fact, change and development are inevitable and necessary parts of language history. A language that doesn't develop is dead, fit for study but not likely to be used for speech except in special circumstances. Arguably, no language has developed further and more dynamically than English. Some of the reasons for that global success are examined in this book.

THE WORLD'S MOST POPULAR LANGUAGES?

But first we might ask what underlies the claim that English is the closest thing to a world language yet achieved. What criteria are to be used in assessing the popularity of any language?

The ranking of the world's languages – the top tongues, the most significant ones – is not as straightforward as it might at first appear. Does 'top' or 'most significant' apply to the languages that are most widely used around the world or to those with the greatest number of speakers? To what extent ought secondary speakers to be included (secondary speakers are those making regular or even primary use of a language which is not their own)? What weighting should be given to the economic power and cultural status of particular countries, since these factors will obviously have a marked effect on the spread, accessibility and popularity of a language? A complicating element is the unreliability of the statistics, especially those for secondary speakers.

The problem was tackled in the 1990s by linguistic expert George Weber, who compiled figures and drew up tables in which the relative positions of the 'ten most influential languages' varied according to the criteria used. Although the overall number of speakers of all of these languages will have increased since then, this does not affect their positions vis-à-vis each other.

In simple numbers of primary users, Chinese comes out on top with well over a billion speakers. English is in second place, with roughly half a billion, followed by Hindi/Urdu, Spanish and Russian. This ranking is based on the most generous estimates of speakers for each language. However, when secondary speakers are added, the list changes slightly. Although Chinese and English

Language is a city, to the building of which every human being brought a stone.

RALPH WALDO EMERSON, *LETTERS AND SOCIAL AIMS* (1876)

ESPERANTO

Esperanto, the most enduring of the artificial languages, was created in 1887 by Dr Ludovic Zamenhoff, a Polish eye specialist living in Bialystock, then under Russian control. Zamenhoff was familiar with the tensions caused by the linguistic divisions of the city among four languages (Russian, Polish, German and Yiddish) and his creation of an artificial language seems to have sprung from the philanthropic desire to foster harmony and understanding – in every sense – between people. The name of the language was Zamenhoff's pseudonym for his first text-book, with the literal meaning of 'the hoping one'.

Although an estimated million and a half people scattered round the world have a working knowledge of Esperanto and despite being on the school curriculum of countries such as Hungary and Bulgaria, the heyday of Esperanto was in the early part of the 20th century. It was perceived as enough of a threat by totalitarian regimes for its use to be regarded with suspicion in Hitler's Germany and Stalin's Russia. Esperanto is reputedly less difficult for English speakers to learn than French or Spanish, although it has something of a 'Spanish' feel to it, as indicated by the opening lines of the Lord's Prayer: 'Patro nia, kiu estas en la chielo, sankta estu via nomo; venu regeco via; estu volo via, tiel en la chielo, tiel ankau sur la tero.'

Poster for an Esperanto convention in London in 1930, organized by the SAT – the Sennacieca Asocio Tutmondo, or 'World Non-National Organization'.

remain first and second, Spanish, Russian and French now occupy third, fourth and fifth places respectively.

The explanation for this shift lies largely in the expansionist histories of Spain, Russia and France. All three were countries with 'empires', whether or not they were officially acknowledged as such, and so they had a significant impact in areas of the world sometimes far removed from their own territories.

The French language, for example, survives in countries like Vietnam or Algeria because of its colonial past, while for the same reason Spanish is dominant in South America (and Portuguese in Brazil). By contrast, the related forms of Hindu and Urdu are spoken in densely populated India and Pakistan but do not have much of a linguistic role in the world outside their borders, leaving aside their scattered immigrant communities.

Using a different criterion, based on the number of countries in which a language is used, English comes out comfortably ahead with a figure of 115 countries, more than three times that of the next language, French (at 35). Arabic, Spanish and Russian occupy places three to five, respectively. The use of English in the majority of the world's countries does not mean that it is widely understood by a majority in any country, apart from those that are Anglophone. Rather, it means that English will be spoken by a substantial minority and be important as a language of commerce and tourism. Any traveller will be able to confirm that.

Taking other factors into account, such as economic power and 'socio-literary prestige', George Weber came up with the following ranking for the top ten most influential languages: 1. English; 2. French; 3. Arabic; 4. Spanish; 5. Russian; 6. German; 7. Mandarin (Chinese); 8. Portuguese; 9. Hindi/Urdu; 10. Bengali.

Recent evidence for the global dominance of English can be found in everything from its use as the international language of aviation (see opposite) to the linguistic breakdown of articles on Wikipedia, the on-line encyclopedia created by users. There are more than three times as many articles in English as in the next most popular language, which is German. French comes third, with Japanese, Italian and Polish users contributing a lesser but roughly equal number. Users from the United States provide more than half of all contributions in English.

KEYWORD

OK

English is the closest the world has yet come to a universal language, at least in the sense that even those who cannot speak it – admittedly, the large majority of the world's population – are likely to be familiar with the odd English expression. One term that is genuinely global as well as genuinely odd is *OK* (or *O.K.* or *okay*), originating in America in the 19th century. An astonishingly adaptable word, it works as almost any part of speech from noun to verb, adjective to adverb, though often just as a conversation-filler – 'OK, what are we going to do now?' Depending on the tone of voice, *OK* can convey anything from fervent agreement to basic accquiescence. It may be appropriate that such a truly universal term has no generally agreed source. Attempts to explain where it came from don't so much show variety as a high degree of imaginative curiosity. So, *OK* is created from the initials of a deliberate misspelling, *oll korreket*, or from a campaign slogan for a would-be US president in the 1840s who was known as Old Kinderhook because he came from Kinderhook in New York State. Or it is a version of a word imported from Finland or Haiti, or possibly one borrowed from the Choctaw Indians. Or it is older than originally thought and derives from West African expressions like *o-ke* or *waw-ke*. Enough explanations, OK?

AIR-TRAFFIC CONTROL

Although other languages are sometimes used, English is the default choice of worldwide aviation. Internal flights may employ the language of that particular country but it is obviously vital for pilots and air-traffic controllers handling international journeys to be on the same linguistic wavelength. At least three major crashes have been blamed partly on poor communication and misunderstanding. The worst was in 1977 at Tenerife airport, on the Canary Islands, when confusion arose between the pilots of a KLM (Dutch) Boeing 747 and the control tower. Use of ambiguous non-standard phrases (including 'OK' by the ground controller) led the Dutch pilots to assume they had received clearance for take-off. Their plane collided with another 747 taxiing on the runway, with the loss of 583 lives. Conditions in an emergency are aggravated by the fact that non-English speakers may have only a limited repertoire of English terms which breaks down under pressure, while English speakers easily fall back on slang or colloquial usages. Speaking some English is

The primacy of safety in the skies prompted the ICAO to require standardized English phraseology in aviation.

not enough. It has to be the right kind of English, one agreed on by all flying nations.

In 2001 the International Civil Aviation Organisation (ICAO) accepted proposals to standardize the English used for aviation communication. Some countries were happy to comply. Japan – accustomed to English as a lingua franca – has a single-language policy for all its air-traffic control. But others saw it as an attempt to impose a monoglot solution. France, always sensitive over encroachments on the primacy of the French language, protested at the ICAO proposals. It was not the first time. In 2000 French pilots had been vocal in their opposition to the order that, when approaching Charles de Gaulle airport in Paris, they should talk in English to the controllers whom they gracefully termed *les aiguilleurs du ciel* ('the signalmen of the sky'). In the 1970s there were protests in Canada over the same issue, since that country is officially bilingual.

Early English

The Celts and the Romans
c.750 BC–c.AD 410

The Anglo-Saxons
c.410–800

The Viking Effect
800–1066

Stone carving of a helmeted Viking warrior from the National Historical Museum in Stockholm, Sweden.

hgeneratio

The original inhabitants of the British Isles before the arrival of the Romans were Celtic-speaking tribes. Celtic itself was one of the many offshoots of the earlier Indo-European language. The Roman invasion – prepared by Julius Caesar's short-lived military expeditions of 55 and 54 BC but only beginning in earnest when the legions of Emperor Claudius landed in AD 43 – subdued large areas of Britain. Together with their laws, customs and roads, the conquerors imported the imperial language of Latin.

THE CELTS AND THE ROMANS

The first people who can properly be called British were part of the Celtic migration that spread westwards from central and southern Europe thousands of years ago. By the 5th century BC they were established in tribal groupings across the British Isles. They had their own religion and a language that would inevitably have proliferated into different dialects in different parts of the country. It is from Celtic that various later and related tongues developed. These include Breton (in the Brittany region of France), Cornish, Manx (in the Isle of Man), the forms of Gaelic connected to Scotland and Ireland, and Welsh. These are now minority languages, if they have survived at all.

The Celts should not be regarded as a unified people, let alone a nation living within defined borders. Although the term was applied by Greek and Roman writers to groups in western Europe, it is not recorded in English until the early 17th century. The following years saw an awakening of interest in the Celtic past of Britain, significantly in regions – or countries – which wanted to assert their own identity and preserve their indigenous languages. The so-called Celtic Revival was especially strong in pre-20th-century Scotland and Ireland.

In England, however, there was not much left to preserve or rediscover. Successive invasions, particularly the incursions and settlements of the various

Monogram from the Book of Kells, *a Latin manuscript of the Four Gospels produced in the British Isles in around 800 by Celtic monks. This page (folio 34) shows the* chi rho, *a traditional Christian symbol comprising the first two letters of Christ's name in the Greek alphabet.*

Germanic tribes known collectively as the Anglo-Saxons, had erased most Celtic traces from England, and it was once thought that this extended to the Celts themselves. It now seems that they enjoyed – or endured – a form of co-existence with the Anglo-Saxons from the fifth century AD onwards, either living among them or establishing themselves in separate pockets of territory. Long before that, however, the Celts had of necessity learned to live with the Roman *imperium* which controlled most of the known world.

THE ROMANS IN BRITAIN

The Roman conquest of most of Britain was rapid and overwhelming. The emperor Claudius (r.41 – 54) took part in the landing of an estimated 40,000 men in AD 43 – or at any rate arrived by the time his army reached the Thames – and led the triumphal entry into Colchester, the tribal capital of the region. Within four years, the Romans had consolidated their power as far as the Fosse Way, a road that they themselves built in the west of England and which was eventually to run diagonally across the country on a southwest–northeast course from Topsham (Devon) to Lincoln. It took a little longer to subdue the Welsh tribes but before the end of the first century AD, Wales was dotted with legionary fortresses.

Scotland – or Caledonia – was more of a challenge to the Romans. Despite some early victories, they soon gave up the attempt to control the Highland region. Hadrian's Wall, planned during the emperor's visit to Britain in AD 122 and extending about 74 miles (118 km) from modern Newcastle upon Tyne to the Carlisle area, was intended as much to mark the northern limit of the Roman empire as it was a piece of extended fortification. A slightly later emperor, Antoninus Pius (r.138 – 161), attempted to extend the bounds of the empire with the building of a 37-mile (59-km) wall further north between the Forth and Clyde rivers. The Antonine Wall was abandoned in little more than 20 years and the Lowlands were largely left to themselves, despite frequent raids south by the Picts (literally the 'painted ones' in Latin) as well as Roman punitive expeditions that crossed Hadrian's Wall in the opposite direction.

The Romans, seemingly concerned mostly with pacification and tax revenues, allowed their subject peoples a fairly high degree of autonomy as long as they behaved themselves. The invaders did not seek to impose their language, at least by force. They didn't have to. They taught tacitly and by example, backed up with overwhelming military and civil power. Many native Britons, or at least the more ambitious ones, would naturally have chosen to learn Latin in the early years following the AD 43 invasion. Some would have grown up in Latin-speaking households, as the Celts were assimilated into the world of the conquerors, whether through involvement with the colonial administration or through commerce or by intermarriage.

Despite almost four centuries of Roman occupation and settlement, the impact of Latin was surprisingly small in the period after their departure. The most evident linguistic marker is arguably in the *-chester*, *-cester* and *-caster* suffixes to many English place names (e.g. Winchester, Cirencester or Doncaster) coming from the Latin *castra* or 'camp'. The Romans left signs of their physical presence everywhere, particularly in the siting of towns and in the network of roads, some of whose routes are still followed today. But the great legacy of Latin dates principally from three later periods, the one following the arrival of the missionary St Augustine in 597, the Norman invasion of 1066 and the Renaissance era, when Latin came back into English by indirect paths.

The people who laid the foundations of the English that we still speak today began to arrive in the British Isles at about the time the Roman occupation finished, early in the fifth century AD. The Romans were not driven out of Britain; rather, they abandoned it when their empire was in the later stages of disintegration and there were more pressing concerns than safeguarding a remote colonial island. From before the time when the Roman troops started to withdraw there were, crowding on the northwestern fringes of Europe, various tribes and peoples looking to spread westwards. They would not be as tolerant of the native Celts as the Romans had been.

Naturally I am biased in favour of boys learning English; and then I would let the clever ones learn Latin as an honour, and Greek as a treat.

WINSTON CHURCHILL, *MY EARLY LIFE*

A section of Hadrian's Wall, a striking physical reminder of the Roman occupation of Britain. The linguistic legacy of Latin is still with us, though much of it comes from a far later period.

LATIN AND MONEY

One Latin legacy with which English speakers and others have daily contact is to be found in the hard cash in their purses and wallets. The image of Queen Elizabeth's head on the obverse of all British coins is garlanded with the mystifying legend ELIZABETH II DG REG FD, followed by the year of production. The II is, of course, the traditional Latin way of indicating that she is the second Elizabeth to sit on the throne. DG is an abbreviation of the Latin tag *Dei gratia* ('by the grace of God') and REG is the shortened form of *Regina* (Queen), while FD stands for *Fidei Defensor* or 'Defender of the Faith' – a title originally conferred by the Pope on Henry VIII in 1521 for his defence of Catholicism but later reinterpreted to signal the link between the crown and the new Church of England. Round the milled rim of the £1 coin is an obscure

A pile of £1 coins. Another Latin inscription on the rim is the Scots motto Nemo me impune lacessit – '*No one attacks me with impunity*'.

quotation from the Roman poet Virgil: DECUS ET TUTAMEN, meaning 'an ornament and protection'. It indicates that the milled edge is a safeguard against counterfeiting, and first appeared on coins struck during the reign of Charles II. After that, it comes as something of a disappointment to learn that there is no equivalent use of Latin on British banknotes.

In the US, the application of Latin to currency is even more widespread. The very term 'cent' is from the Latin word for 'hundred'. On the one-dollar coin is the US national motto E PLURIBUS UNUM ('One out of many'). On the one-dollar bill is the Great Seal, with the Eye of Providence symbol atop a pyramid plus the Latin phrases ANNUIT COEPTIS ('He [i.e. Providence or God] approves our enterprises') and NOVUS ORDO SECLORUM ('new order of the ages'). Nor is it hard to recognize the Latin – or rather the imperial Roman – influence in the buildings that grace some of the US notes: the grand pillared porticoes of the US Treasury ($10), the White House ($20), and on the $50 note the Capitol, the seat of US government. The term 'Capitol' derives from the temple to Jupiter on Rome's Capitoline Hill, just as the US Senate borrows its name from its Roman archetype.

THE CELTIC LEGACY

Celtic has left only a tiny legacy to current English, terms mostly restricted to landscape features or place names. These include London, the Thames and another river name, the Avon. The 'tor' (meaning 'hill' or 'high rock') in Torquay or Glastonbury Tor is Celtic, as is the '-combe' or 'cwm' element of place names like the Devon resort of Salcombe or the Welsh town of Cwmbran ('comb' or 'cwm' being a hollow or valley). The fact that these topographical expressions refer to an up-and-down landscape suggests that their survival is because the Germanic language speakers who displaced Celtic did not have an adequate vocabulary to describe hills and valleys. Coming from the flat lands of northwest Europe, they did not require such words.

These place terms apart, there is very little to show in the English language for the centuries-long inhabitation of the British Isles by the Celts. *Bard* and *glen* and *colleen* (from Irish *cailin* –'girl') come to us from Gaelic but they are distinctly un-English in their associations. More interesting, perhaps, is the case of *whisky* or, to give it its Irish and US spelling, *whiskey*. This derives from the Gaelic *uisgebeatha*, which itself comes from the happy union of two words for 'water' and 'life' (compare the medieval Latin *acqua vitae*, which was a generic term for spirits and which is echoed in turn in the modern Swedish and Danish *akvavit*).

But the most surprising of all Celtic relics are two terms that sound absolutely contemporary. The first, 'slogan', is irrevocably linked to the world of contemporary advertisers and political spin-doctors. Yet the slogan originally defined a Gaelic war-cry, from *sluagh* (army/host) and *gairm* (cry). And it is possible that there was in Old Celtic the word *karros*, meaning 'cart', which Latin turned into *carra* and which, after a diversion through Norman French, entered English as *carre*. Hence we may (possibly) derive the *car* from a word dating back more than two millennia.

However poorly Celtic fared in England, it managed to hang on beyond its borders and, as already indicated, its descendants include Welsh and the forms of Gaelic that were widely spoken, until quite recently, in parts of Scotland and Ireland. The Celtic language with the highest profile is unquestionably Welsh.

A Celtic cross. The word 'cross' is itself a Celtic term, deriving from the Irish Gaelic crois. *It was brought over to England by Christian missionaries from Ireland and for a long time existed alongside the Old English term* rood *before supplanting it.*

WELSH

Modern Welsh is a descendant of the Celtic tongue originally spoken in Britain and pushed to the margins of the country by two sets of invaders, the Romans and the Anglo-Saxons. It is related to the languages of two peninsulas, Brittany in northwest France and Cornwall (in the far southwest of England). Those who

DRUID

It was Julius Caesar who gave the most complete account of the *druids* in Gaul (France) and Britain, describing them as a priestly class. Their association with magic and soothsaying or prophecy comes from old Welsh and Irish legends. The word *druid* is from Latin but the term derives from a Celtic root that can still be seen in modern Gaelic (where *draoidh* signifies 'magician'). Interest in Druidism revived in the early 18th century, coinciding with the beginnings of the study of ancient monuments like Stonehenge.

can speak Breton are still numbered in the tens of thousands, although they are concentrated among the older part of the population. The last speaker of Cornish as a mother tongue – that is, someone who did not deliberately set out to learn it – died more than two centuries ago. When considered alongside these linguistic cousins, Welsh is therefore a success story and can claim to be increasing the number of speakers, even if they do not use it regularly.

About 20 percent (*c.*600,000 people) of the population of Wales can speak Welsh, and there are pockets of speakers elsewhere, most notably in Argentine Patagonia where a band of Welsh immigrants was encouraged to settle in the 1860s. In the home country, Welsh speakers are concentrated in the less populated areas in the west and northwest, a pattern that repeats the earlier migration of Celtic to the remote fringes of a territory.

While other minority languages have withered, Welsh has survived and even prospered because of the determination of nationalist and cultural groups, usually maintained in the face of government indifference or outright hostility. At the end of the 19th century Welsh children could be beaten for daring to speak Welsh in Welsh schools. Happily, decades of campaigning by, among others, the political party Plaid Cymru (literally 'Party of Wales') and a more enlightened attitude from the British government now ensure that Welsh has equal status with English, at least in the public sector.

A bilingual signpost in Welsh and English. Unlike English, which is fraught with inconsistencies in its pronunciation, Welsh is entirely regular and phonetic.

The most obvious sign of the language for the visitor is, literally, a matter of signs. Road signs and destinations are displayed in Welsh as well as English. There is a Welsh-language television channel (S4C) and a regional BBC radio service. More importantly, study of the language is compulsory in schools. Without young speakers a language will inevitably die, and it is education more than anything else that will ensure the survival of Welsh even if it can never again become the majority language of the country.

As with the Irish, the Welsh have made a distinctive and valuable contribution to English. Their style when using the language has been called

CELTIC FAKERY

James Macpherson (1736–96) was a Scottish poet who hit on a neat way of capitalizing on the fashion for 'primitivism' and a simpler way of life that characterized some of the more educated and sophisticated circles of 18th-century society. At the age of 24 he published *Fragments of Ancient Poetry Collected in the Highlands of Scotland*, supposedly translated from old Gaelic originals.

The book did so well that only a year later Macpherson uncovered and translated another treasure, an epic poem about the Celtic hero Fingal (or Finn) allegedly written by his son Ossian and dating back to the third century. This he published in two instalments. They were immensely successful not just in the British Isles but across Europe. Years later, Napoleon carried an Italian translation of Ossian on his campaigns and even had scenes from the story painted on the ceiling of his study.

One of the first people to cast doubt on the authenticity of these works was the always-robust Dr Samuel Johnson (1709–84). Macpherson threatened him with physical force, so Johnson kept a great oak stick to hand in case the Scot made good his boast. A committee set up after Macpherson's death established that the Ossian works were largely fraudulent, a combination of real early Gaelic poems but with plenty of invented additions from Macpherson himself. Even so, many people continued to believe in their authenticity, demonstrating a hunger for any material out of the misty and romantic Celtic era.

flamboyant. The Swansea-born Dylan Thomas (1914–53) stands out among modern poets for his ornate, sensuous writing. Nor is it a coincidence that actors such as Richard Burton (1925–84) and Anthony Hopkins (b.1937) – both hailing from near Port Talbot in South Wales – are famous for the musicality of their voices and the crystal clarity of their diction.

Modern Welsh draws on old Celtic words such as *buwch* (cow) or *brenin* (chief or king) and its feminine form *brehines*, or borrows from English or Latin originals, as in *ffenestr* for 'window' (compare Latin *fenestra*, French *fenêtre*, German *Fenster*). When it comes to contemporary terms, a Celtic modification or twist is often applied: 'ambulance' is *ambiwlans*, 'taxi' is *tacsi* (or *car hurio* – 'car to hire') while 'television' is *teledu* and 'computer' is *cyfrifydd* (*cyfrify* – 'to reckon').

I am always sorry when any language is lost, because languages are the pedigree of nations.

Dr Samuel Johnson, *Tour to the Hebrides* (1785)

The various groups from the northwest fringes of Europe who reached Britain in the centuries following the departure of the Romans made the greatest contribution of all to the English language. Indeed, they could be said to have created it. They provided the bedrock of words which, with some relatively small modifications, we still use most frequently today. At least in linguistic terms, they are the most significant visitors – and later inhabitants – in English history.

THE ANGLO-SAXONS

These expanding groups were the Angles, the Saxons and the Jutes. They came from regions of what is now Denmark, northern Germany and northern Holland. In his history of how Christianity came to Britain, written in Latin around 730 (*Historia ecclesiastica gentis Anglorum*), a Northumbrian Benedictine monk called Bede (see Bede, page 30) described those who came over as being from 'the three most powerful nations of Germany', even if they were members of tribes rather than what we would regard as 'nations'. But unlike the Roman landings, this was no systematic invasion. Instead it was a repeated and piecemeal process of incursions, which resulted in a patchwork of settlements that eventually came to dominate the country.

Some of the 'occupiers' were probably present before the Romans left, simply as immigrants or possibly as auxiliaries in the Roman army. Some were actually invited over – a case of fire being used to fight fire. They were required to help the native British counter threats from other enemies overseas or from the Picts in the far north. There was resistance to the Anglo-Saxon newcomers – the legends of King Arthur date from this time (see King Arthur's Cross, page 33) – but less than 100 years after the departure of the Romans, the new 'English' had control of a great triangle of land consisting of the southeast of England and East Anglia and parts of Northumberland.

Although there were differences between the language variants spoken by the Angles, Saxons and Jutes, to the extent that it is not known how easily they could have understood each other, they did share a linguistic heritage. Their branch of the

Ceremonial helmet from the early seventh-century Anglo-Saxon Sutton Hoo ship burial in Suffolk. The Old English epic poem Beowulf *opens with the funeral of a king in a longship laden with treasure.*

THE ANGLO-SAXONS

language tree was one of three collectively called Germanic. North Germanic gave birth to languages such as Icelandic, Swedish and Danish; East Germanic produced a tongue (Gothic) which is long extinct; while West Germanic was the foundation for English, Dutch and German (see A Universal Language?, page 10).

It is tempting to see the movement of languages and peoples as a neat, timetabled affair. The Romans go, leaving the door half open for the Angles, Jutes and Saxons to come in. The native population of British is pushed steadily back to the western fringes of the island while the new arrivals set themselves up in the bit of country appropriate to them (the Angles in East Anglia, etc.). In reality, things would have been much more haphazard. Some of the original British speakers would probably have been assimilated by the new arrivals, while others would have been displaced altogether. Others might have coexisted, uneasily or not, with the Germanic-speaking groups.

But a couple of related questions remain. How was it that those British who stayed put were assimilated by the invaders rather than the other way round? And why did the Germanic language of the new arrivals, which was oral rather than written, prevail over the native forms of Celtic? After all, the Norman invasion of England produced exactly the opposite results. It may have taken a couple of hundred years after the arrival of William the Conqueror in 1066 but the Normans ended up being absorbed by the people they had conquered just as they ended up speaking English (although with a multitude of French additions). So why didn't something similar happen after the Anglo-Saxon invasion?

There are no definitive answers. It has been suggested that, following the death of some charismatic leader such as King Arthur, the British areas fell to squabbling among themselves, offering no united resistance to the newcomers. Perhaps any mingling between the races was confined to intermarriage at the top, for which there is some evidence in the choice of Celtic names by the Anglo-Saxon nobility. On the other hand, the displacement mentioned earlier might have been so systematic and thorough as to indicate a dismissive, even contemptuous, attitude towards Celtic culture on the part of the Anglo-Saxons. A very different interpretation is that the new arrivals, feeling themselves not superior but *inferior* to a people who had been shaped and polished by nearly four centuries of Roman rule, wanted nothing to do with the Romano-Celtic heritage.

Whatever the causes, the result was that (Old) English became the dominant tongue while, over the long term, Celtic speakers chose or were forced to retreat to the more remote areas of Britain. Just as Hadrian's Wall had marked the northern limits of Roman control under the emperors, so the construction in 757 of Offa's Dyke, a line of defensive earthworks along the boundary of the kingdom of Mercia and present-day Wales, made for a literal division of the Britons and the English.

The success of English was all the more surprising in that it was not really a written language, not at first. The Anglo-Saxons used a runic alphabet, the kind of writing J.R.R.Tolkien recreated for *The Lord of the Rings*, and one more suitable for stone inscriptions than shopping lists. It took the arrival of Christianity to spread literacy and to produce the letters of an alphabet which, with a very few differences, is still in use today.

THE ROOTS OF ENGLISH

It would be a mistake, though, to think that Anglo-Saxon culture, with its oral traditions and remote pagan origins, was a crude affair. The world reflected in the famous Old English poem *Beowulf* (see Beowulf, pages 40–1) which is a fusion of Viking and Saxon cultures, may be hard, even unrelenting, but it is far from crude either in its themes or its language. *Beowulf* and other Old English poems like *Dream of the Rood* ('rood' meaning Christ's cross) are as ornate in their style or imagery as some of the artefacts recovered from Anglo-Saxon burial sites like Sutton Hoo.

But the skeleton of a language is not to be found in elaborate or poetic inventions. Rather, it is in the basic words that are used for everyday things. It is here that Old English triumphed and continues to do so. It has been calculated that almost all of the 100 most frequently found words in English, wherever it is used now around the world, come from Old English. These include *a* and *the* and *and* itself, as well as pronouns (*I, you, she*), prepositions and conjunctions (*from, with, when*), and the various forms of the verbs *to have* and *to be*. The very word 'word' is Old English. Slightly more elaborate but still very commonplace terms also have their roots in Old English: *ship, sheep, field, earth, wood, work*. Like all vocabulary, these give us an insight into the way of life, in this case a largely agricultural one, that would have been standard for the settlers.

As far as the language was concerned, the two most important historical events in the lengthy period of Anglo-Saxon domination were the arrival of the Vikings or Danes (shorthand terms covering all the Scandanavian groups who began raiding England towards the end of the seventh century) and the earlier arrival of Christianity in England with St Augustine in 597. This could more

---

KEYWORD

MEAD-HALL

The *mead-hall* (in Old English, *meduheall*) was not simply the equivalent of the pub in the world of the Anglo-Saxons. True, it was the communal hall where they might consume mead, made of fermented honey, and other drinks besides, but the *mead-hall* was primarily a refuge from a hostile world. It was a place where stories and riddles were told, reputations made or lost, and tribal identity fostered. At least it is so in the great Anglo-Saxon poem *Beowulf* and today's reader will find such scenes echoed in Tolkien's *The Lord of the Rings*. There is a wonderfully poignant line in the poem *Beowulf* describing how the light from the hall gleams out across distant lands (*'lixte se leoma ofer landa fela'*), which conveys to us more effectively than pages of history the fragile but tenacious sense of community and civilization that the *mead-hall* helped to sustain.

BEDE

Visitors to Durham Cathedral today can gaze at a plain tomb in the west-facing Galilee Chapel which contains the remains of a man who lived in the middle of the Anglo-Saxon era. The 'Venerable' Bede (he did not become St Bede until 1899 when he was canonized) may not be much more than a name to us. But he was the first great historian of England and in the years following his death he became famous in scholarly circles as copies of his writings were disseminated across Europe. Bede wrote a variety of texts and he is credited with devising the chronological structure which is still in world-wide use, by dating events from the year of Christ's birth, or *anno domini* (AD).

Bede, who was born in around 673, began his education at the monastery of Wearmouth

Woodcut of the Venerable Bede, from the Nuremberg Chronicle *of 1493.*

in the northeast at the age of seven and within a few years moved to the nearby monastery at Jarrow. There he remained until his death in 735. His most important work, the *Historia ecclesiastica gentis Anglorum* ('Ecclesiastical History of the English People', written, in Latin, towards the end of his life), gives an account of the arrival of Christianity in Britain. He was very careful to establish dates and to provide an accurate narrative, going so far as to get a fellow-priest to consult the papal archives in Rome. He was the first to give expression to the idea that the English were a unified people, and it is surely no coincidence that King Alfred – likewise concerned with ideas of national identity and unity – should have overseen a translation of the *Historia ecclesiastica*.

accurately be termed a second coming, since there was already a vigorous Celtic Church, which had been driven westwards by the pagan Anglo-Saxons. By 550 Christianity survived in England only in Cornwall. However, the new missionaries dispatched from Rome not only brought back religion, but also fostered literacy and produced a new crop of concepts and words, many deriving from Latin.

THE RETURN OF CHRISTIANITY

The Christian conversion of England operated at both ends of the country. In the south, Augustine together with a band of missionaries began by converting Ethelbert, the king of Kent, who even at his first meeting with Augustine seems to have shown a remarkably open-minded attitude towards beliefs that were new to him. A little later in the north, Aidan – originally from Celtic Ireland and a monk on the Scottish island of Iona – worked to convert Northumbria. The principle that Augustine adopted was to convert a king or queen, on the reasonable assumption that their people would follow. It didn't always work.

Some kingdoms relapsed from Christianity and some rulers hedged their bets: the king of East Anglia, for example, maintained pagan altars as well as Christian ones in the same building.

A trace of this double standard lies innocently hidden in the names for days of the week, most of which are derived from ancient Norse or Germanic gods like Woden (*Wodnes daeg* – Wednesday) or Thor (*Thors daeg* – Thursday). Similarly, *Easter* may be derived from a spring festival in honour of the Germanic goddess Eostre, and it has often been remarked that the Christmas season was superimposed on older pagan practices celebrating the mid-winter period.

But the Christian influence was felt in a slew of words brought in during the years following the conversion of England, however much parts of the country may have stayed attached to older forms of worship. Concepts such as *heven* and *hel* were already familiar from Old English but hierarchical terms like *bisceop* (bishop) or *nonne* (nun) now entered the language, ultimately from Latin or Greek. The *deofol* (devil) came out of Latin *diabolus*, although Old English already knew all about the *feond* (fiend), which had its modern sense of 'devil/monster' as well as meaning, simply, 'enemy' (cognate with the modern German word for enemy, *Feind*). Other imports included *altar* (connected to Latin *altus* – 'high'), *engel* (angel, from Greek *angelos* meaning 'messenger') and *ymen* (hymn, from Latin *hymnus* or 'song of praise to gods or heroes').

In some cases, a direct translation from Latin produced word-forms that have lasted to the present day. *Spiritus sanctus* became *halig gast* or *Holy Ghost*. The Latin *evangelium*, meaning 'good news', became *god-spell* (literally 'good story') which turned into *gospel*. 'Judgement' was *dom* in Old English so 'Judgement Day' became *Domesday* or *Doomsday*. William the Conqueror's Domesday Book – which was so thorough a summary of English property and possessions in the 11th century that it was said not 'one cow nor one pig escaped notice in his survey' – acquired its slightly puzzling name because it was thought to be as definitive as Judgement Day.

The essential vocabulary of religion already existed in Old English before these imports. In the Anglo-Saxon version of the Lord's Prayer there are only a handful of terms which differ from the famous version established in the King James translation of the Bible. They include *rice* instead of '[Thy] kingdom [come]' (compare modern German *Reich*) and *syle* for 'give [us this day]' (*syle* is related to 'sell' in its present-day sense, which in Old English would have been expressed by the formula *sellan wip weorpe* or 'give with worth'). Even though the basics were already there, the long-term effect of the return of Christianity to England was to add about 400 new words to the language.

Dating from the mid-eighth century, the Spital Cross at Hexham Abbey in Northumberland is a rare example of the Crucifixion in Anglo-Saxon art. It indicates that Christianity had been widely adopted by the Germanic invaders by this period.

ANGLO-SAXON ATTITUDES

*'I see somebody now!' she exclaimed at last.' But he's coming very slowly –
and what curious attitudes he goes into!' (For the Messenger kept
skipping up and down, and wriggling like an eel, as he came along,
with his great hands spread out like fans on each side.)
'Not at all said,' said the King. 'He's an Anglo-Saxon Messenger – and those
are Anglo-Saxon attitudes.*

(Lewis Carroll, *Through the Looking Glass*)

The popular image of the Anglo-Saxons is of primitive and often ferocious tribal groups who pushed aside the original Celtic Britons as they spread across England. The newcomers were obviously warlike, as suggested by the possible derivation of the term Saxon from an old Germanic word for 'knife'. But the wider reality is that, while Anglo-Saxon society was not as sophisticated or highly ordered as the civilization brought by the Romans more than four centuries earlier, it possessed its own intricate culture, rituals and social organization.

Apart from their provision of English as the bedrock of the modern language, the idea of the Anglo-Saxons lives on in ways that are sometimes slightly 'curious', to quote Lewis Carroll's Alice.

Not so curious perhaps in the case of the Church of England or Anglican Church, whose alternative title derives from the medieval Latin *Anglicanus,* which in turn comes from the Angles who began to arrive in Britain in the fifth century. The name of the people which was eventually bestowed on the established Church recalls the well-known story of sixth-century Pope Gregory's encounter with a batch of boys about to be sold as slaves in Rome. Struck by their fair complexions, Gregory asked where they were from. When told they were Angles, he punned in Latin: '*Non Anglii, sed angeli*' ('Not Angles, but angels'). The legend goes that after this he resolved to bring Christianity to their pagan country.

*Non Anglii, sed angeli
('Not Angles, but angels').*

POPE GREGORY, ON BEING TOLD THAT BOYS ABOUT TO
BE SOLD AS SLAVES IN THE ROMAN MARKETPLACE
WERE ANGLES, AN EVENT THAT SUPPOSEDLY LED TO
THE CONVERSION OF ENGLAND TO CHRISTIANITY

Not all applications of the Anglo-Saxon idea are so high-minded. At one end of the spectrum, the heavy-metal band Saxon – from Barnsley in Yorkshire – presumably acquired their name through a desire to be seen as basic and primitive, a head-banging force straight out of the Dark Ages. At the opposite end of the spectrum, the ancient Anglo-Saxon kingdom of Wessex, which covered much of south and southwest England, was revived by Thomas Hardy (1840–1928) as the setting for the great sequence of novels he wrote in the closing years of the 19th century. There was a fashionable interest in the Anglo-Saxon era in the Victorian period and both people and streets were given Old English names (e.g. Hereward, Athelstan, Alfred) in a style that is somewhere between the whimsical and the nostalgic. But Thomas Hardy went much further and created an entire world in Wessex, which he described as 'partly real, partly dream'. He rechristened many existing towns, of which

KING ARTHUR'S CROSS

In 1190 the monks of Glastonbury Abbey excavated a site which, it was claimed, contained the remains of King Arthur and Queen Guinevere. At a depth of some 5 metres (16 feet) beneath the abbey grounds was discovered a hollowed-out log full of bones, some of which were of unusual size. Halfway between ground level and the primitive coffin was a cross made of lead around 0.3 metres (1 ft) in length, with the Latin inscription *HIC IACET SEPULTUS INCLITUS REX ARTURIUS IN INSULA AVALONIA* ('Here lies buried the renowned King Arthur in the Isle of Avalon').

Replica of 'King Arthur's Cross', from William Camden's original sketch of the artefact.

The royal bones were eventually interred in a more fitting style near the high altar in the great abbey church. The cross rested on top of the tomb. So things remained for several centuries until the dissolution of the monasteries (1536–9) under Henry VIII. Almost everything was destroyed or lost but the Arthurian cross survived and was sketched by the antiquarian researcher William Camden (1551–1623) for his *Britannia*, the first guide-book to Britain. After passing into the possession of an official at nearby Wells Cathedral, the cross disappeared in the early 17th century and remains lost to this day.

The monks' claim to have discovered the remains of Arthur and Guinevere has been treated sceptically, if not with outright dismissal. Glastonbury Abbey needed money for rebuilding after a catastrophic fire and the discovery was conveniently timed. Such legendary relics would have attracted plenty of visitors and donations, although in practice it doesn't seem as though the abbey capitalized much on its finds. The leaden cross, which was seen and depicted by reliable witnesses hundreds of years later, is a reminder of the Romano-Celtic tradition in Britain, one that fiercely resisted the arrival of the Germanic tribes with their pagan religion and their new language.

Casterbridge for Dorchester is the best-known example. Hardy's explanation shows how potent was the folk-memory of an Anglo-Saxon regional kingdom:

> *... the press and the public were kind enough to welcome the fanciful plan, and willingly joined me in the anachronism of imagining a Wessex population living under Queen Victoria; – a modern Wessex of railways, the penny post, mowing and reaping machines, union workhouses, lucifer matches, labourers who could read and write, and National school children.*

A final illustration of the survival of the Anglo-Saxon idea is the US acronym WASP standing for 'White Anglo-Saxon Protestant' and characterizing the upper-middle class group (particularly in the northeastern states) which is descended from the earliest settlers or which claims to embody their values.

The arrival of people from the Scandinavian countries, beginning in the late eighth century and continuing for more than 300 years, started as a series of raids and ended in a combination of conquest and colonization. There were two waves of Viking settlement and triumph, one leading to their effective control of half the country (known as the Danelaw) and the second, briefer one marked by the accession of the Danish king Cnut (Canute) to the English throne in 1016. Overall, the Viking impact was felt most strongly in the northeast of England, where even today there are signs of their presence in place names and dialect terms. The contribution of Scandinavian words to general English was also considerable, although it took many years for them to percolate through to general use.

THE VIKING EFFECT

For about 200 years before the arrival of the Vikings, England had enjoyed relative peace. Although there was sporadic fighting among the various Anglo-Saxon kingdoms as well as a continued threat from the Welsh and Scottish borders, there was also a general stability which allowed for the Christian conversion of the country. All this was to change, beginning in the year 793 when, according to the *Anglo-Saxon Chronicle*, dreadful portents of doom appeared in the skies over Northumbria (lightning, dragons). The portents, or at least their imaginative interpretation, may have been retrospective but they more than hinted at the destructive impact of the Vikings.

The reasons behind the sudden migrations/incursions from Scandinavia are obscure. It may have been a growing population in northwest Europe that pushed people westwards across the North Sea. It was certainly facilitated by the seafaring skills of the Vikings, one of several generic terms for the inhabitants of present-day Sweden, Norway and Denmark. The very origin of the term 'Viking' is something of a mystery too. It has been traced back to the Norse *vik* (creek or inlet) or to the Old

A carved stone depicting Viking warriors wielding swords and battleaxes, at a ruined abbey in northern England. In the eighth and ninth centuries, England's coast was ravaged by Norse attackers.

English *wic* meaning 'camp', because of the Viking practice of setting up temporary bases. An alternative derivation is another Old English term, *wicing* or 'pirate'.

To this day there is some uncertainty about what to call these aggressive settlers. To the Anglo-Saxons they were Danes, irrespective of their place of origin. They were also called 'Norsemen' (signifying 'men from the North') and their language Old Norse, which is the usual term applied today. Popular imagination thinks of them as Vikings, perhaps because of its faintly exotic associations, summoning up a world of beak-prowed longships, of ale-quaffing, manly combat and general rapine.

Whatever the precise meaning of the word 'Viking', their early raids were certainly piratical. The northern monasteries of Lindisfarne, Jarrow and Iona were plundered one after the other in the years between 793 and 795. No coastal part of the country was immune, and during the first half of the next century Viking attacks and encampments were recorded from the Thames estuary to Cornwall. These pin-pricks turned into a full-blown assault on northeast England and by the second half of the ninth century half of the country was under Viking control. They might have overrun the rest of it had it not been for the resistance and eventual victory of the forces led by King Alfred. After that there was a lengthy period of coexistence between the two sides.

KING ALFRED THE GREAT

Alfred is one of the handful of decisive rulers in English history. As far as the survival and spread of English are directly concerned, he is the most important. Had he and his army not driven back the invading Viking forces and then made peace with them, there would have been no English-speaking kingdoms left and the dominant tongue would almost certainly have been Norse, the common language spoken with some variations by the inhabitants of Sweden, Denmark and Norway.

Alfred (849–99) inherited the kingdom of Wessex in 871 after his brother died fighting against the Danes. For several years the Danes overran increasingly large areas of Wessex until Alfred and his followers were forced into refuge on the Somerset Levels, a low-lying area of marshes and islands near the Bristol Channel. It was here on the island of Athelney, close to modern Bridgwater, that the probably apocryphal incident of the cake-burning occurred. According to the legend, which first surfaced in the tenth century, an old woman left a disguised Alfred in charge of the cake-baking but the king was so preoccupied with the woes of his kingdom that he neglected the simple domestic task.

Whatever the fate of the cakes, Alfred succeeded in the more important job of saving his kingdom by mustering an army and defeating the Danes in 878 under their leader Guthrum at the Battle of Ethandune (present-day Edington in Wiltshire). The white horse carved into a nearby hillside at Westbury supposedly commemorates his victory. The Treaty of Wedmore (878) resulted in the withdrawal of the Danes and, effectively, the splitting of the country roughly along the line of Watling Street, then a still-passable Roman road that ran northeast from London to Chester. The area above this line was under Danish law, hence 'Danelaw' ('law' comes from the old Norse *lagu*).

After his victory, Alfred set about consolidating control over the south and southwest. He seems to have been the first English ruler to employ language for political ends, as a way of cementing the union of his realm. The old knowledge of Latin had been lost, putting religious and other texts out of reach. Translation into Anglo-Saxon was required. In a preface to one such book Alfred wrote:

> *Our ancestors [...] loved wisdom, and through it they created wealth and left*
> *it to us. Here we may yet see their footprints, but we cannot follow their*
> *tracks after them [...]Therefore it seems better to me [...] that we translate*
> *certain books, which are most needful for all men to know, into that*
> *language that we all can understand.*

Alfred's dedication to learning was notable. He started learning Latin when he was almost 40 and he then oversaw or instigated the translation of works such as Bede's *Ecclesiastical History of the English People*. He was concerned too with secular history as it reflected national identity, and he was the first to bring together the writings known as the *Anglo-Saxon Chronicle*, a kind of diary-cum-history of events that started in 55 BC, with the arrival in Britain of Julius Caesar and continued well beyond another more significant invasion, that of William the Conqueror in 1066. Copies of the *Chronicle* were made and sent to monasteries, where they were updated. The king earned his respectful soubriquet of Alfred the Great, the only English monarch with such a title.

The statue of King Alfred the Great in Winchester, capital of the former kingdom of Wessex, was sculpted by Hamo Thornycroft in 1899 to commemorate the 1000th anniversary of Alfred's death. Alfred won a number of key victories against the Danish Viking invaders and helped ensure the survival of Old English.

KEYWORD

SKY

It took several hundred years for the Norse word *sky* to establish itself in English with its current application to everything that lies above our heads. In old Norse it meant no more than 'cloud' and was related to an older root-word signifying 'to cover'. The cloudy sense continued until the late Middle Ages. Geoffrey Chaucer writes of the wind blowing so hard that it 'left not a skye in alle the welkene.' *Welkin* or *heaven(s)* were the Old-English-derived equivalents for sky and they lasted into Shakespeare's time, with the addition of *firmament*. 'Sky' is so simple and expressive a word that it lends itself naturally to more than two dozen compound terms (e.g. sky-dive, skyscraper, sky-writing).

DANISH PLACE NAMES

Not surprisingly, there is a preponderance of place names in the northeast of England that show the influence of Danish settlement and the Old Norse language. The simple *by*, for example, signifies a farmstead and provides the suffix to many places, small and large, that would once have been part of the Danelaw. An area of a few square miles around Grimsby on the River Humber yields more than a dozen, including Aylesby, Keelby, Grainsby, and even a double helping in Ashby-cum-Fenby.

Anglo-Saxon already had a word to describe a valley or area of low ground in *dæl*, but the reinforcing effect of the Old Norse *dalr* combined with the up-and-down geography of the north of England, accounts for the number of '-dale' names there, from Arkengarthdale to Wharfedale. The equivalent valley suffix in southern and western England is the Celtic *-comb(e)*, although it tends to describe less spectacular landscape features.

Thorp(e), Old Norse for 'village', is a frequent place name in the east and northeast of England, almost always as part of a longer title (Thorpe Bassett, Burnham Thorpe). Although Old English also had the word, in two slightly differing forms, there are virtually no 'thorps' to be found in the south or west, areas beyond Danish influence. A similar pattern is evident with *-thwaite* (Old Norse *thveit* meaning 'clearing' or 'reclaimed land'), either standing by itself or more usually as a suffix (Bassenthwaite, Braithwaite). In addition to place names, the Danish influence extended to people's surnames, for example in the case of the Scandinavian *-son* suffix (Johnson, etc.) which had a much higher frequency in the east of the country according to early records.

WHAT THE VIKINGS BROUGHT US

Like any invader-colonizer, the Vikings brought their language with them. Old Norse was a Germanic language, as was Old English or Anglo-Saxon. The two tongues had much in common, to the extent that it is sometimes difficult for specialists to tell which language contributed which word to later English expressions. One of the principal markers for the Old Norse effect on England, and one that demarcates the areas under their control, consists in place names (see Danish Names, above).

But for all their shared linguistic background, it is unclear how far the two sides – Anglo-Saxon and Norse/Danish/Viking – would have been capable of understanding each other at first in the areas they were compelled to share. If there was a gap in understanding, the onus would have been on the indigenous inhabitants, the Anglo-Saxons, to come to linguistic terms with newcomers who were, after all, their conquerors.

In the long run, however, it was the Old Norse speakers who ceded to the English language. There was still a large proportion of native speakers in Danelaw, and within a few years of King Alfred's death in 899 his son Edward had begun a campaign to restore English rule over the whole country. For most of the tenth century under leaders such as Athelstan – the first ruler who could justifiably be referred to as the king of all of England – the Vikings were defeated or kept at bay. Additionally, the fact that Old Norse was an oral rather than a written culture would have weakened its chances in the 'battle' with English. Nevertheless it did leave a considerable mark on the English language.

There are a number of current English words that can definitely be traced back to Old Norse. They include very familiar terms such as *skin, skull, skill, egg, husband* and *sister*. This does not mean, of course, that the Anglo-Saxons did not already possess words for these everyday items. For them, 'skin' was rendered by *hyd* (hide), while the concept of 'skill' was expressed by *cræft* (craft) while 'skull' required the more elaborate and characteristically Anglo-Saxon formation of *brægnpanne* (brain-pan). In some cases, Norse eventually pushed out Old English but in others, like 'skin/hide' or 'skill/craft', it added to the general stock of words.

Another effect of Norse additions was to produce words that are related but not absolutely synonymous. For example, the Old English for 'to die' was *steorfan*. Norse had its own word: *deya*. Rather than ditch one of these terms, English kept both while giving *steorfan* a twist to particularize a type of death. We can see the word in transition during the Middle Ages, when *steorfan* could be used to mean both 'die' and 'starve', the exclusive sense in which it has been used ever since. Another addition was the Norse *skyrta*, originally a 'shirt', but a garment which the English pushed down the body and transformed into a 'skirt'. Similarly related pairs are 'wish' and 'want' (OE *wyscan*, ON *vanta*); 'sick' and 'ill' (OE *seoc*, ON *illr*); 'rear' and 'raise' (OE *ræran*, ON *reisa*).

An important Norse contribution was to make clearer the distinctions between pronouns. The Old English for 'they' was *hie*, not very different from the singular *he* (he), while *hiera* (their) was close to *hiere* (her). The modern 'they', 'their', etc. are descendants of original Scandinavian forms, although it took a long time for them to filter into standard English (Chaucer was still using *hem* for 'them' in the late Middle Ages). It is also likely that the use of an *-s* ending in the third person singular (e.g. 'he talks', 'she sings') came from contact with Old Norse. It eventually replaced the Anglo-Saxon form *-eth*, even though this old ending also hung on for several centuries – Shakespeare used *singeth* once (in *Hamlet*) but otherwise he wrote *sings*.

Viking coins set against the backdrop of a page from the late ninth-century Anglo-Saxon Chronicle, *detailing the transition of the Vikings from raiders to settlers. This document is the most important source for the history of England in the Anglo-Saxon period.*

But the linguistic and cultural legacy of the Norse/Danish/Viking settlement of Britain was not restricted to individual words or word-endings. It is also visible in literature, especially in the most famous poem of the Anglo-Saxon era, *Beowulf*.

BEOWULF

Hwæt! We gar-dena in geardagum,
þeod-cyninga, þrym gefrunon,
hu a æþelingas ellen fremedon.
[Modern English: 'Lo, praise of the prowess of the kings of the spear-armed Danes in days long gone by, we have heard, and what honour the princes won!']

A popular story throughout Viking lands was that of Sigurd, a warrior-hero who slew the dragon Fafnir. The scene is portrayed here on the portal of a church at Hylestad, Norway. This motif recurs in the Old English tale of Beowulf.

So begins the most famous surviving poem written in Old English, *Beowulf*. It is usually dated to the eighth century, but survives only in a tenth-century manuscript. The language of the poem appears daunting and even some of the letters used will be unfamiliar – the runic þ and ð symbols represent a 'th' sound – but the story it tells is timeless and still has great appeal. So much so that it was turned into a computer-generated-imagery feature film in 2007, starring Ray Winstone and Angelina Jolie.

The story tells of the beginning and end of the heroic life of Beowulf, a warrior from the Geatish people in Sweden. In his young days Beowulf slays Grendel, a monster that has attacked the Danish king's mead-hall (see Mead-Hall, page 29), and then Grendel's equally monstrous mother, who is seeking revenge for her son. The second part recounts Beowulf's own death in mortal combat with a dragon many years later after he has become king of the Geats. The story ends with Beowulf's ceremonial burial.

The world of the poem is highly ritualized and formal but also precarious, a world constantly threatened by darkness and the monsters who live there. In his *Ecclesiastical History* (completed *c*.731) the Venerable Bede made a comparison between human life and the flight of a sparrow through a great dining-hall in the middle of winter. Inside, there is warmth, food and company; outside is the rain and snow and the unending night. The sparrow's time in the light is soon over. This is the context of the *Beowulf* poem. The complicated warrior-culture needed to face the darkness is reflected in the elaborate diction. The poem is full of complex language (such as the many compound terms for the 'sea' like 'whale-road') using the favourite Anglo-Saxon linguistic device of coupling two words together to make a new one. Indeed, the name of the hero is an example. Beowulf means 'bear' from 'bee-wolf', and reminds us of a time when bears roamed northern Europe – and raided hives.

GOING BERSERK

Several bellicose words in modern English can be traced back to the Viking era, and testify to the fearsome reputation of these Scandinavian warriors.

Berserk(er), to describe a frenzied fighter, is not recorded in English before the early 19th century but was retrieved from Old Norse *berserkr*. This has a probable literal meaning of 'bear-sark' which, in turn, designates a coat or upper garment made of bearskin. An alternative explanation is that the term means 'bare-shirt' and indicates that such fighters were so reckless and hardy that they fought without armour.

Ransack originally suggested making an authorized search of a place or person (for stolen property) but, by the Middle Ages, the word had done an about-turn and acquired its modern sense of 'rob', 'plunder'. Given the piratical nature of the early Viking raids, it is not inappropriate that ransack also derives from Old Norse (*rann*=house+*sækja*=to seek). Curiously – and confusingly – the noun/verb 'sack', also meaning 'destruction' or 'to plunder', is not a shortening of 'ransack' but comes from a different source altogether, the French *sac* (into which you might put your looted goods).

The Old English *cnif* was probably a simple adaptation of the Old Norse *knifr* (knife). As a word it displaced the Old English *seax* (hip-sword, dagger) from which, it is thought, the Saxons themselves may have been named, presumably on account of their own warlike habits. Similarly, 'club' derives from a Scandinavian word, *klubba*. As does 'slaughter' (the Old Norse *slatr* denoted 'butcher's meat'), which was originally applied to the killing of livestock but was extended to human beings by the Middle Ages.

In common with some later Middle English poetry such as *Sir Gawain and the Green Knight* (see The Gawain Poet, pages 68–70), *Beowulf* is structured in blocks of alliterative words. *Gawain* and *Beowulf* are linked too in that the manuscripts survived a near-disastrous fire in the 17th century in the Cottonian Library in Ashburnham House in London. The Library, named for its founder Sir Robert Cotton (1571–1631), was made up largely of works that had been salvaged at the time of the Dissolution of the Monasteries by King Henry VIII in 1540. The *Beowulf* manuscript was damaged by fire and seems to have been neglected for many more years until it was transcribed by an Icelander called Grímur Thorkelin – fortunately just in time, since its fire-charred edges were already crumbling away. Thorkelin was looking for stories of Danish heroes in British archives. His relative ignorance of Anglo-Saxon prevented him from filling gaps in the manuscript, as had been the practice of medieval scribes. The original of *Beowulf* and other Old English manuscripts are now in the British Museum, but at one point the survival of almost all Old English poetry hung by a thread.

MIDDLE ENGLISH

THE NORMAN CONQUEST
1066–1345

CHAUCER'S ENGLISH
1345–1475

*The visible power of the Norman invaders epitomized by the
towering stone keep of Cardiff Castle. Linguistic hegemony,
though, was never achieved, with English eventually
supplanting Norman French even as the language of the court.*

The violent arrival of the Normans, relatively few in number but profound in their impact on English life, was ultimately to work to the benefit of the English language. New words and phrases were added in profusion to the existing stock, while the inevitable interchange between the indigenous population and their new overlords produced a simplification in linguistic structures. The gains for Old English and Norman French speakers were mutual, but by the time the process was complete there were no longer two languages. It took more than 200 years after the Battle of Hastings in 1066 for English to be reinstated as the language of law, education and government, but by then the reverse conquest was complete.

THE NORMAN CONQUEST

King Harold (?1020–66) was the last of the Anglo-Saxon kings of England and the last English-speaking king for almost three centuries. Harold's predecessor on the throne, Edward the Confessor (?1005–66), had no heir and William, duke of Normandy (?1028–87), was among the various claimants. William claimed to have been promised the succession by Edward, whose mother was Norman and who had spent much of his early life in Normandy. In addition Harold himself had sworn – or been made to swear – an oath to the same effect while he was a 'guest' in William's court. Despite this, Edward apparently made Harold his successor on his deathbed.

While William was assembling an army on the other side of the Channel, the new English king was facing a threat at the opposite end of the country from King Harald Hardrada of Norway (1015–66), who also claimed to have been offered the English throne (though not by Edward the Confessor). Harold made a forced march north and defeated the Norse invaders at the Battle of Stamford Bridge in Yorkshire. In the meantime the Normans under William landed at Pevensey, near Hastings. King

King Edward the Confessor, seated on his throne, holds an audience with Harold Godwinson, his successor. Scene from the Bayeux Tapestry, which was commissioned in c.1076 to commemorate William's successful invasion.

Harold and a portion of his army returned south in haste. The famous battle ensued, with Harold fighting courageously, although it is debatable whether he died from an arrow through the eye, as depicted in the Bayeux Tapestry. But die he did, after one of the briefest reigns in British history, taking with him the Anglo-Saxon title to the throne. William, the duke of Normandy, had won, and the future of England and the course of the English language were to be changed for good.

WILLIAM'S RULE

The Norman Conquest could have been the death-knell for the form of language known as Anglo-Saxon or Old English. If English had perished, there might have been a certain poetic justice to it, since the Angles and other invading tribes had themselves turned Celtic into a minority language hundreds of years before. At first glance it seems strange that English didn't die out or at least become a marginal language. The triumph of William of Normandy, after his defeat of King Harold at the Battle of Hastings, was swift and absolute. The battle was fought in mid-October and William was crowned king at Westminster Abbey less than three months later, on Christmas Day 1066.

William established his authority rapidly and, where necessary, with brutality. The so-called 'harrying of the north' was his response to attempted revolts in Northumbria, during which the majority of the population either died or fled. The same period saw resistance in the fenlands of East Anglia led by Hereward the Wake (Wake meaning 'vigilant'), a near-legendary figure with a touch of King Arthur to him. The Norman victory over Hereward and other rebels consolidated the new king's authority. But his ascendancy was not merely military. It extended over every important area of life.

Durham Cathedral, begun in 1093 and completed in 1128, was one of many imposing new buildings, both ecclesiastical and secular, that the Normans constructed to assert their authority over their new domain.

A Norman abbot was appointed Archbishop of Canterbury, replacing the Anglo-Saxon one, and other senior church posts were similarly filled. Court positions were given to the French-speaking nobility who accompanied William and they were also rewarded with great swathes of land. The result was the first great age of castle-building in England. The Tower of London was started in 1078, and by the Elizabethan period had become such a hallowed feature of the city that it was believed to have been built on the orders of Julius Caesar. At the other end of the country, the imposing Norman castle and cathedral of Durham, which continue to stand high above the River Wear after almost a millennium, are potent reminders of the might of William's new, triumphal culture, as well as an indication of the need to put his stamp on the rebellious north of England.

French-speaking clerks and officials dominated the apparatus of government, which some 20 years after the Conquest drew up the Domesday Book. This statistical record of national property was far more thorough than anything yet attempted, and remained unequalled in its scope until the 19th century. It served less as a census than as a guide to prosperous land-holders and their taxable status. Meanwhile French merchants and craftsmen moved across the Channel seeking fresh opportunities for trade. The original English, the Anglo-Saxons, were reduced to walk-on roles in their own country, whether as labourers and servants or as minor tradesmen and functionaries.

England became a bilingual land, with the upper classes speaking and writing their brand of Norman French and the lower ones continuing to speak Anglo-Saxon. As far as written language was concerned, England was trilingual, since Latin was widely used in the church and in administrative circles, including the composition of the Domesday Book. But the conquerors' variety of French was not only the language used by those who pulled the levers of power, it would also have been the fashionable way to speak. Indeed, the connection between French and fashionability may date from this time. French has a centuries-old link to fields such as cookery and diplomacy and, of course, the world of *haute couture* itself. Even today the deployment of terms like *chic, savoir-faire, je-ne-sais-quoi, sangfroid* and dozens of others may be considered sophisticated among some English speakers.

King William himself never learned to speak English. Although there is a story that he tried to master the language, he was either insufficiently dedicated to the task or too busy putting down trouble in his newly acquired kingdom. Perhaps he was simply too busy elsewhere; William spent about half of his reign (1066–87) back in Normandy and sometimes did not visit England from the end of one year to another. This was an absentee pattern followed by several of the kings who succeeded him, like his son William Rufus (1087–1100).

MIDDLE ENGLISH

1066 Battle of Hastings, death of King Harold, accession of William I

1086 William orders information to be gathered for the *Domesday Book*

1087 Death of William the Conqueror while on campaign in France; England 'bequeathed' to his second son William Rufus

1154 Accession of Henry II, great-grandson of William I, and founder of the Plantagenet line, the longest-lasting English monarchical house to date; Henry's 'empire' incorporates swathes of France, including duchy of Aquitaine, which he acquired through marriage to his new wife Eleanor

1187 King Richard I joins Third Crusade, mounted as reaction to Saladin's capture of Jerusalem; like many of the early Plantagenet kings, Richard saw England as part of a larger empire, and spent much of his reign out of the country

1203 King John, youngest son of Henry II and Eleanor of Aquitaine, loses control of Normandy and other French lands; weakening of traditional links between England and Normandy, and growing sense of English identity

1215 John signs Magna Carta ('Great Charter'), drawn up by hostile barons; includes right for freemen to be judged by their peers (i.e., trial by jury) and a clause against imprisonment without charge

1327 Accession of Edward III, longest reigning of the Plantagenet monarchs; Edward fosters cult of chivalry at court

1337 Outbreak of sporadic conflict with France later known as the Hundred Years' War

A NEW LAYER OF LANGUAGE

Whatever the movement of the kings, the words they brought with them stayed put in England. Many of these words were associated with notions of honour and chivalry, which were absolutely central to the self-image of the medieval world, or at least to those who occupied its upper echelons. The Anglo-Saxon world, too, had placed great emphasis on honour and the warrior's code, as the *Beowulf* poem demonstrates. But the centuries following the Conquest saw not just a refinement but a reinvention of these ideals; significantly, the role of women was highlighted. Courtly manners were brought to England and promoted by the Normans, particularly by such influential figures as Eleanor of Aquitaine (1122–1204), wife of Henry II (1133–89) and queen of England.

Over time, an estimated 10,000 verbal terms shifted from Norman French and became assimiliated, taking on a new English identity. But the newcomers were building on solid, earthy foundations. Expressions describing physical movement and body parts, basic foods and domestic interiors, these were Anglo-Saxon and remained so. The English ate bread, cheese and fish, and they drank ale. All the while they lived in houses with doors, floors, windows and steps. They used words which, allowing for small differences in spelling (*brede, chese*), are still in use to today. As important as the terms for basic actions and objects was the survival of the nuts and bolts of speech: *I, you, we, a, the, and, but, if, however...*

It has sometimes been said that the difference between the two languages – Anglo-Saxon and Norman French – is shown by the distinction between the (Old English) names given to animals when they were wandering around alive and the different (Norman) names given to them when they were cooked and served up at table. Hence the *sheep* in the field turns to *mutton* on the table, the *cow* to *beef*, the *swine* to *pork*. An extra level to this distinction is provided by the idea that the poor old English were out in the field tending the Anglo-Saxon flocks and herds while the Norman interlopers were being served the prepared French meats indoors. The notion, which was aired by Sir Walter Scott in his medieval romance *Ivanhoe* (1819), may be a bit cut-and-dried but it does

The Domesday Book (above) was a comprehensive record of land-holdings and taxes compiled at the behest of William I in 1086. The Anglo-Saxon Chronicle *records the zeal with which this task was undertaken:* 'So very narrowly did he [*i.e. William*] commission them to trace it out, that there was not one single hide, nor a yard of land ... not even an ox, nor a cow, nor a swine was there left, that was not set down in his writ.'

England's on the anvil – hear the hammers ring –
Clanging from the Severn to the Tyne!
Never was a blacksmith like our Norman King –
England's being hammered, hammered, hammered into line!

RUDYARD KIPLING, 'THE ANVIL' (1911)

convey something about the distribution of power between the two national groups.

Far from driving out Anglo-Saxon, Norman French became a very rich stratum laid on top of the native tongue. Not surprisingly, most of the words connected to law, governance and rank derive from the Norman: *justice, perjury, attorney, prison, parliament, prince, baron, duchess*. Sometimes there was a kind of marriage between English and French. In this process, the French *gentil* was added to English roots to produce *gentleman* and *gentle-woman*. The mirror phrases *law and order* and *ways and means*, in which each part means essentially the same as the other, are literal evidence of a fairly harmonious coexistence. *Law* is Old English (originally from Norse) as is *ways*, while *order* and *means* derive from French.

KEYWORD
CURFEW

William the Conqueror was reputed to have introduced the *curfew* to England as a means of imposing civic order. Although there is no reliable evidence for this tradition it does reflect something of the tight grip that he exercised over his conquered land. *Curfew* comes from the old French *covre-feu* ('cover-fire') and originally applied to the evening bell rung in towns as a signal that fires should be extinguished. This was less an arbitrary display of power than a way of minimizing the danger of a blaze in tightly packed streets of houses made of combustible materials like wood and thatching. In its current use, a *curfew* describes a ban on the inhabitants of a place being out on the streets for a specified period, usually after dark. Whether or not King William I introduced the *curfew*, he might be gratified to know that this feudal measure is still employed by dictatorships and panicking authorities everywhere.

WHY ENGLISH SURVIVED

So what were the reasons behind the survival of English? Why did the Normans not succeed in eradicating the tongue spoken by those they had conquered? Put simply, they didn't try. Whatever their attitude towards the English as a subject people, there was no hostility towards English as such. William the Conqueror was brutal in putting down dissent, particularly in the north of the country, but there was no conscious attempt to replace one language with the other, no explicitly nationalistic sense that French was a superior tongue. Some of the earliest documents issued by William after the Conquest were actually in English, even if the king himself would not have been able to understand them.

There was a startling disparity in numbers between the Norman arrivals and the original inhabitants of the country, with estimates of William's soldiers ranging from 15,000 men to as low as 5000. (Whichever figure we take, this was substantially fewer than the estimated 40,000 legionaries and auxiliaries who landed under the emperor Claudius in AD 43.) The English population of the late 11th century, by contrast, stood at around one and a half million. In addition, there was already a well-established spoken and written English culture, which would have been almost impossible to dislodge. This was a very different situation from the one obtaining centuries earlier when the Angles, Saxons and other tribes poured in and drove the Celts to the margins of the island. Over the years the Anglo-Saxons came in much greater numbers than the Normans and overwhelmed the Celts, who had little in the way of a written tradition of language. Even if no other advantage remained with the English after 1066 they had a tremendous superiority in numbers.

Another reason for the persistence of English was intermarriage between the two sides. Most of those who accompanied William across the Channel were, unsurprisingly, male rather than female. A high-ranking Norman soldier or administrator planning to stay and in search of a wife would almost inevitably have to look for one among English women. Their children, spending time with mothers and nurses, would have grown up if not bilingual then with a working knowledge of two languages. Meanwhile the French speaker, once he moved outside his military, court or professional circles, would have been dealing with English-speaking servants or minor officials such as stewards. In order to keep control or simply to conduct his day-to-day business, he would have had to acquire some of the language. Of course, this must have been a two-way process, with those English speakers in regular contact with the French picking up some of *their* language also.

But perhaps the most significant factor behind the eventual triumph of English is that it didn't take very long, in historical terms, for the Norman conquerors to go native. Less than 150 years after the Conquest, William's great-great-grandson, King John (1167–1216), lost control of Normandy. Within a few years the French nobility were no longer able to have a foot in both camps – possessing estates and owing loyalties both in France and England – and were compelled to declare their allegiance to one country or the other. By the time of Edward I (1239–1307), the monarch could use the threat to 'our' language as a rallying-cry against the enemy on the other side of the Channel, claiming that it was the French king's 'detestable purpose, which God forbid, to wipe out the English tongue'. The outbreak of the Hundred Years' War in 1337 set the seal on the antagonism between France and England and confirmed the value of all things English, including its evolving language.

An intriguing footnote is that this was not the first time the Normans had adapted to the language of an area they had conquered. In the late 9th century, when Alfred the Great's England was threatened and nearly overrun by Viking invaders, the area of France around the mouth of the Seine and present-day Cherbourg had also been attacked and settled by Scandinavian tribes. The first duke of Normandy was actually a Norse chieftain, given the dukedom by a French king in 912 as a way of buying off trouble. The original settlers (or 'pirates', as the French called them) therefore spoke Norse but within a couple of generations they were using French. This has been called one of the quickest language shifts on record and is a foreshadowing of the rather slower development by which the descendants of the Norman invaders of 1066 adjusted to their new-found Englishness. Looked at in another light, it could be said that the Norman Conquest was a second, and even more successful, Viking invasion.

CHIVALRY

For all the ruthlessness, even brutality, that marked the arrival of the Normans under William the Conqueror, the following centuries witnessed the emergence in England of high-minded conceptions of duty and honour that had originated in France.

The term *chivalrye* starts to appear in English in the early 12th century, and traces its roots through French before reaching back to the Latin *caballus*. By a slight irony, *caballus* was a slang term for a Roman cavalryman's horse. It was the equivalent of 'nag' while the regular Latin was *equus*. Yet it is the old nag rather than the noble horse which has given us not just *chivalry* but, later on, *cavalry* and *cavalier*. The link was between the fighter on horseback, the knight, and the brave and honourable behaviour that he was expected to display.

Similarly, the expression 'knight' has unassuming origins. In Old English *cniht* meant no more than 'boy', but then the word took a step up to signify a male servant before getting a further promotion to indicate a man owing military service to the king or other feudal

Saint George (c.1510) by the German painter Lucas Cranach the Elder. The legend of the knight who became the patron saint of England epitomizes the idea of chivalry; he was called upon to slay a dragon and rescue a king's daughter from its clutches.

lord. Since a knight might receive land in return for his services, it is easy to see how his status could grow even more. By the Middle Ages, the *knight* had taken on all the familiar connotations of bravery, decency, modesty, etc. After that the word became dated, except as a title given by the crown to this day to British subjects, as in Sir Mick Jagger. Interestingly, Jane Austen in her novel *Emma* (1816) gives the surname of 'Knightley' to the most perfect and gentlemanly of all her heroes.

Another significant concept from French is that of *curteisye*, gracefulness and politeness. The adjective *curtois* ('courteous') came first and its primary definition links it to the sort of well-mannered behaviour that would be expected in the court of a prince (in Middle English, *curt* = court). Later on, *courtesy* lost a couple of letters to provide us with *curtsy*, the 'bending of the knee' or little bobbing motion, which is a sign of deference. Less respectably, *court* is also the root of *courtesan*, a court-mistress or high-class prostitute.

SUBTLE LINGUISTIC NUANCES

The blending of Norman French with Old English greatly increased the store of vocabulary and in that way enhanced the variety and complexity of language. Sometimes French achieved this by serving as a kind of conduit for expressions which had travelled further than across the English Channel. *Lute, orange, amber, saffron*, all come from Arabic via French. In other cases, where one word had existed for a single concept, two might now be available, as in the already noted *law/order* or *ways/means*.

The process extended far beyond simple synonyms. More words meant greater suppleness and subtlety. For example, from Old English we have *ask*, while from Norman French we get *demand*. In modern French, the infinitive form *demander* means the same as *to ask*, but the two words have acquired distinctly different senses in English, with *demand* being altogether more insistent than *ask*.

Sometimes there might be no surface difference between the words. *Axe* (OE) and *hatchet* (Fr) are synonymous, as are *seek* (OE) and *search* (Fr). Yet even here there are quite fine distinctions: the comparatively rare *axeman* is generally used in its literal sense of 'someone with an axe' (or is modern slang for '[rock] guitarist') while *hatchet man* is always metaphorical and describes one who does other people's dirty work, destructive and even illegal. Similarly with *seek* and *search*; the first may carry overtones of looking for something higher (seeking truth, enlightenment) while the second tends to be found in a more mundane context (searching for lost car keys).

Speak in French when you can't think of the English for a thing.

LEWIS CARROLL, *THROUGH THE LOOKING-GLASS* (1871)

THE LANGUAGE SIMPLIFIED

However, the impact of Norman French was not just to give English a richer, larger vocabulary. Over time, it also simplified the ways in which words could be used and sentences put together.

Take the vexed business of gender. Norman French had two genders for nouns, masculine and feminine, as modern French still does. Old English went one better with three genders, having a neuter form to add to the other two: in pronoun terms the equivalent of *he, she* and *it*. Adjectives in both languages were inflected – that is, they took different endings according to the gender of the noun they were describing. To complicate things further, a French 'masculine' noun might have a 'feminine' equivalent in English, or vice versa. A speaker trying to bridge the gap between the two languages and doing his or her translation on the spot would first have to choose the right word for the occasion and then work out the right gender-ending for the adjective.

It was simpler to do away with gender altogether or, if that makes the process sound too conscious and deliberate, then it can be said that gender just disappeared. This is what had happened by the 14th century, establishing a pattern that remains unchanged to this day.

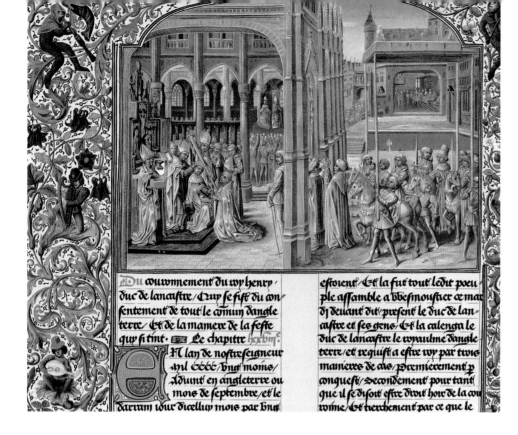

The great majority of nouns in modern English are gender-free or neuter. And even for those that are not – *mother, policeman* – there is no change in the qualifying adjective. If the policeman is *happy* then the mother is *happy* too. But in modern French not only do the definite and indefinite articles change according to gender, so too do the qualifying adjectives (e.g. *le gendarme heureux, la mère heureuse*).

Another significant change to Norman French practice was in the distinctive word ordering whereby the noun is followed by its adjective, as remains the case in modern French (so that the *White House* becomes *la Maison Blanche*). This was modified by the encounter and then the union with Anglo-Saxon. English usage had put the adjective in front of the noun for hundreds of years and here was a preference that stuck. The only exceptions in current English are a few French-derived terms like *court martial* and *body politic*, anomalies such as the title created by King Charles II, *Astronomer Royal*, and occasional adjective–noun inversions produced for the sake of rhetorical emphasis (*He took an early interest in things mechanical*).

The arrival of French also helped to standardize and simplify other things, particularly the endings of verbs. (Most nouns in both languages already shared the addition of 's' in the plural.) A little grammar history is necessary when it comes to explaining what happened to verbs, and the distinction between the so-called 'weak' and 'strong' verbs. The '-ed' ending is now applied to the great majority of English verbs when they shift from present to past: *help/helped, work/worked, pick/picked*. These are so-called 'weak' verb formations, ones which change in a regular way. That this is a predictable pattern is shown by a young child's attempt to form a new past tense by saying things like 'I see-ed her', using an '-ed' parallel which in this case is logical but wrong.

The term 'strong' is used to describe those verbs which, in the past tense, do not add '-ed' but change their shape in a more irregular fashion: *cling/clung, light/lit, sell/sold*. Sometimes they are stubborn and register no change at all between past and present (*burst, hit, put*). A neat contemporary illustration of the difference is provided by the verb application of the word *dive*: the past tense in the US is *dove* (strong formation), while in British English it is *dived* (weak formation). Sometimes the strong and weak forms continue to survive side by side, as in *strived* and *strove, weaved* and *wove*, although the weak '-ed' form in both these cases tends to be less common.

After the arrival of the Normans in 1066 there was an increasing tendency to regularize verbs by using the '-ed' ending, particularly when words moved across from French and became assimilated into English. This had already begun to occur under the Danish influence in the north of England but it was speeded up by the impact of the Normans. It is not difficult to see how this might have occurred. Rather than fiddling around with various possibilities – whether to change the middle of the word or to leave it as it was or to chop it off early – it was more straightforward to apply a standard rule and fasten the simple '-ed' on to the end. The general implication of this is that surviving irregular 'strong' verbs are descended not from French stock but from Old English (*do/did, run/ran, see/saw*). Their shape is a little piece of archaeology or linguistic carbon-dating. And because these verb forms are among the more commonly used English words, we probably assume that there is a greater degree of irregularity in the language than actually exists.

Your Roman-Saxon Danish-Norman English

DANIEL DEFOE, *THE TRUE-BORN ENGLISHMAN* (1703)

THE ENGLISH CONQUEST?

It took about 200 years for the Norman Conquest to become the English Conquest. In 1356 the order went out that law-court proceedings in London be conducted in English, not French. At the beginning of the same century, teachers in schools had used the language of William the Conqueror. Well before the century's end, all instruction in the grammar schools was carried out in English. Although children thereby lost touch with the French part of their inheritance, one of the advantages of the switch to English was that it took the same children less time to learn their grammar. No doubt, the simplifying of verb endings and the dropping of genders and agreements all helped.

Change was slowest at the top. It was not until the coronation of Henry IV in 1399 that a new English king delivered a speech in *English* claiming his right to the throne. Henry had deposed his predecessor Richard II (1367–1400) and after his accession he had Richard murdered. Perhaps Henry wanted to make his claim to the throne crystal-clear because it was actually rather tenuous. Whatever the reason, at his coronation he spoke to his fellow-countrymen in their own tongue. Better late than never.

KING LUD'S GATE

A 14th-century map of the area of London around St Paul's shows the hotch-potch of cultural, historical and linguistic influences that had marked the city in the more than 1000 years since its founding. Many of the street names are a roll-call of London's activities and occupants. Some are named simply for their proximity to a natural feature: Thames Street is obvious while Holborn comes from the 'old burn' (stream) that ran there. Fleet Street takes its cue from the River Fleet, which once flowed from Hampstead to the Thames and which now, entirely covered, serves as a sewer.

The London name with the claim to be the oldest is likely to be Ludgate, originally a gated entrance between Fleet Street and St Paul's. This was supposedly named for the legendary King Lud, a warlord in the pre-Roman era who may also have provided London with its name. Watling Street, on the other side of St Paul's, was (and is) a fragment of one of the major cross-country roads constructed by the Romans, its present name deriving from Anglo-Saxon.

Cornhill is self-explanatory as the site of a corn market but the nearby Leadenhall commemorates an oppressive mansion that stood there in the 14th century. East Cheap and West Cheap (now Cheapside) have more ancient origins, since Old English *ceap* meant 'barter' and hence denoted a marketplace. Budge Row has nothing to do with moving on – that sense came much later – but is adapted from an old French word (*bouchet*) and in Middle English signified a kind of lamb's skin and hence the area where the skins were treated. The growing cosmoplitan nature of London in the early medieval period is shown by what would have been a more recent name, Lombard Street. Foreign merchants were permitted to trade in England if they paid extra taxes to the Crown. Lombardy in northern Italy was a centre for trade and finance.

Map of London (1593) by the topographer John Norden. Many ancient names of streets were retained after the Great Fire of 1666 that razed much of the medieval city.

Of prides, than ye han herd bifore
Comprehended in this litel tretys heere
To oidone with, theffect of my matere
And though I nat the same wordes
As ye han herd, yet to yow alle I prey
Blameth me nat, for as in my centini
Shul ye nowher, fynden difference
ffro the sentence, of this tretys lyte
After the which, this mirye tale I
And therfore, herkneth what that I shal
And lat me tellen, al my tale I prey

¶ Explicit

¶ Heere bigynneth Chaucers

A yong man called Mel...
up on his wyf that
which that called was
he for his desport is
his wyf and eek his doghter, hath he
the dores, weren faste yshette thre
and setten laddres to the walles of
hem criyed, and beten his wyf
fyue mortal woundes in fyue sondri
hir feet, in hir handes, in hir eiys,
and leften hir for deed and wenten
tornned was in to his hous, and whan
was man seyinge his clothes...

In the 14th century, England was a patchwork of different dialects. Speakers from one part of the country would have had difficulty understanding each other, although they were speaking the same basic language and lived within the boundaries of the same nation. By the end of the medieval period, the situation was quite different. One dialect – that of the East Midlands used by the poet Geoffrey Chaucer – had become dominant and was to form the basis for the English that we still speak and write today.

CHAUCER'S ENGLISH

It is coincidental that the poet Geoffrey Chaucer (1345–1400) wrote in the East Midlands form that was to become the dominant style of English. Chaucer used that dialect because it was the one that came naturally to him. What is certain is that had Chaucer written in a different dialect – that is to say, had he been born and bred and worked in a different part of England – he would not be as widely read as he has been in the past and even today. Because Chaucer's words look relatively familiar, he makes the rise of the East Midlands dialect look inevitable, but there were other factors involved, most of them pre-dating Chaucer's birth.

The principal factors had to do with the increasing centralization of the country, the power and magnetic allure of London, and the growing wealth of the Midlands, the southeast and East Anglia. Later in the medieval period came the invention of printing, a discovery with consequences that were both global and invaluable. As far as the development of English was concerned, printing was to become a key element in the standardization of written English.

CAXTON AND THE EGGS

The printer and publisher William Caxton (*c*.1422–91) recounts an intriguing story concerning regional differences in English in his prologue to the translation of the Latin poet Virgil's *Aeneid*. The passage is given as it appears in Middle English:

The earliest known depiction of Geoffrey Chaucer, an illustration from the Ellesmere manuscript of the Canterbury Tales, *which includes 22 other equestrian portraits of the narrators of the tales.*

In so moche that in my dayes happened that certayn marchauntes were in a shippe in tamyse [Thames], for to have sayled over the see into zelande [Holland], and for lacke of wynde, thei taryed atte forlond, and wente to lande to refreshe them. And one of theym named Sheffelde, a mercer [dealer], came in-to an hows and axed [asked] for mete [food]; and specyally he axyed after eggys. And the good wyf answerede, that she coude speke no frenshe. And the marchaunt was angry, for he also coude speke no frenshe, but wolde have hadde egges, and she understode hym not. And thenne at laste a nother sayd that he wolde have eyren. Then the good wyf sayd that she understod hym wel. Loo, what sholde a man in thyse dayes now wryte, egges or eyren? Certaynly it is harde to playse every man by cause of dyversite & chaunge of langage.

It may be that Caxton played up the story for effect. It doesn't seem very likely that a woman selling eggs on the banks of the Thames would have been able to make sense only of the southern version of the word, *eyren*, rather than the form deriving from old Norse, *egges*, which she apparently mistook for French and which eventually became standard English. Perhaps she was having fun at the expense of the man asking the question.

Nevertheless, Caxton's story points to the real problems of understanding between people who occupied the same country and spoke what was technically the same language. It was more than a matter of linguistic curiosity; it was a significant commercial question for a translator and printer. Caxton wanted his books to appeal to as wide an audience as possible and would be wary of usages that might baffle sections of his readership. (Hence the somewhat defensive tone of the remark above: 'Certainly it is hard to please everybody because of the diversity and change in the language.')

In an age of standardized English it may be difficult to imagine such gulfs of incomprehension, but they can still occur. When a preview of Ken Loach's film drama *Kes* (1969) was shown to an American executive from the film's backers, the broad Yorkshire dialogue left him confused and indifferent. 'I would have preferred it in Hungarian,' he said afterwards to the producer, and the film was not released in the US.

Despite William Caxton's comments, by the time he came to write the prologue to the *Aeneid* translation in 1490, the question of the dominant form of English had more or less been settled. This can be seen by looking at the very passage quoted above. It is relatively simple to understand because its use of language is so close to our own. The biggest difference between Caxton's account and modern English lies in the spelling. Leaving aside a couple of insignificant exceptions, the word order is as it would be today and almost all the words are identical. Even where a meaning has been lost or changed it is easy to see how an expression relates to modern English: *mercer* is used by Caxton interchangeably with *merchant*; the Old English *mete* has the generalized sense of food, still surviving in *mincemeat*; while *wyf*, also Old English, means simply *woman*, although it can also denote a 'married woman' or 'housewife'. The least familiar words are probably the geographical ones: *tamyse* and *zelande*.

THE DIALECT QUESTION

If we go back a century or more the situation was much less clear-cut than in Caxton's day. There were four principal dialect forms of English in the country during the medieval period, each dominating in one of four roughly rectangular blocks of territory that corresponded to the principal regions. The Northern form, still much influenced by Old Norse, held sway in the area stretching from the River Humber to the lowlands of Scotland. Central England was parcelled up between two related dialects, the East Midland and the West Midland varieties, with the East Midland also affected by the remnants of Old Norse (with the north, it had formed part of Danelaw). Meanwhile, the southern area of the country was given over to the Southern and Kentish forms of the language.

The difficulties of a person from one part of the land understanding another may have been sharpened by regional hostility or plain unfamiliarity, but they were genuine. At the end of his poem *Troilus and Criseyde* (completed *c*.1385), Geoffrey Chaucer lamented the confusing variety of his own language and the errors that could result:

*And for there is so gret diversite
In Englissh and in writyng of oure tonge,
So prey I God that non myswrite the,
Ne the mysmetre for defaute of tonge.*

In an age before the invention of printing and the resulting 'fixing' of language, Chaucer's anxiety about mistakes is understandable. Scribes copying his work could have got words wrong or caused the verse to scan incorrectly (*mysmetre*). They might have done this through carelessness or perhaps because they were not accustomed to Chaucer's own usages.

An observation made by the scholar John of Trevisa (*c*.1342–1402) at about the same time as Chaucer's comment in *Troilus* pointed towards the eventual solution to the problem of competing dialects. John described how 'the Mercians, who are men of middle England and as it were partners of the ends [of the country], understand better the language to their sides, the Northern and Southern, than the Northerners and Southerners understand each other'. In other words, the people in the heart of the country had a more than slight advantage over those in the far north and south in that they had some understanding of both 'ends'. This in itself might suggest that the dialect form likely to emerge

Dialect areas in 14th-century England. In Chaucer's time, localized forms of English made it almost impossible for somebody from the north of England to understand a person from the south.

GENTILESSE

A key word in English literary and cultural history, *gentilesse* is related to other significant medieval concepts such as honour, chivalry and courtesy, all deriving from Norman French. Signifying gentleness of birth (i.e. coming from a noble or upper-class family), *gentilesse* then spread to encompass notions of how people from that kind of background ought to behave. For women it implied delicacy, refinement, the capacity for sympathy. For men, honourable deeds and words, chivalry and tact. For both sexes, self-restraint and honesty are required. *Gentilesse* is not the same as the modern 'gentleness', although it is a related idea. Geoffrey Chaucer's Knight in *The Canterbury Tales* is an energetic fighter in foreign lands – he appears on the Canterbury pilgrimage still wearing his battered coat of mail – but he is also 'a verray, parfit gentil knight'. Elsewhere Chaucer goes to some lengths to demonstrate that you don't have to be well-born to possess *gentilesse*. It is a state of mind and a correct way of feeling rather than a matter of blood and breeding. The concept survives in *gentleman* and the rarely found *gentlewoman* as well as in *genteel*, once a term of approval but now pejorative (because a genteel person is aping the surface manners of someone higher up the social scale and doing it badly).

as the dominant one would derive from the 'men of middle England'.

First of all, though, the question has to be answered: why was a standardized form of English required, when people in different regions had got by with their different dialects for such an extensive period? French and Latin had long been available to the most educated groups as a means of communication and, while that situation persisted, there was less need for a standard English. But French began to disappear in the 14th century, and was no longer used for formal instruction in schools or for proceedings in the law-courts. Classical Latin was regarded by scholars as the purest form of language but the well-springs of such purity, to be found in authors like Horace and Cicero, were up to 1500 years old. Latin had an indisputable but largely indirect influence on English. It was the natural language of the church and of scholars but, as it had survived across the centuries, it was seen as having fallen away from the classical gold standard.

The real impetus for a standard English came not so much from the inadequacy of the fading tongues of the educated classes as from the need for a form of language to suit an increasingly centralized society. England at the height of Middle Ages was a country in which the laws emanated from one place, a state in which the collection of taxes was arranged centrally, and a nation where culture and business were at their most energetic and profitable in a single region.

The distribution of wealth in medieval England was concentrated in the central and eastern areas. The flourishing wool trade with Flanders brought prosperity to East Anglia, the remote effects of which can be seen even today in the number and the echoing size of the churches there. Norwich was second in population only to London. Significantly, the wider East Midlands area was also home to the universities of Oxford and Cambridge. But it is the capital city that always exerts the biggest pull, and London must have been an enticing prospect for outsiders. Even then it had its tourist sites and sights, such as the famous 20-arched bridge (the sole crossing-point on the Thames until 1750) weighed down with shops and houses, whose rentals were required for its upkeep, and the towering wooden spire of St Paul's Cathedral, reputedly the highest in Europe.

The lure of London was especially strong after the devastating outbreaks of the Black Death (see The Black Death, page 64) in the middle and later parts of the 14th century when people flooded to the city in search of employment. In London was to be found the royal court at Westminster as well as the court of Chancery and Parliament, with all the legions of clerks and administrators that these instituitions required.

GEOFFREY CHAUCER

London was not only the administrative centre but also the country's busiest port, and it was at the heart of the port area that the poet Geoffrey Chaucer (1345–1400) was brought up in the appropriately named Vintry Ward. As a child, he probably lived in its principal thoroughfare, Thames Street, which still – as Upper and Lower Thames Street – runs parallel to the river between the Tower of London and the area around Blackfriars. Geoffrey's father John was a vintner or wine wholesaler, supplying tavern-keepers with products that were mostly imported from France. (Incidentally, it is around this time that surnames become properly established in English, frequently drawn from people's trades. *Vintner/Vinter* and *Taverner* are two examples still current.)

Although he came from a middle-class background, Chaucer had very close links with the royal court. His sister-in-law Katherine Swynford was mistress, and eventually wife, to John of Gaunt, a younger son of Edward III. Chaucer went on diplomatic missions to Genoa and Florence, during which he may have met the writers Petrarch and Boccaccio whose fame was spread across Europe. Throughout his life he was a high-ranking public servant, whether as a Member of Parliament for Kent or later as the Clerk of the King's Works, a post that made him responsible for the financing of the repair of royal buildings. When he died in 1400 he was buried in Westminster Abbey. Ironically, this was not because of his literary achievements or his government work but because in 1399 he had taken out – somewhat optimistically – a 53-year lease on a house in the abbey precincts.

Geoffrey Chaucer, from a 19th-century engraving. Chaucer's English was close to the standardized form that was beginning to evolve from a mixture of Midlands and London dialects. Only in The Reeve's Tale does he employ a slightly different dialect for two northern characters.

The worshipful father and first founder and embellisher of ornate eloquence in our English, I mean Master Geoffrey Chaucer.

WILLIAM CAXTON IN PREFACE TO CHAUCER'S TRANSLATION OF BOETHIUS (1478)

But it as a poet that Chaucer is remembered, specifically for the extraordinary variety of *The Canterbury Tales* (see below) and for *Troilus and Criseyde*, the story of a pair of star-crossed lovers who come from opposite sides during the Trojan War. The narrative of Middle English sometimes makes it appear that Geoffrey Chaucer was personally responsible for the 'triumph' of the East Midlands form of dialect. He was the most famous writer of his day and remains, arguably, the best-known English poet after Shakespeare. His work was printed and reprinted down the centuries and, until recently, was quite widely read in British schools. So he is popularly – and misleadingly – regarded as the 'creator of English'. But no writer is that influential. The English that Chaucer wrote in, the London/East Midlands form, would have become the standard one even if he had never penned a word.

It should also be noted that there are aspects of Chaucer's work that make it hard to claim that he was setting an absolute linguistic standard. For one thing, he was writing poetry, and poetic and literary English will always be different from the language of the woman in the street or the shop. It was not an era of consistency, either. Writing in a pre-dictionary age, he sometimes spelled the same word differently on different occasions. In addition, no manuscript in Chaucer's hand survives. Before the advent of printing, he was copied and re-copied by scribes who no doubt added their own mistakes or verbal preferences to Chaucer's originals.

What Chaucer did was to add enormously to the prestige and significance of the form of English that he, as a life-long Londoner, naturally used. We can see in it the skeleton of modern English. Even so, his language is still quite distant from us. A passage of Chaucer requires a bit of effort from the reader, and for a close translation a glossary and notes are likely to be needed. He is not as easy to understand as, say, William Caxton writing 100 years later (see pages 57–58). But, once the effort has been made, much of his work is as readable and enjoyable as it ever was.

THE CANTERBURY TALES

Late on an April day in the closing years of the 14th century a group of 30 or so pilgrims are gathering at the Tabard Inn in the London borough of Southwark, south of the Thames. Next morning they will start on a journey to Canterbury to pay their respects at the shrine of Thomas Becket (1118–70), the Archbishop of Canterbury murdered two centuries earlier on the orders of King Henry II (r.1154–89) and a celebrated saint and martyr almost from the instant of his death. Thomas's shrine is the most popular pilgrim destination in the country.

Harry Bailly, the Tabard landlord, volunteers himself as a guide-companion to the party. He suggests that to pass the time while they are travelling each pilgrim should tell four stories, two on the way to Canterbury, two on the way back. Harry will be the judge of who tells the best tale and the winner will earn a supper paid for by the others. The landlord is an expansive man, large and good-humoured, but one who won't tolerate disagreement.

Anyone who goes against his judgement will pay the expenses for everyone else. He is shrewd too. His proposal means that the entire group will have to come back to the Tabard Inn when the pilgrimage is done.

The next morning the group sets off from Southwark soon after daybreak. The pilgrims reach the first watering-place for the horses, a brook that flows near the second milestone on the Canterbury Road. Now that they have shaken off the effects of sleep and are properly on their way, Harry reminds them of their agreement. Given the number of people on the pilgrimage, the fairest method of deciding who tells the first story is to draw lots. By apparent chance the lot falls to the most senior member of the party, a knight. He begins to tell a tale of chivalry, love and death.

So begins the great sequence of poems and stories by Geoffrey Chaucer called *The Canterbury Tales*. Chaucer did not complete his wildly ambitious scheme of providing each pilgrim with four stories, if that was ever a serious proposition. Even so, the two dozen contributions making up *The Canterbury Tales* give an unmatched view of England in the Middle Ages.

A heavily romanticized vision of Chaucerian England, in Canterbury Tales: Tabard Inn *(1897) by Edward Corbould (1815–1905). The Victorians vaunted Chaucer as the Father of English Literature, producing sanitized children's editions of his tales, but deplored his 'indelicacy and filthiness'.*

THE BLACK DEATH

The Black Death had a devastating effect on the British Isles as on the rest of Europe. The population of England was cut by anything between a third and a half. Probably originating in Asia, the plague arrived in a Dorset port in the West Country in 1348, rapidly spreading to Bristol and then to Gloucester, Oxford and London. If a rate of progress were to be allotted to the plague, it was advancing at about one-and-a half miles a day. The major population centres, linked by trading routes, were the most obviously vulnerable but the epidemic had reached even the remotest areas of western Ireland by the end of the next decade. Symptoms such as swellings (the lumps or buboes that characterize bubonic plague), fever and delirium were almost invariably followed within a few days by death. Ignorance of its causes heightened panic and public fatalism, as well as hampering effectual preventive measures. Although the epidemic petered out in the short term, the disease did not go away, recurring in localized attacks and then major outbreaks during the 17th century which particularly affected London. One of them disrupted the preparations for the coronation of James I in 1603; the last major epidemic killed 70,000 Londoners in 1665.

The term 'Black Death' came into use after the Middle Ages. It was so called either because of the black lumps or because in the Latin phrase *atra mors*, which means 'terrible death', *atra* can also carry the sense of 'black'. To the

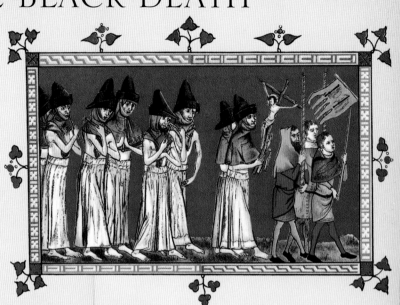

Members of a religious order, the Brothers of the Cross, scourge themselves to try to rid the world of the Black Death at Doornik in Holland in 1349.

unfortunate victims, it was the plague or, more often, the pestilence. So Geoffrey Chaucer calls it in *The Pardoner's Tale*, where he makes it synonymous with death. The words survive in modern English even if with a much diminished force in colloquial use: 'He's a pest.' 'Stop plaguing us!' Curiously, although *pest* in the sense of 'nuisance' has its roots in *pestilence*, the word *pester* comes from a quite different source, the Old French *empêtrer* ('entangle', 'get in the way of').

The impact of the pestilence on English society was profound. Quite apart from the psychological effects, there were practical consequences. Labour shortages meant a rise in wages and a more fluid social structure in which the old feudal bonds began to break down. Geographical mobility would also have helped in dissolving regional distinctions and dialect differences.

Chaucer, who introduces himself as one of the pilgrims, was not the first writer to create a sequence of stories by using a narrative pretext to bring his characters together. Giovanni Boccaccio had done just this in his *Decameron* (*c.*1349), in which ten inhabitants of Florence escape the plague in their city and spend time telling each other stories in country villas. Nor was Chaucer the first English writer to offer a panorama of his society. William Langland had presented a kind of generalized view slightly earlier in *Piers Plowman* (*c.*1367). But *Piers* is a fundamentally religious work while Chaucer's writing, apart from the odd piece, is solidly secular. And Chaucer deals less with broad types than with recognizable individuals. Literally so in one case, since there really was a Southwark inn-keeper called Henry Bailly.

In the *Prologue to the Canterbury Tales* Chaucer provided a physical description of many of the pilgrims, picking out telling details such as the bright scarlet leggings worn by the Wife of Bath or the Friar's cope (top garment) which is as 'rounded as a bell' and which indicates that he is far from being an abstemious churchman. Socially, the pilgrims run the gamut from the nearly noble (the Knight) to the nearly criminal (the Pardoner). They come from a variety of regions of England and they tell a variety of stories.

Some of the pilgrims reveal a great deal about themselves. The Wife of Bath describes how she got the upper hand over each of her five husbands and then throws in her story as an afterthought, while the Pardoner revels in giving details of how he tricks simple country congregations into giving him money and goods in exchange for absolving them of their sins. There is rivalry between the travellers. Because the Miller tells a story in which a carpenter emerges as a fool, the Reeve – a steward on an estate but a carpenter by training – retaliates in his account of a cheating miller. Some of the tales are very high-minded, full of honour, chivalry and the nobler side of human nature (*The Knight's Tale, The Franklin's Tale*). Others are crudely humorous (*The Merchant's Tale* and *The Reeve's Tale*).

Manuscript illustration of the eponymous narrator of The Parson's Tale, *a straightforward reflection on sin and repentance.*

CHAUCER'S ENGLISH

As an example of the gap between Chaucer's English and its more familiar forms from the following century (the 1400s) and later, look at this passage from the closing stages of *The Merchant's Tale*, one of the most readable and bawdy stories from the Canterbury collection. Briefly, the narrative concerns a wealthy old knight, symbolically named January, who marries a young and attractive woman, May. Dissatisfied, even repelled, by her aged husband, May falls for a young squire called Damyan. January becomes absurdly jealous of her, particularly after he is struck blind, and he insists on keeping his hands on his wife all the time, literally. By pre-arrangement, Damyan climbs up a pear tree in January's private garden and waits for the arrival of May, escorted by her husband. When they reach the tree, she says she'd like nothing better than a pear. This is what happens next:

'Allas,' quod [said] *he, 'that I ne had heer a knave* [servant]
That koude clymbe! Allas, allas,' quod he,
'For I am blynd!' 'Ye, sire, no fors [no matter]*,' quod she;*
'But wolde ye vouche sauf, for Goddes sake,
The pyrie [pear tree] *inwith youre armes for to take,*
For wel I woot [know] *that ye mystruste me,*
Thanne sholde I clymbe wel ynogh,' quod she,
'So I my foot myghte sette upon youre bak.'
'Certes,' quod he, 'theron shal be no lak
Mighte I yow helpen with myn herte blood.'
He stoupeth doun, and on his bak she stood
And caughte hire by a twiste [branch]*, and up she gooth.*
Ladyes, I prey yow that ye be nat wrooth [angry] –
I kan nat glose [gloss over this]*, I am a rude* [ignorant] *man –*
And sodeynly anon this Damyan
Gan pullen up the smok, and in he throng [thrust]*.*

Although the overall sense of the passage is clear, there are several challenges in it for the modern reader. First of all, there are the words that have slipped right out of use. Examples include:

• *quod* (past tense form of *quethen* – 'to say' – and still found extensively in Shakespeare but only in the present tense *quoth*);
• *pyrie* for 'pear tree' (similar to the modern French *poirier*);
• *twiste*, last recorded in the sense of 'twig' or 'branch' in 1622;
• *anon*, which during Chaucer's time meant 'straightaway' and then shifted to mean 'in a moment', in which sense it is still used for rather strained comic effect ('I'll see you anon.').

There are also terms that are either dated or have changed meaning:

• *wrooth* for 'angry', surviving only in the archaic noun *wrath* (*Grapes of Wrath*);
• *rude* for 'uneducated' and not necessarily carrying any pejorative sense;
• *knave* which here has the plain sense of 'boy' or 'servant', but which like the similar low-grade terms *churl* and *villein/villain* was also beginning to acquire the meaning of 'rogue' (modern German *Knabe* keeps the original sense of 'boy').

Then there are the unfamiliar verb forms. *Woot* is the first person singular of the verb *witen* ('to know'). *Stoupeth* and *gooth* are the third-person singular present-tense forms of *stoupen* and *goon*, 'stoop' and 'go'. Although it persisted for several centuries, this *-th* or *-eth* ending was eventually replaced by the standard modern *-s/-es* ending ('stoops', 'goes') which originated in the north of England. There are also oddities like the adverbial *certes* ('certainly') or the unfamiliar splitting of words that now form one unit, *vouche sauf, kan nat* (vouchsafe, cannot).

JOHN WYCLIF AND THE BIBLE

John Wyclif (or Wycliffe; c.1330–84) was an early radical figure in the English church. Born in Yorkshire and educated at Oxford, Wyclif held various church livings until he caused such a reaction that he was prevented from preaching and his manuscripts were burned. He argued against the prestige of bishops and the supremacy of the pope. He was convinced that the Bible, rather than any of the established institutions of religion, was the only authority for the word of God. What made him particularly dangerous was his belief that the Bible should be available to the people in the language that they knew, i.e., in English rather than Latin. He drew on the example of Christ, writing (in a modern translation): 'Christ and His apostles taught the people in the tongue that was best known to them. Why should men not do the same now?'

The idea was not completely new. There had been partial attempts at translation, the earliest known of which was literally written between the Latin lines of the text of the *Lindisfarne Gospels* and probably dates back to the tenth century. But Wyclif wanted to do the thing wholesale. This was shocking to a

Wyclif's second Bible translation appeared in c.1400. This first page of the Gospel According to St Mark opens with the words: 'The bygynynge of ye gospel of Jesus Christ ye sone of God...'

religious establishment which demanded that the interpretation of God's word be kept safely in its own hands. The chronicle-writer Henry Knighton, a canon at an Augustinian abbey in Leicester, complained in Latin a few years after Wyclif's death that:

Master John Wyclif translated from Latin into the English language – the language of the Angles not of angels – the gospel which Christ gave to the clergy and doctors of the church [...] As a result it has become more common and open to ordinary people and even to women who know how to read ...

Wyclif was behind two translations of the Bible, one of which was produced shortly before his death, while the other appeared a few years later. He also inspired a group of followers, the Lollards (from Middle Dutch *lollen*, to 'mutter'), but their attempts to spread the translated versions were banned. Wyclif's work on the Bible perhaps had more symbolic significance than actual effect: it was the first known attempt at a complete translation of the Gospel into a language that would be familiar to everyone.

For all the unfamiliarity of Chaucer's writing, the bulk of it is quite easy to understand once the reader has got used to the slightly strange look of it on the page. Reading aloud sometimes helps, without paying much attention to what Chaucer's pronunciation would have been (anyway, a contested subject). It would be surprising, in a sense, if Chaucer were even less accessible than he is, since it is his East Midlands/London English that leads directly to the English we see, speak and read every day.

It shouldn't be thought, however, that Geoffrey Chaucer or other writers of the period knew that they were setting a standard. This is demonstrated in the only one of *The Canterbury Tales* in which the poet has his characters speak in a style which is different from the East Midlands dialect. *The Reeve's Tale* is a farcical and bawdy story of the mistaken identities and bed-hopping which occur when a pair of Cambridge students stay the night at a miller's house.

Interestingly, Chaucer gives to the better-educated students what would now be regarded as the dialect speech – they come from the north – while the miller and his wife and daughter speak in the standard speech of the south. The Northerners use an 'a' in some words where the Southerners would use an 'o', as in *banes* or *ham* or *tald* (*bones, home, told*). On the other hand, some of the Northern usages recorded in *The Reeve's* Tale are actually those that eventually became standard for the whole country: as already mentioned, the singular verb form '-eth' in the south of England (*goeth, speketh*) was to be pushed aside by the Northern '-s' (*says, makes*). Similarly, the Northern pronoun form *thair* (*their*) is closer to modern English than the Southern form of *hir*. There is no suggestion in the story that one style of speech is superior to the other and *The Reeve's Tale* captures a short period in English history when all dialects were, in effect, equal.

Geoffrey Chaucer is the best-known but not the only medieval poet. Apart from Langland and his *Piers Plowman*, there is the author of one of the most romantic narratives of chivalry ever written, the tale of Sir Gawain, which is significant not only because it represents one of the highpoints in the medieval love-affair with chivalry and everything connected to King Arthur but also because it emanates from a quite different area of the country, hundreds of miles from the hub of London.

THE GAWAIN POET

The author of the narrative poem *Sir Gawain and the Green Knight* is unknown. He was writing in the late 14th century, at about the same time as Chaucer was composing *The Canterbury Tales*. The style and diction of *Sir Gawain* are noticeably different from anything that Chaucer wrote because the anonymous poet was using a different dialect from Chaucer's East Midlands one. *Sir Gawain* and three religious poems that survive in the same manuscript were written in a style that has been located as originating in an area somewhere around north Derbyshire and south Lancashire. Even nowadays, this is a region distant from London, both geographically and culturally, and in the Middle Ages it might almost have seemed part of another country. Although *Sir Gawain* reflects the

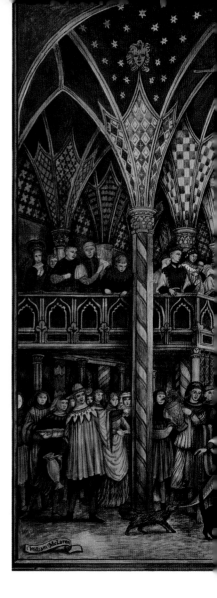

near-obsession of the period with chivalry and right behaviour, the outlook of the poem is a long way removed from Chaucer's easy-going, metropolitan stance.

We are back in the court of King Arthur at Camelot. It is New Year's Day and a feast is in progress for the élite of Arthur's knights and their ladies when 'there rushed in through the hall-door a dreadful man, the tallest on the earth ... and this man and his clothes were all covered in green'. This terrifying knight – he is riding a horse that is also green – issues a challenge. He will take a stroke from any of the knights assembled there, provided he is given the right to retaliate with another blow in a year's time. Sir Gawain steps forward and deals the kneeling knight such a great blow that it severs his head from his body. This is what happens next:

> The blod brayd fro the body, that blykked on the grene;
> And nawther faltered ne fel the freke never the helder,
> Bot stythly he start forth upon styf schonkes,
> And runyschly he raght out, there as renkkes stoden,
> Laght to his lufly hed, and lyft hit vp sone;

An interpretation of the tale of Sir Gawain and the Green Knight by the 20th-century illustrator William McLaren (1923–87). This late 14th-century romance, by an unknown author, is written in a northwest Midland dialect of Middle English.

And sythen bowes to his blonk, the brydel he cachches,
Steppes into stelbawe and strydes alofte,
And his hede by the here in his honde haldes.

[In Modern English, this passage reads: 'The blood, spurting from his body, shone against the green, and the man neither faltered nor fell any further but stoutly set out on firm legs and fiercely reached out, where the men were standing, took hold of his fine head and lifted it up. And then he goes towards his horse, catches the bridle, puts his foot in the stirrup and steps up, while in his hand he holds his head by the hair.']

Leaving aside the drama for the moment, the language of the passage is slightly different from what would be found in the East Midlands dialect. There are two words for 'man', *freke* and *renke*, which Chaucer does not use (he would have put *wight* or *man*). The green knight's horse is a *blonk*, a word that sounds odd to modern ears. But the horse fairs in Sheffield used to be held in Blonk Street, and Sheffield is at the heart of the area where *Sir Gawain* was composed. *Blonk* derives from the French *blanc* and was originally applied only to a white horse. Appropriately enough for a poem concerned with chivalry, *Sir Gawain and the Green Knight* contains plenty of terms borrowed from French, something that shows the countrywide spread of the language. Like the earlier *Piers Plowman*, the poetry is alliterative, with the lines built up from blocks of words beginning with the same letters on which the stress falls – usually two in the first part of the line and one in the second (Step*pes* into stel*bawe* and stry*des* alofte,/And his hede *by the* here *in his* honde *haldes*).

What happens next to Sir Gawain? The Arthurian knight, a model of chivalry, sets off in quest of the green knight after a gap of almost a year. On the way, he stays at the castle of the mysterious Sir Bertilak. Following an interlude in which a complex bargain is struck between the two men, and Lady Bertilak attempts in vain to seduce Gawain, the hero rides off to fulfil his promise to the green knight. The 'twist in the tale' is that the knight (who only inflicts a flesh wound on Gawain) turns out to be Bertilak, who has been engaged in a game organized by King Arthur's sister Morgan le Fay.

William Caxton (left)
presenting his incunabulum
(early printed book) of
Dictes and Sayings of
the Philosophers, *which he*
produced in 1477, to King
Edward IV.

WILLIAM CAXTON AND PRINTING

Much more important than any medieval poet, however significant his contribution to the English language, was the arrival of printing in the British Isles. Johannes Gutenberg had introduced movable type – originally invented in

China – to Europe in 1458 but the first book in English was not produced until 1475, when William Caxton (c.1422–91) printed a history of the Trojan War. Caxton, born in Kent, was working in Bruges at the time as a merchant and entrepreneur, and his decision to publish books in English was the act of a businessman rather than a language missionary. It was a risk, too, since the reading population was small. Nevertheless, Caxton must have scented success for, within a year, he had returned to England and set himself up near Westminster Abbey, producing over 100 books before his death. His business acumen is shown in a choice of publications that included books about gaming and chivalry, as well as editions of Chaucer's *The Canterbury Tales* and Sir Thomas Malory's *Morte d'Arthur*, the romance that consolidated the fashion for all things Arthurian.

Caxton had help, notably from the assistant who took over the business after his death, the aptly named Jan Wynkyn de Worde. But he seems to have operated as something of a one-man band, frequently translating the work that he was publishing as well as casting a careful editorial eye over all of it and writing extra material such as prefaces to the volumes. He also contemplated the problems of producing books in a language that was far from fixed (see the 'eggs' story at the beginning of this chapter).

William Caxton was followed by other printers who established themselves in London before the end of the 14th century, and slowly a standard of printed English began to emerge, one in which conventions of spelling and punctuation were largely shared between different presses. The more widespread the circulation of printed material, the more there would be conformity in usage. Conformity, but not absolute uniformity. Even now, publishers differ. Every newspaper has its own 'house-style', which will dictate, for example, whether double or single quotations marks are used or which nouns are capitalized. There are dozens of spelling variations between US and British English, to say nothing of different verbal usages and punctuation traits. And, publishers' conventions and preferences aside, the printed word will change as the language changes.

Nevertheless, the establishment of English-language printing in 1475–6 is a seminal moment, however long it may have taken for its full effects to filter through. It matters because, before the advent of radio and television, printing was the prime means of disseminating news and information – as well as gossip, entertainment, etc. The commercial circulation of printed material both assumes and encourages a literate population across a broad canvas, usually a national one. It helps to standardize usages and so brings about the 'universal' written English which we have today. The very fact that there are arguments over quite minor topics, like the value of the apostrophe or the use of Americanisms, is paradoxically a testament to these near-universal standards.

> *The three great elements of modern civilization: Gunpowder, Printing and the Protestant Religion.*
>
> THOMAS CARLYLE, *ESSAYS* (1838)

DEVELOPING ENGLISH

THE AGE OF SHAKESPEARE
1552–1616

FAITH AND SCIENCE
1603–1700

A NEW-FOUND LANGUAGE
1600–1787

A key text of the Scientific Revolution: title page of Isaac Newton's Principia Mathematica *(1687), in which he expounded his laws of motion and universal gravitation.*

PHILOSOPHIÆ

NATURALIS

PRINCIPIA

MATHEMATICA.

Autore *JS. NEWTON*, *Trin. Coll. Cantab. Soc.* Matheseos
Professore *Lucasiano*, & Societatis Regalis Sodali.

IMPRIMATUR.
S. PEPYS, *Reg. Soc.* PRÆSES.
Julii 5. 1686.

LONDINI,

Jussu *Societatis Regiæ* ac Typis *Josephi Streater*. Prostat apud
plures Bibliopolas. *Anno* MDCLXXXVII.

Mr. WILLIAM
SHAKESPEARES

COMEDIES,
HISTORIES, and
TRAGEDIES.

Published according to the True Originall Copies.

Martin Droeshout sculpsit London.

LONDON

Shakespeare's lifetime (1564–1616) saw the rise of England under Queen Elizabeth I (r.1558–1603) and the first stirrings of an empire-building culture that was to last for the best part of 400 years. Despite external threats and internal political and religious dissent, some of which was violently suppressed, this was an era of relative tranquillity that witnessed an explosion of creativity and innovation. The English language was to be one of the main beneficiaries.

THE AGE OF SHAKESPEARE

In the Elizabethan period the English language flexes its muscles. It begins to experiment, to play around, to show off. It finds innovative ways of saying old things. It creates fresh expressions. There was even a word for those new words that were considered too flashy or contrived. They were 'ink-horn' terms, an ink-horn being, unsurprisingly, a container for ink. Presumably they were called this because writing them required more ink or perhaps because of the association between a desk-bound man and pedantry. 'Ink-horn' words were generally derived from Latin or Greek. Examples from the Elizabethan period that have not survived include *cohibit* (restrain), *concernancy* (concern), *eximious* (excellent) and *illecebrous* (enticing).

The 'ink-horn' word was only used as a criticism and never as a compliment. The implication behind the jibe – another Elizabethan coinage – was that English did not require these new-fangled and sometimes ugly expressions. There were already good old English terms, literally Old English in many cases. What was wrong with the Anglo-Saxon roots of language? Why did writers have to go ransacking the classical tongues when better and shorter words were available?

The simplest answer is that writers used these words because they wanted to, either to impress their readers or to baffle them (sometimes the two overlap), or because they were simply exploring what could be done with the language. In response, some of the objectors deliberately revived Anglo-Saxon words that had fallen out of use.

England's national poet William Shakespeare left an indelible stamp on the language; the Oxford English Dictionary *credits him with the introduction of nearly 3000 words.*

THE AGE OF SHAKESPEARE

1552 Revision of Archbishop Thomas Cranmer's *Book of Common Prayer*, which remains standard Anglican liturgical text for the next four centuries; Cranmer burnt at the stake in 1556 for heresy during Queen Mary's reign (1553–8)

1558 Accession of Elizabeth I

1562 English involvement with slave trade begins as John Hawkins makes first voyage taking slaves from West Africa to the Caribbean

1564 Birth of William Shakespeare

1576 James Burbage founds the first purpose-built theatre in Shoreditch, London

1587 Execution of Mary, queen of Scots, Elizabeth's cousin and rival

1588 Defeat of Spanish Armada through combination of bad weather and English attacks; confirms Queen Elizabeth's almost sacred status in England; she delivers famous *'I have the heart and stomach of a king'* speech at Tilbury

1594 Shakespeare joins acting company of Chamberlain's Men (later King's Men under James I), with whom he will remain associated as shareholder and playwright throughout his career

1601 Rebellion led by earl of Essex, ex-favourite of Elizabeth; uprising fails but highlights unease over who is to be ageing Elizabeth's successor; around this time *Hamlet* is first performed

1603 Death of Elizabeth I; she names James VI of Scotland as her heir; he accedes to throne as James I

1616 Death of Shakespeare

The protests made no difference. Some new words survived, some died. The choice was made by the users of language even though the process must have been more instinctive than deliberate. Nor was there any obvious logic to the process, since it does not seem to have been based on the simplicity or the sound of a word.

Take the case of *impede* and *expede*, words deriving fom Latin and having related though opposed meanings. The verb *impede* has been part of English for more than 400 years, while the now obsolete *impedite* was recorded even earlier, in 1535. It might be assumed that the more cumbersome word, *impedite*, was compelled to give way to the shorter, more convenient one, *impede*. Perhaps so. Yet the opposite happened with *expede*, which is noted as a Scottish usage in the early 1500s but does not seem to have enjoyed much of a life. It is the synonymous but slightly more complicated *expedite* – in the sense 'to clear of difficulties' and so 'to hasten or make easier' – which has not merely survived but even become something of a commercial buzz-word.

Sometimes a word might be permitted to join the Elizabethan English lexicon even if others with identical or similar meanings already existed. This is obviously the case with examples such as *absurdity* or *assassin* or *external*, all of which are first recorded within a few years of each other in the mid-16th century. By contrast, other words for which there were synonyms did not last the course. For instance, terms deriving from the Latin *mittere* (to send) such as *transmit* and *remit* are standard modern vocabulary, yet *demit* was never allowed to gain a foothold by its pre-existing synonym, *dismiss*. It is rarely if ever possible to say why one word should flourish and another fail to catch on.

Whatever the arguments of the time over the eligibility of new words, there is no doubting that the imports into English between the late 1400s and the early 1600s – roughly speaking, the Renaissance period – added richness and variety to the language. The confidence of writers and others in using new vocabulary is paralleled by the growing confidence of England itself as the country emerged as a significant European power under Elizabeth I, and as explorers and commercial imperialists began to expand the very boundaries of the nation. From new words to new worlds ...

NEW WORLDS, OLD RELIGION

Despite the stress on the new and unfamiliar in the Elizabethan period, there were some legacies from earlier years and centuries that would not be banished. Many of these legacies were religious. It was under Elizabeth's father, Henry VIII (r.1509–47), that the English Church had broken away from Rome. During the reign of Mary I

The Book of Common Prayer, *first published in 1549 during the brief reign of Edward VI, was the first prayer book to contain the forms of service in English. The 1549 version was rapidly succeeded by a revision in 1552.*

(1553–8), Henry's daughter by his first wife Catherine of Aragon, there was a shortlived realignment of England with the Catholic Church. Even though Elizabeth I, daughter of Henry by his second wife Anne Boleyn, maintained a kind of truce with English Catholics after coming to the throne in 1558, she reverted to the Protestant dispensation of her father. The expression *Protestant* had itself come into English around the time of the Dissolution of the Monasteries (1536–9). It derived from a dissenting 'Protestation' made by German rulers against Catholic edicts.

At least in the early part of her reign, Elizabeth showed tolerance towards adherents of the 'old religion' (i.e., Catholicism), rejecting enquiry and persecution by saying that she had 'no desire to make windows into men's souls'. But later challenges to her power, ranging from the Catholic Mary, queen of Scots to the perpetual threat from Spain (realized most directly in the Armada of 1588) to various conspiracies against her life, hardened the queen's position. She was also facing dissent from the other side, from those who believed that religious reform in England had not gone far enough, a group generally referred to as the Puritans.

The term Puritan, from the Latin for 'pure' or 'purity' (*purus, puritas*), enters the language during the last quarter of the 16th century. The Puritans' campaign for a 'purification' of the church from excessive ceremony, as well as their austere morality and plain style of dress, made them obvious targets for mockery and the 'puritan' expression was more often used *about* them than *by* them. Minorities they may have been, and often derided, but the various dissenting factions that can be grouped under the Puritan banner were historically significant in two ways: they were a key component in the early settlement of America and they were the victors in the English Civil War.

Another significant consequence of Queen Elizabeth's religious allegiance was the revival of the *Book of Common Prayer*. This had been compiled by Thomas Cranmer, Archbishop of Canterbury for more than 20 years until he was burnt at the stake for heresy in 1556 under the Catholic Queen Mary. The Prayer Book was banned during Mary's brief reign but reissued in slightly modified form at the beginning of her half-sister's rule. The *Book of Common Prayer* counts as one of the most influential volumes in English history since, following another revision after the English Civil War (1642–51), it was used for Anglican services for more than three centuries. Designed to be spoken aloud as much as read, many of its phrasings and rhythms entered popular consciousness. This was not only because they were heard during regular weekly services but because words from the Prayer Book were used for the rites of baptism, marriage and burial. Even though the language of the liturgy has been modernized and church congregations in Britain are now only a small fraction of what they once were, expressions from the *Book of Common Prayer* have proved extraordinarily durable, as the brief selection below demonstrates.

KEYWORD

POLITICIAN

Politician first appears in English in Shakespeare's time and is an obvious spin-off from the Middle English adjective *politic*, originally equated with 'political' (as in the 'body politic') or meaning 'shrewd'. But *politic* gradually assumed the more dubious senses of 'crafty' or 'prudently self-serving'. *Politician* was a two-faced word from the start, with the respectable sense of 'one versed in the science of government' first recorded in 1588 but with the meaning 'schemer' occurring a year earlier. Shakespeare's use of the term is generally uncomplimentary. For King Lear, a *politician* is 'scurvy' (worthless), while Hamlet takes great delight in the graveyard scene in speculating that he might be looking at the skull of a *politician*, now tossed around by the irreverent grave-digger. Although in contemporary use *politician* often comes with an inbuilt sneer, this is a word that has become slightly more respectable – and respectful – over the centuries.

We have erred, and strayed from thy ways like lost sheep

We have left undone those things which we ought to have done; And we have done those things which we ought not to have done; And there is no health in us.

Give peace in our time, O Lord.

Deceits of the world, the flesh and the devil.

To have and to hold from this day forward, for better for worse, for richer for poorer, in sickness and in health, to love and to cherish, till death us do part.

In the midst of life we are in death.

Earth to earth, dust to dust, ashes to ashes.

Like the King James version of the Bible, first published in 1611, the *Book of Common Prayer* did not add to the resources of the English language in terms of fresh words. Indeed, it would have been surprising if a text intended to be solemn and authoritative had employed much new terminology. Rather, the style of the Prayer Book is vigorous and plain. The references are immediate and easily understood (*like lost sheep, dust to dust*). The language often rests on the oldest vocabulary, words deriving from Old English and not from Norman French or Latin. It is frequently monosyllabic. The excerpt above from the General Confession beginning '*We have left undone those things ...*' uses only one word of two syllables and not a single word that does not derive from Old English.

SHAKESPEARE — THE MYTH AND THE MAN

There is more mystery than fact in the life of William Shakespeare. Or perhaps it is the case that, because what is definitely known about him is quite ordinary, people feel the need to see shadows and create mysteries where none exist.

The biggest (and most unnecessary) mystery is over the authorship of the plays. For more than 200 years disputes have raged over whether Shakespeare actually penned the dramas that bear his name. Rival candidates range from the philosopher Francis Bacon (1561–1626) to aristocrats like the earl of Derby to the playwright Christopher Marlowe (1564–93). The fact that Marlowe was murdered in a brawl at a tavern in Deptford in 1593 – shortly before Shakespeare published his poem *Venus and Adonis* – is no obstacle to this theory, since it is claimed that Marlowe faked his death with the help of influential friends. To avoid trouble from the Privy Council over his blasphemy and declared atheism, Marlowe was spirited away to France after his 'death', only to return in secret to England to write 'Shakespeare's' plays while secluded in the country estate of an admirer.

The common factor in these alternative Shakespeares is that they were either better born or better educated than the man from Stratford-upon-Avon, whose father was (probably) a glove-maker and who, unlike the Cambridge-educated Christopher Marlowe, never went to university. There is more than a touch of snobbery in the assumption that a mere provincial would not have been capable of imagining scenes in the palaces of English kings or Venetian doges.

The key and undisputed facts in Shakespeare's life could be listed on a single sheet of paper and still leave room to spare: his birth (1564); his marriage (1582) to a woman who was eight years older than her teenage husband and who bore him three children; a sneering reference to him in a pamphlet which

Shakespeare's contemporary and fellow playwright Christopher Marlowe, to whom the former's works are sometimes attributed. Marlowe's great legacy to the language of English drama was his innovative use of the unrhymed ten-syllable line – blank verse – a form that Shakespeare also employed extensively in his plays.

Stock characters on stage at the Red Bull Playhouse in Clerkenwell, from a print of 1672. In Shakespeare's time, numerous theatres both public and private were established in London, catering for the great popular demand for plays. Theatres were closed by the Puritans in 1642, during Cromwell's Commonwealth, but reopened with the restoration of the monarchy in 1660.

is important only because it shows that by 1592 he was living and writing in London; his involvement with the Chamberlain's Men, later the King's Men, soon after their foundation in 1594, a connection that lasted throughout his career; his purchase of a large house in Stratford in 1597; his death in 1616. Seven years later John Heming and Henry Condell, two of Shakespeare's fellow shareholders in the King's Men, published the First Folio containing all but one of the plays that Shakespeare wrote.

Stories and rumours did circulate about Shakespeare during his life or shortly after his death, some of them faintly scandalous (including one that he was the father of a natural son by the beautiful wife of an Oxford innkeeper, the said son growing up to become Sir William Davenant, a playwright around the time of the Civil War). But none of the stories ever suggested that William Shakespeare was not the author he claimed to be or that he was any kind of trickster. Indeed, when he was referred to, it was in a tone of admiration touched with affection. John Aubrey (1626–97), living and writing only a couple of generations later, said of him: 'He was a handsome, well-shaped man: very good company, and of a very ready and pleasant smooth wit.'

A QUESTION OF CLASS

William Shakespeare used a range of styles of speech in his plays to suit characters across the social spectrum, from foppish courtiers through bluff soldiers to simple country-dwellers. But the dominant manner of his speakers is elevated and rhetorical. Even when it is not outright poetry, it is closer to poetry than it is to everyday speech. Devices that Shakespeare uses widely, such as alliteration, assonance, rhythm and the extensive use of metaphorical language, may be seen as more typical of verse than of prose.

This high style is appropriate to Shakespeare's settings and situations. In his plays he is fleshing out the lives of kings and queens, of princes and senators, bishops and generals. They are no different from other human beings in their passions and dilemmas but they are much more likely to be found debating in the council chamber than drinking in the local tavern. When Shakespeare does deal with working-class urban characters he tends to make them speak in prose and, although they may be quick-witted like the Roman citizens who appear in *Julius Caesar*, they are usually a bit ridiculous too. The social grouping that is notable by its absence in Shakespeare's writing is the middle-class, although he himself was an archetypal member of it.

It is the lower-class urban figures who are more reliably the object of Shakespeare's linguistic humour. The more sophisticated and complex a language, the more it can be played with, and by Shakespeare's time English was very sophisticated indeed. However, Shakespeare's jokes at the expense of his lower-class characters are somewhat one-note. They choose the wrong words, saying the opposite of what they mean. Dogberry, the watchman or constable in *Much Ado about Nothing*, makes remarks like 'O villain! thou wilt be condemned into everlasting redemption for this' and 'Does thou not suspect my place? Dost thou not suspect my years?' The grave-digger in *Hamlet*, generally a smart fellow capable of holding his own with the Prince of Denmark, mangles his Latin, coming out with *argal* when he should be saying *ergo* (the final term in a logical argument, meaning 'therefore'). Definitely a joke for the better-educated who were occupying the more expensive seats in the playhouse.

This is one aspect of Shakespeare that has not worn well, and the laughter that greets these remarks in the theatre tends to be respectful – or, as Dogberry would probably say, suspectful – rather than prolonged. But before we start accusing the playwright of being patronizing we should remember that a large

SHAKESPEARE AND DIALECT

Because Shakespeare rarely uses dialect or accent in his plays, the few examples tend to stand out. Like the introduction to a joke, the cast of *Henry V* includes among the minor characters a Scotsman, an Irishman and a Welshman, all serving as officers under the king at the time of Agincourt. Part of their function is to show that it is Britain, rather than England alone, which is fighting against the common enemy, France. Shakespeare reproduces something of their accented English, as when the Scots Captain Jamy says: 'By the mess, ere theise eyes of mine take themselves to slumber, aile do gud service, or I'll lig i' the grund for it.' He has some fun too with the volubility of Captain Fluellen, though at the same time he stresses the Welshman's good sense and bravery.

The only time Shakespeare gives us a full-blown version of a country dialect is in *King Lear*, when Edgar is protecting his father from being attacked. A typical passage from this brief scene runs: 'Nay, come not near th'old man, che vor ye [I warn you], or ise try whether your costard [head] or my ballow [cudgel] be the harder.' In fact, Edgar is in disguise – his father has been blinded and does not know him – and he is no closer to being a country yokel than is 'th'old man', the earl of Gloucester. Edgar's words are as stagy as the utterances of some forelock-tugging peasant in an old-time farce or whodunnit, a theatrical style commonly known as 'Mummerset'. When Shakespeare portrayed 'real' country characters he provided them with elevated, romantic diction, as with the lovelorn shepherd Silvius in *As You Like It*.

part of the audience in the Globe Theatre and elsewhere was made up of exactly those same urban working-class figures being guyed on stage. If the 'groundlings' didn't mind it, neither should we. Besides, they would always have had the manners and language of their betters to laugh at. Shakespeare was very ready to mock the elaborate diction employed by courtiers or the fantastically complicated excuses and justifications of the nobility, such as the speech from the Archbishop of Canterbury at the beginning of *Henry V* arguing that it is morally right to go to war against France. Here is a case of language being (mis)used in a style any contemporary political spin-doctor would recognize.

SHAKESPEARE'S LANGUAGE

Even though he is concentrating on the nobility, Shakespeare's poetry is wonderfully flexible and, one might say, mongrel. He draws on all the resources of English vocabulary, whether its roots are in Anglo-Saxon or Norman French or Latin or elsewhere. As an example, take a few lines from the 'Scottish' play, *Macbeth*. These occur after the tragic hero-villain has murdered his way to the throne, spurred on by the witches' prophecies, the taunting of his wife and his own ambition. Deep in blood, Macbeth begins to envy those he has put to death including Duncan, the late king. Halfway through the play, when he has had enough but cannot undo his crimes, he says to his wife:

> *Duncan is in his grave;*
> *After life's fitful fever he sleeps well;*
> *Treason has done his worst; nor steel, nor poison,*
> *Malice domestic, foreign levy, nothing*
> *Can touch him further.*

This is heartfelt stuff. It reveals Macbeth's despair, his longing for oblivion. To convey these emotions, Shakespeare uses a mixture of basic monosyllables (*grave, life, sleeps, steel*) and more complex expressions (*fitful fever, malice domestic, foreign levy*). The most simple terms of all are found in almost identical form in Old English: *is, in, he, his, him, after, well, can, further* have been with us for well over 1000 years. Slightly more complicated but still everyday words also derive from Old English: for example, *life* from OE *lif* and *grave* ultimately from the verb *grafen* meaning 'to dig'. The more elaborate words tend to be French-derived – *treason, poison, malice, levy* – or from Latin, in the case of *domestic*.

Shakespeare also added to the stock of English words. There are approximately 2000 terms that first appear in his plays. This does not mean that he invented them but a fair proportion – perhaps as much as three-quarters – are likely to be his own coinages. Some of these have fallen by the wayside (*adoptitious, aidance*) but others are long established (Macbeth was the first to talk of *assassination* and Othello refers to *accommodation*).

Even when Shakespeare was employing familiar English vocabulary, he had a genius for phrase-making. People who have never seen one of his plays regularly use expressions that he created, from 'cold comfort' to 'all Greek to me', from 'blinking idiot' to 'good riddance'. He has always been a good provider of titles for books and films, plays and poems. A short monologue from the end of *Macbeth* throws up several examples from the 20th century: *The Way to Dusty Death* (a thriller by Alistair MacLean), *Brief Candles* (short stories by Aldous Huxley), *The Sound and the Fury* (a literary novel by William Faulkner), *Out, Out* (a poem by Robert Frost). Finally, *All Our Yesterdays*, which comes from the same speech, was the title of an episode from *Star Trek* as well as the name of a long-running documentary series on British TV, and has been used at least once as a book title. All this from a single speech of 12 lines!

But Shakespeare's impact on English lies not only in individual words and phrases. He was also daring in the way he employed those words. He was and is famous for his puns and word-play – or notorious for them. In the 18th century Samuel Johnson, who was not afraid to take Shakespeare to task, said of him: 'A quibble [pun] was to him the fatal Cleopatra for which he lost the world and

> *His [Shakespeare's] mind and hand went together: And what he thought, he uttered with that easiness, that we have scarce received from him a blot.*
>
> JOHN HEMING & HENRY CONDELL *FIRST FOLIO* (1623)

was content to lose it'. There are whole books on Shakespeare's use of bawdy and *double entendres*. When Gratiano at the very end of *The Merchant of Venice* reflects that 'while I live, I'll fear no other thing/So sore as keeping safe Nerissa's ring', it is not only his betrothed's engagement gift he is talking about. Shakespeare did not shy away from using puns at moments of high tension, either. When Lady Macbeth plans to smear with blood the faces of the sleeping bodyguards of King Duncan, to make it appear that they are responsible for his murder, she snatches the bloody daggers from her husband's trembling hands and says: 'I'll gild the faces of the grooms withal/For it must seem their gilt.'

MASTER MANIPULATOR

Shakespeare made words do what he wanted them to do. Adjectives were turned into verbs: 'Thank me no thankings, nor proud me no prouds', says father Capulet to his daughter Juliet. Another father lecturing his daughter – Prospero to Miranda in *The Tempest* – coins the phrase 'the dark backward and abysm of time', casually transforming an adverb (*backward*) into a noun as he talks about the distant past. In Shakespeare's most famous play, Polonius warns his daughter Ophelia to keep away from Prince Hamlet by playing on a series of noun/verb meanings attached to the word *tender* (a bid made without payment, to treat with respect, to offer as a present) while, ironically, avoiding any genuine tenderness in his words to her.

Words were Shakespeare's business. Sometimes his characters might seem weary of them, as when Hamlet is asked what he is reading and replies, 'Words, words, words.' At other times words assume a magical force, as in the witches' spells in *Macbeth*. And in his last completed play, *The Tempest*, Shakespeare dealt head-on with the power of language, both for good and bad. Prospero, the one-time duke of Milan, has been exiled to the nameless island where the entire plays unfolds. Until his enemies are shipwrecked on the island, Prospero is alone with his daughter Miranda, and two semi-human creatures Ariel and Caliban. Caliban is 'a savage and deformed slave', an original inhabitant of the island, tutored and protected by Prospero until he attempted to rape Miranda. (All this has occurred before the play begins.) Given the power of speech by Prospero, Caliban announces:

> *You taught me language; and my profit on't*
> *Is, I know how to curse.*

And curse he does, both his master and his miserable condition. But Caliban is also gifted with some of the most strange and moving lines in the play:

A Victorian engraving of Caliban, Prospero and Miranda from The Tempest *(1610–11). This play is renowned for its lyrical, almost spellbinding language, as in Prospero's famous speech in Act IV:* 'The cloud-capp'd tow'rs, the gorgeous palaces,/ The solemn temples, the great globe itself,/Yea, all which it inherit, shall dissolve,/ And, like this insubstantial pageant faded,/Leave not a rack behind. We are such stuff/As dreams are made on; and our little life/Is rounded with a sleep.'

CODED SHAKESPEARE

If you open the King James version of the Bible and go to the forty-sixth psalm – the one beginning 'God is our refuge and strength, a very present help in trouble' – you will find that the forty-sixth word is 'shake'. If you go to the end of the same psalm and, leaving out the formulaic term 'Selah' which probably indicates a pause, count forty-six words the other way you reach 'spear'. Put the two words together and – abracadabra! – you get Shake-spear. Is this proof that the greatest English writer of all time had a hand in what has been called the most influential prose work of all time? Quite a few people think so. Is the clinching detail the fact that William Shakespeare had reached the age of 46 in 1610 when the finishing touches were being put to the Bible? Yes, the same people will seize on this as incontrovertible evidence.

More legends attach themselves to Shakespeare than any other great writer, perhaps because what little is known about him is so tantalizingly ordinary. Much time and ingenuity have been wasted in poring over his and others' words to prove all sorts of things about Shakespeare. The way in which the English language lends itself to word games, including codes and ciphers, has been very helpful to conspiracy theorists. For example, Shakespeare uses the word 'honorificabilitud-initatibus' in his early play *Love's Labour's Lost*.

Francis Bacon, one of several figures advanced by conspiracy theorists as the 'true' author of Shakespeare's plays.

Although it has a meaning to do with honour, it's a joke word thrown in by a clownish character. Yet 'honorificabilitudinitatibus' has been taken very seriously indeed by those who believe that Shakespeare's plays were written by the Elizabethan writer and philosopher Francis Bacon (1561–1626). For this long and nonsensical word can be rearranged to spell out, in a rough sort of Latin, *hi ludi, F.Baconis nati, tuiti orbi*, translating as 'these plays, the children of F. Bacon, are preserved for the world'. However, a quick search of an online anagram-finder shows that the word can also be rearranged in a further 37,000 ways, none of them making much sense.

Some believe that Shakespeare was a practising Catholic at a time when it was dangerous to adhere to the 'old religion' in Protestant England. One commentator has decoded his plays to suggest that references to being 'sunburned' or 'tanned', like his heroines Viola, Imogen and Portia, symbolize being close to God and so a true Catholic. The fact is that none of these theories can be proved in any meaningful sense, and that most of them are created by people who decide what they want to find before they go looking for 'evidence'. Even so, the theories – whether half-reasonable or completely crackpot – make for entertaining reading.

Be not afeard: the isle is full of noises,
Sounds and sweet airs, that give delight, and hurt not.
Sometimes a thousand twangling instruments
Will hum about mine ears, and sometime voices
That, if I then had waked after long sleep,
Will make me sleep again: and then, in dreaming,
The clouds methought would open and show riches
Ready to drop upon me that, when I waked,
I cried to dream again.

Shortly before this, in graphic language Caliban has been describing how Prospero might be murdered (his skull battered with a log, a stake driven through his paunch, his windpipe cut). One moment language is being deployed to provoke violence, the next to evoke a vision of paradise.

Shakespeare was pre-eminent in the Elizabethan/Jacobean period for his capacity to make language do things that were fresh and forward-looking. His rival and fellow playwright Ben Jonson (1572–1637) could write very generous praise of Shakespeare after he was dead – saying that he was comparable only to the Greek classical dramatists, that he was 'not of an age, but for all time' – but the man from Stratford was just one of dozens of playwrights and poets who were enriching the language with their coinages and linguistic daring.

THE ELIZABETHAN UNDERWORLD

There were other kinds of language apart from those uttered on the public stage. At the opposite end of the spectrum was the specialized slang used in the shadowy spaces occupied by vagrants, conmen and criminals. Yet the gap between the Shakespearean world and the criminal underworld was not so great, for all that Shakespeare's company performed regularly for Queen Elizabeth and was later under the patronage of King James I.

The Globe and other playhouses were situated on the south bank of the Thames, an area of London which was outside the control of the city authorities. In addition to the theatres, the district was host to a bevy of brothels and a pit in which bears and bulls were baited for public amusement, as well as several prisons. Much of the area was under the control of the bishop of Winchester, whose London residence was in Southwark, and the local prostitutes were accordingly known as 'Winchester geese'. No doubt many of the more prosperous inhabitants of north London who paid their one-penny fees to be rowed across the Thames or who came on foot across London Bridge experienced a pleasant *frisson* as they contemplated the dodgy *demi-monde* around them.

This interest in the culture of the underworld extended to its language, sometimes called thieves' cant. Almost all the words used then have dropped out of use but knowledge of them survives because, from the early 16th century onwards, writers interested in language set about collecting examples. Thomas Harman was a magistrate who produced a guide to the Elizabethan underworld.

He focused on one of the biggest criminal/social problems of the age, the large number of beggars and vagrants who practised violence or trickery to get money.

Harman and others defined such figures as the 'counterfeit crank', a trickster who feigned illness by covering himself with simulated sores or by chewing soap so as to produce foaming at the mouth in imitation of the 'falling sickness' or epilepsy. The idea was that the passer-by would be moved by pity to reach into his purse. The term *crank* does not describe an eccentric individual but is related to the modern German *krank* ('sick'). Other underworld characters in the rogues' gallery included the 'prigger of prancers' or horse-thief, the 'curber' or 'hooker', who carried a long hook with which to retrieve clothes from open windows, and the 'cutpurse' who literally cut the strings fastening the purse to the victim's belt. To cut the string, the thief might employ a 'horn-thumb', a sliver of sharpened horn attached to the thumb.

Once arrested and brought up before the 'Queer-cuffin' (Justice of the Peace), the felon might find himself doing time in a prison like the Counter near Cheapside. Here, if he could offer enough 'garnish' (bribes), he would be put in a cell in the Master's Side, where straw bedding and candle-stub illumination provided the highest grade of prison accommodation. When the money ran out or he could no longer prevail on his friends outside to supply him with more, the luckless prisoner would be shifted to the Knight's Ward, the middle grade of lodging, or put into the self-explanatory Hole.

The Elizabethans would have been very familiar with prisons, at least from the outside. There were three within a quarter of a mile of St Paul's alone. It is not surprising that the dictionaries of thieves' cant sold well. These underworld guides were ostensibly produced as warnings to the gullible – Thomas Harman's had the word *Caveat* (a Latin injunction meaning 'Take Care') in the title. Their purpose was also to give out titillating information about a level of society closed to law-abiding people, beginning a fascination with criminal slang and jargon that continues to the present day.

The Globe Theatre (left) and the bear-baiting pit on the disreputable south bank of the Thames at Southwark. This part of London was also home to the infamous Clink Prison, which gave us the slang phrase 'in the clink'.

The Queen's English at Tilbury

Despite the religious divisions within the country and the threats from outside, there was also a growing sense of national identity and self-confidence. The language boom was clear proof of the latter. England was no longer a sliver of an island on the edge of a continental landmass but an increasingly powerful kingdom, one with foreign ambitions that combined the imperial and the commercial. The principal continental threat came from Spain, in the vanguard of Catholic Europe and immensely wealthy because of its possessions in the New World. It was 30 years into Elizabeth's reign before the turning-point of the Armada but it was a decisive moment: Spain endured the worst naval defeat in its history while England seemed to have been preserved by some special act of divine providence.

In 1588, the year of the Spanish Armada, the nation also faced an invasion threat from forces under the command of the duke of Parma, an ally of King Philip of Spain. With thousands of troops massing on the other side of the English Channel, Queen Elizabeth ignored the advice of her councillors and went to the port of Tilbury on the Thames estuary to rally her troops. Wearing a silver breastplate, she delivered the most famous speech of her reign.

Her words were as calculated, as forceful and as brilliantly effective as anything later created by Shakespeare, whose playwriting career was, coincidentally, just beginning at around this time. The best-known part of the queen's speech includes the lines:

> *I know I have the body of a weak and feeble woman, but I have the heart and stomach of a king, and a king of England too, and think it foul scorn that Parma or Spain, or any prince of Europe, should dare invade the borders of my realm; to which, rather than any dishonour shall grow by me, I myself will take up arms …*

As if to emphasize her through-and-through Englishnesss, Elizabeth employed a majority of expressions that come ultimately from Anglo-Saxon, although with a smattering of Latin- and French-derived terms (*multitudes, concord, valour*). There are several examples of those couplings of near-equivalent or mirror expressions that make English such a richly expansive language: *faithful and loving, strength and safeguard, recreation and disport, weak and feeble, noble or worthy.*

When she smiled it was pure sunshine, that everyone did choose to bask in, if they could: but anon came a storm from a sudden gathering of clouds, and the thunder fell in wondrous manner on all alike.

Sir John Harrington (1539–1613) on Elizabeth I

A contemporary painting on wood shows Queen Elizabeth I and her retinue arriving at Tilbury. In the background, a great conflagration engulfs the ships of the Spanish Armada.

Robert Dudley, the earl of Leicester, had ordered the speech to be taken down by one of the queen's chaplains and copies of it were widely circulated. In its defiant and stirring rhetoric, Elizabeth's call to arms is the 16th-century equivalent of Winston Churchill's famous broadcasts during the Second World War, which use a similar mixture of the simple and the high-flown. For Elizabeth's hearers – and later for the readers of the circulated speech – the power of language and the appeal to patriotism are fused. Dudley was in no doubt of the impact of the Tilbury oration which, he considered, 'had so inflamed the hearts of her good subjects, as I think the weakest among them is able to match the proudest Spaniard that dares land in England'.

THE
HOLY
BIBLE,

Conteyning the Old Teſtament,

AND THE NEW:

Newly Tranſlated out of the Originall
tongues: & with the former Tranſlations
diligently compared and reuiſed, by his
Maieſties ſpeciall Comandement.

Appointed to be read in Churches.

Imprinted at London by Robert
Barker, Printer to the Kings
moſt Excellent Maieſtie.

ANNO DOM. 1611.

In contrast to the relative stability of Elizabeth's reign, the next 80 or so years were a period of great turmoil. The 17th century brought the English Civil Wars (1642–51), the execution of Charles I, Cromwell's Commonwealth, the restoration of the monarchy under Charles II, the end of Stuart rule and the 'Glorious Revolution', ushered in by William III.

FAITH AND SCIENCE

Elizabeth's successor, James I (James VI of Scotland), was a very different ruler from England's Virgin Queen, but like her he was preoccupied with image, both on a personal and a national level. As a Scottish incomer, he was particularly sensitive to questions of nationality and the boundaries of the realm. He manoeuvred for a full political union between England and Scotland but could not whip up enough enthusiasm for it in either country. In common with other monarchs from the Middle Ages onwards, James was fascinated by the legends of King Arthur. On his accession, he had wanted himself styled king of Great Britain, wishing to be seen, like Arthur perhaps, as a monarch embracing the whole circle of the island, even if in name only.

James had succeeded to the Scottish throne in 1567 at the age of one when his mother Mary, queen of Scots, had been deposed. He would have had no conscious memory of his mother – Mary saw him for the last time when he was scarcely ten months old. James was baptized a Catholic but given a Protestant coronation, another event which he could hardly have recalled. His education was at the hands of severe Scottish Presbyterian governors. He later described his predicament, a privileged but poignant one, when he wrote: 'I was alane, without fader or moder, brither or sister, king of this realme, and heir apperand of England.'

As he grew up, James found happiness in two, seemingly opposed, pastimes. He loved hunting. And he loved reading, writing and intellectual debate. He was a word-man, who dictated royal proclamations himself rather than merely signing them. James composed poetry, he translated the Psalms, he wrote a guide on kingship for his son Prince Henry and a book about witchcraft, he even penned an anonymously published

Title page of the first edition of the King James Bible *(1611).*
A prime concern of the 47 translators was to produce a text that
would sound dignified and authoritative when read in public.

pamphlet on the 'shameful imbecility' of smoking in which he pointed out the expensive and addictive quality of the habit (*A Counterblast to Tobacco*). His royal status allowed him to pursue these activities to the full. He supposedly spent about half his waking life out hunting. Much of the rest was given over to more scholarly pursuits. His authority and his authentic intellectual gifts meant that his opinions were listened to and his ideas taken up.

James I was not some ideal philosopher-king. Although he was welcomed with enthusiasm in England after the eclipse of Elizabeth's final years, his treatment of his male favourites and his extravagance were soon cause for comment ('The King [...] dwelleth on good looks and handsome accoutrements') and there were serious disputes with Parliament later in his reign. But in the beginning all was, almost, sweetness and light. So it is no coincidence that the start of James's reign in England in 1603 sees the most significant linguistic enterprise of the entire period: the proposal for a new translation of the Bible.

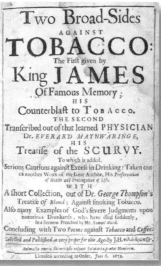

King James's A Counterblast to Tobacco *(1616). In this polemical tract, the king inveighed against the 'filthy novelty' of smoking, which he condemned as:* 'loathsome to the eye, hateful to the nose, harmful to the brain, dangerous to the lungs, and in the black stinking fume thereof nearest resembling the horrible stygian smoke of the pit that is bottomless'.

THE BEGINNING OF THE BIBLE

There had been several translations of the Bible into English before the one authorized by King James, including the ground-breaking version done under the direction of John Wyclif (see page 67). The book that had been used for most of Elizabeth I's reign was the *Bishops' Bible* (1568), so called because the translation was the work of 14 bishops. The *Bishops' Bible* was officially approved and, for that reason, didn't please everyone. For example, it was not to the taste of those anti-authority Puritans who preferred the translation made by English Calvinists in Geneva in the 1550s, a translation whose small-printed pages would be found in private homes rather than public churches, and whose numerous annotations took sideswipes at 'tyrants'.

In the closing decades of the 16th century the divisions within the church had clarified, with the Puritan tendency well entrenched against a more traditional majority that retained links with the older Catholic forms of worship. Of course there were extremists on both sides but such people were beyond the pale. Those Catholics who went so far as to plot against the state would, after the 1605 Gunpowder Plot, be hunted down. Some of those Puritan Separatists who believed only in the authority of Scripture and turned their backs on every aspect of church hierarchy would soon make the Atlantic crossing to establish a new order of things in America. But at the centre of the English Church there remained an uneasy alliance of moderates from both wings.

James I had some experience of extremes. The son of an executed Catholic but brought up Protestant by devout adherents to the Scottish Kirk, James had responded by searching for the middle way. He made no secret of his open-mindedness. Both religious wings, radical and conservative, took the opportunity of a fresh incumbent on the throne to launch their petitions for the future of the church.

A conference was convened in 1604 at Hampton Court Palace with the king in the (velvet-covered) chair. Apart from the fact that James naturally favoured the pro-monarchist and traditionalist side, it wasn't exactly an equal match. The bishops, led by John Whitgift, Archbishop of Canterbury, thoroughly outnumbered the four representatives of the Puritan party. On the other hand, the two sides had more in common than they had dividing them. They were all part of the establishment. The 'radicals' were churchmen too, and two of them were heads of Oxford or Cambridge colleges.

Although the Puritans were in the minority and on the defensive, it was one of them who suggested a new translation of the Bible from its original Hebrew, Greek and Latin sources. The king was interested. He claimed that he had never yet seen a 'well translated' Bible. He particularly disliked the Geneva version because of its 'dangerous and traitorous' annotations. He wanted a plain translation with no editorializing, as it would now be called. With his deep interest in study, King James demanded that 'the best learned of both the Universities' be involved, as well as the bishops. Then there would be two more levels to go through – the Privy Council and the king himself – to ensure that everything was approved.

When the king commanded, action followed quickly. Within six months six companies of translators had been established and given a portion of the Bible to work on. They were based at Westminster, Oxford and Cambridge, two companies to each centre. The number of translators in any single group varied between seven and eleven. With a single exception (Sir Henry Savile, the provost of Eton), all of them had taken holy orders. The learned and pious Lancelot Andrews – reputed to spend five hours at prayer every morning – was director of the Westminster company which was responsible for the first books of the Old Testament (Genesis to 2 Kings). The largest group was the Oxford company, which had the task of translating the Gospels, the Acts of the Apostles and the Book of Revelation.

The translators relied heavily on previous translations, including the *Bishops' Bible* and the version produced by William Tyndale in the 1520s. They did not regard their job as producing something new since they were, after all, dealing with the word of God. In the preface to the first published edition (1611) Miles Smith, the Bishop of Gloucester and a member of one of the Oxford companies of translators, compared their task to the polishing of gold so that it should shine more brightly.

When the individual companies had done their work, a committee of their representatives gathered in London in 1610 to weigh up the results. They sifted

FAITH AND SCIENCE

1603 Accession of King James I of England (James VI of Scotland)

1604 New translation of the Bible is commissioned

1605 Gunpowder Plot

1611 First edition of the *King James Bible* published

1616 Death of William Shakespeare in Stratford-upon-Avon

1628 William Harvey publishes his theory of circulation of the blood

1642 Civil War breaks out in England after King Charles I tries to arrest his parliamentary critics; first battle between Roundheads and Cavaliers at Edgehill

1649 Charles I executed at Whitehall in London; under Oliver Cromwell England becomes republic; Cromwell conducts ruthless campaign in Ireland

1653 Cromwell becomes Lord Protector and assumes king-like authority

1658 Death of Cromwell

1660 Charles II proclaimed king; return of British monarchy

1666 Fire of London; most of City area destroyed

1667 John Milton publishes epic poem *Paradise Lost*

1689 Accession of William III of Orange and his wife Mary as joint king and queen

KEYWORD

CABAL

Cabal enters English in the early 17th century via French from a Hebrew word, originally *qubbalah* and now *kabbala* (or any one of five other variants). *Kabbala* describes the mystical teaching and interpretations of Jewish rabbis and, by extension, any secret doctrine. Appropriately for an era that witnessed the Gunpowder Plot and the outbreak of the English Civil war, a *cabal* is a small group of intriguers. It is a term with shady associations, although in the reign of Charles II (1660–85) it was applied to what would now be known as a council or kitchen cabinet. Curiously – as was noted at the time – the initial letters of the names or titles of those who made up the inner council which signed a treaty with France in 1672 formed the word *cabal* (Clifford, Arlington, Buckingham, Ashley, Lauderdale).

through the text again, and over the course of about nine months decided on the best and final form of words. Judging the authorized version purely as a literary artefact and leaving aside its religious content – a viewpoint that the translators would not have accepted – this is perhaps the only time in history that a masterpiece has been composed by committee.

The language the revisers chose was often slightly old-fashioned and elevated, partly because they were turning towards translations that had been made over the previous century but also because they wanted the English of their Bible to be distinct from the English of everyday use. The sacred words had to be understood by ordinary people when they were read aloud in church every Sunday but those same words had to be imposing, they had to move through the Sabbath air with assurance, even majesty. Nor was the majesty God's alone. This Bible was the divine word but it was also a royal production, initiated by the king, approved by him, fulsomely dedicated to him.

The result of the translators' labours was a book that has endured for more than four centuries. The *King James Bible* has been replaced by more up-to-date translations such as the *New English Bible* (1970), but whenever a comparison is required for a new translation, it is almost always the King James one that is cited as the template, for its musicality, its dignity and grace. It is still part of the fabric of English, as is shown by the very brief selection below of sentences and phrases from it.

> And God said, Let there be light: and there was light;
> And they heard the voice of the Lord God walking in the garden in the cool
>   of the day.
> A land flowing with milk and honey.
> Grind the faces of the poor.

The English Bible, a book which, if everything in our language should perish, would alone suffice to show the whole extent of its beauty and power.

EDINBURGH REVIEW, 1828

Repent ye, for the kingdom of heaven is at hand.
Greater love hath no man than this, that a man lay down his life for his friends.
Where your treasure is, there will your heart be also.
The wages of sin is death.
No man can serve two masters.

MICROSCOPES AND TELESCOPES

The 17th century began with the greatest English translation of the Bible ever produced, a version whose language and cadences were to influence English for hundreds of years to come. The same century that witnessed this linguistic triumph of faith also saw what many might regard as the antithesis of faith, the rise of science. There had of course been scientific investigation in earlier centuries but it was only in the early 1600s that science emerged in a style and with a vocabulary that is recognizably modern. It should not be assumed that the scientists and philosophers of the 17th century were anti-religion. If anything, the reverse was true. They were trying to uncover the laws of nature but they saw those laws as being, essentially, created in the first place by God.

Nevertheless, scientific research required individuals with the genius to see further than others and, often, the daring to challenge received opinion and dogma. This was the century in which Galileo Galilei (1564–1642) built a telescope and faced the Inquisition for his pains before being barred by the Church from further research. At about the same time the German astronomer

Galileo demonstrating his telescope to the Doge and senators of Venice, from a fresco in the Museum of Zoology and Natural History (La Specola) in Florence. After being forced by the Inquisition to recant his defence of the heliocentric view of the universe, in which the Earth orbits the Sun, Galileo is reputed to have muttered the defiant rejoinder: Eppur si muove! *('And yet it does move!').*

Johannes Kepler (1571–1630) was formulating his three laws of planetary motion. In 1628 William Harvey (1578–1657), a physician at St Bartholomew's in London, published his discovery of the circulation of the blood. In 1651 the Italian astronomer Giovanni Riccioli (1598–1671) mapped the moon and gave names to its features. Isaac Newton (1642–1727) measured the orbit of the moon, constructed a reflecting telescope and in *Principia Mathematica* (1687) established gravity as the force behind the movement of the planets.

The appetite for science and the hunger for discovery extended to the very top. King Charles II (1630–85) appointed John Flamsteed (1646–1719) as the first Astronomer Royal and funded the building of Greenwich Observatory to rectify: 'the tables of the motions of the heavens, and the places of the fixed stars, so as to find out the so much-desired longitude of places for the perfecting of the art of navigation.' The interest in research and experimentation was reflected in the work of writers, and hence in their language. Ben Jonson penned a satirical play, *The Alchemist* (1610), in which he parodied scientific jargon and mocked the pseudo-science of alchemy and its quest for the magic substance which would transform base metals into gold. In his *Advancement of Learning* (1605) and *Novum Organum* (1620), the philosopher Francis Bacon proposed a new means of studying the world through observation and inductive reasoning (i.e. working from the particular to the general). Experiment should take the place of ungrounded speculation.

The word *experiment* once had the same sense as *experience*. Now the two terms point in opposite directions, *experience* referring to what is already known and therefore familiar, and *experiment* to what has yet to be discovered through trial and error. Increasingly, during the 17th century, *experiment* is to be found only in its modern sense of 'testing a hypothesis'. Indeed, Francis Bacon died in 1626 as the result of an unfortunate scientific test.

According to a story told by the biographer John Aubrey (1626–97), the philosopher/scientist was travelling by carriage on a winter's day towards Highgate (then a village just north of London). Looking out at the snow-covered ground, he suddenly wondered whether extreme cold might be as effective as salt in preserving meat. Bacon got out of his carriage, bought a hen from a woman and, after asking her to kill and gut it, stuffed the carcass with snow. Whatever happened to the chicken, the experiment so chilled Bacon that he had to be taken to a fellow-aristocrat's house in Highgate where, after being put into 'a damp bed that had not been layn-in in about a yeare before', he caught an even worse cold and died within a few days.

The poet John Milton (1608–74) was also stirred by scientific advances. When travelling in Italy as a young man he went out of his way to acknowledge an aged inhabitant of Florence: 'There it was that I found and visited the famous Galileo, grown old, a prisoner to the Inquisition, for thinking in astronomy otherwise than the Franciscan and Dominican licensers thought.' Nearly 30 years later, when Milton was composing his monumental work *Paradise Lost*, he paid tribute to Galileo and his 'optic glass' (telescope) when he refers to:

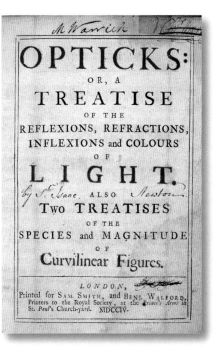

First published in 1704, Isaac Newton's Optics *was written 'not to explain the Properties of Light by Hypotheses, but to propose and prove them by reason and experiment', a clear statement of the new empirically based 'scientific method'.*

JOHN MILTON AND PANDAEMONIUM

The English pamphleteer and poet John Milton (1608–74) was deeply involved in the political life of his time. A strenuous supporter of republicanism, he was given a government post by Oliver Cromwell and briefly put under arrest when Charles II was restored to the throne. But his legacy and influence lie in his poetry, in particular the 12-book *Paradise Lost* (1667), an epic narrative of the story of Adam and Eve in the Garden of Eden, from the Book of Genesis.

To trace out the origins of the human Fall, Milton went back to the earlier fall of Satan from Heaven and as a result much of *Paradise Lost* is set in Hell. It is visualized as a place of horrific grandeur. Milton coined the word *Pandaemonium* to describe the great edifice which the devils construct, half palace, half city. He drew on two Greek words (*pan*=all + *daimon*=spirit), signifying that this was the site for all the devils to gather. So *pandaemonium* came to signify a 'centre of wickedness' and then simply a 'scene full of noise and confusion'. Perversely, the original *Pandaemonium* in Milton's version of hell is well-organized and relatively peaceful, as it is where the fallen angels hold a council to discuss how they can get revenge against God.

Milton was a very influential figure in English literature, arguably second only to Shakespeare. His poetry is elaborate, difficult and musical. It is strewn with references to the classical and biblical worlds, particularly in *Paradise Lost* where he was trying to forge an elevated style fitting the unique subject matter. He uses words in their older Latinate senses (*horrid* for 'bristling', *promiscuous* for 'mixed'). He creates phrases from words that carry contradictory associations: *sad cure, precious bane, darkness visible*. His work has given rise to a host of book titles, from the now unfamiliar *Look Homeward, Angel* (1929; Thomas Wolfe) to *Eyeless in Gaza* (1936; Aldous Huxley) to *His Dark Materials* (1995–2000; Philip Pullman's trilogy of fantasy books). He gave us *trip the light fantastic* and, more seriously, *They also serve who only stand and wait*. And if anyone has ever wondered why, in a very well-known expression, the noun and the adjective appear the wrong way round, the answer is to be found in the last line of Milton's poem *Lycidas: Tomorrow to fresh woods and pastures new*.

... the moon, whose orb
Through optic glass the Tuscan artist views
At evening from the top of Fesole
Or in Valdarno, to descry new lands,
Rivers or mountains in her spotty globe.

Given all this scientific activity and the way in which it permeated culture in general, it is not surprising that we find a great number of technical expressions entering the language during the 17th century. Some of these were created from scratch, while others simply took existing terms and added an extra definition.

Gas was modelled on the Greek word 'chaos' and, unusually, the word can actually be attributed to an individual, the Flemish scientist J.B.van Helmont (1577–1644). *Atmosphere* is another example of a new word and was first used to describe the 'gaseous envelope' which surrounds a heavenly body before it acquired its metaphorical sense of the 'predominant mood' of a place. Like *gas* and *atmosphere*, the *microscope* and *telescope* are drawn from Greek and make their first appearance in the mid-17th century. *Refraction* already had a literal, Latin-derived definition of 'breaking up' but in the early 1600s it acquired a scientific application to describe the way in which rays of light were bent as they passed from one medium to another. Similarly, *spectrum* originally had the sense of 'apparition' or 'spectre' before it was used to characterize the splitting-up of light into a band of colours.

The *barometer* was invented in 1643, and the word created from two Greek terms meaning 'weight' and 'measure'. Latin provided the word *pendulum;* in 1657 the Dutch scientist Christiaan Huygens designed the first pendulum clock (the same year, incidentally, that drinking chocolate was introduced into London and the culture of the coffee-house began). This period also saw the earliest use of *corpuscle* to mean a 'minute body' and the first accurate description of the oxygen-bearing red corpuscles in the bloodstream. William Harvey's earlier description of the principles of (blood) circulation in the body now enabled the same word to be applied to the movement of sap in plants, and eventually the term would be used for all sorts of movement, from newspapers to road traffic. Interestingly, the free and unimpeded flow of such things – whether of information, vehicles, goods, even people – is implicitly seen as a symptom of social health.

In this way the scientific or technological terms of the 17th century broke out of their original contexts and took on additional meanings, often metaphorical. The process goes on to the present day. The invention of the video-recorder in the early 1970s put expressions such as *fast-forward, rewind* and *put on hold* into general circulation. And, of course, the largest contributors of technological terms that have infiltrated the English language in recent years have been the computer and the internet, with expressions like *hard-wired, multitask* and *interactive* being used for all sorts of attitudes and activities.

Ah! my old Friend Dr Harvey – I knew him right well. He made me sitt by him 2 or 3 hours together in his meditating apartment discoursing. Why, had he been stiffe, starcht, and retired, as other formall Doctors are, he had known no more than they. From the meanest person, in some way or other, the learnedst man may learn something.

JOHN AUBREY (1626–97) ON WILLIAM HARVEY, WHO DISCOVERED THE CIRCULATION OF THE BLOOD

SAMUEL PEPYS'S DIARY

The Jacobean era began with the translation of the Bible, which was both a landmark in and a key influence over the development of the English language. Under another Stuart ruler, Charles II (1630–85), a very different style of writing – secular, informal and confessional – began to evolve. Samuel Pepys (1633–1703) was Secretary to the Admiralty and served a term as president of the Royal Society (for the Promotion of Natural Knowledge), a distinguished and still continuing scientific club. But Pepys is remembered and read today as the author of the famous diary that he kept between 1660 and 1669. Written in a kind of shorthand code, it was not deciphered until the early 19th century and a full edition was not published until the 20th century. Pepys's easy-going, even rambling style is shown in this typical passage, for 23 February 1667:

> All the morning at the office, and at noon home to dinner, and thence with my wife and Deb. to the King's House, to see 'The Virgin Martyr', the first time it hath been acted a great while: and it

A page from the diaries of Samuel Pepys. These are an invaluable historical document, giving eye-witness accounts of momentous events like the Plague and the Great Fire of London.

is mighty pleasant; not that the play is worth much, but it is finely acted by Becke Marshall. But that which did please me beyond any thing in, the whole world was the wind-musique when the angel comes down, which is so sweet that it ravished me, and indeed, in a word, did wrap up my soul so that it made me really sick, just as I have formerly been when in love with my wife; that neither then, nor all the evening going home, and at home, I was able to think of any thing, but remained all night transported, so as I could not believe that ever any musick hath that real command over the soul of a man as this did upon me: and makes me resolve to practice wind-musique, and to make my wife do the like.

Pepys's Diaries were first published in expurgated form because of the mildly explicit nature of some of the material. The Deb referred to above was Deb Willett, a servant girl whom Pepys got rid of at his wife's insistence after she came into the room to find him 'embracing the girl con my hand sub su coats [sic]' – as well as using code, Pepys resorted to foreign words when the subject got particularly embarrassing.

For the history of modern English and its global triumph, the key moment occurs towards the end of the 16th century. The tentative beginnings of English imperial and commercial expansion saw the founding of small colonies on the eastern seaboard of America. These, together with the arrival of the Pilgrims, gave English a toehold in the New World. But the language of these settlers was not guaranteed to become the dominant language of the future United States. The Spanish had arrived there before the Elizabethan colonists, and there were French, Dutch and (later) German speakers who occupied substantial swathes of territory.

A NEW-FOUND LANGUAGE

The earliest English-speaking settlers of America arrived before the Pilgrims made their famous 1620 landfall at Plymouth, Massachusetts, from the *Mayflower*. At the end of the previous century, Sir Walter Raleigh (*c*.1552–1618) had helped to establish a colony at Roanoke on the coast of North Carolina. It was so shortlived and its fate so mysterious that it became known as the 'Lost Colony': when one of its founders returned from England after a three-year absence, almost the only trace of it left were the baffling letters 'CRO' carved on a tree. There was a more successful settlement in Virginia at Jamestown, named for the new English king. (The state itself had been named after James's predecessor, Elizabeth I, the Virgin Queen.)

Colonizing the New World was always a perilous undertaking. In the 18 years of settlement in Virginia up to 1625, the survival rate among the colonists was about one in seven. No doubt many of them would have died had they stayed in England, but these fresh territories were hardly a paradise. The Virginians and other colonists were essentially adventurers, brave or desperate enough to be seeking a new start in

The Pilgrims at Plymouth: The First Sermon Ashore, 1621, by the American artist Jean Leon Gerome Ferris (1863–1930). Sheer force of numbers finally saw English assert itself as the dominant language of the emergent United States.

a New World. They would not necessarily have been motivated by the Pilgrims' desire for religious freedom.

THE PILGRIMS

Even at this early stage, however, the New World was not completely unfamiliar with what was to become its dominant language, as the *Mayflower* settlers discovered when they were greeted by a friendly Native American who already knew some English, probably acquired from fishermen out of the European fleets that were increasingly common on the northeastern seaboard of America.

The style of language that the religious separatists carried across the Atlantic was a reflection of their Puritan outlook. It was simple, vigorous and clear. An example is the following excerpt from *Mourt's Relation: A Journal of the Pilgrims in Plymouth,* written by two of the principal settlers in the year following that 1620 Plymouth landfall. A party of armed men is exploring the inland area and also looking for signs of the Indian presence. The spelling has not been modernized but the meaning is about as transparent as it could be:

> *When Wee had marched five or six miles into the Woods, and could find no Signes of any people, wee returned againe another way, and as we came into the plaine ground, wee found a place like a grave, but it was much bigger and longer than any wee had yet seene. It was also covered with boords, so as wee mused what it should be, and resolved to dig it up; where we found, first a Mat, and under that a faire Bow, and there another Mat, and under that a Boord about three quarters long, finely carved and painted, with three Tynes, or broches on the top, like a Crown; also betweene the Mats we found Bowles, Trayes, Dishes, and such like Trinkets; at length wee came to a faire new Mat, and under that two Bundles, the one bigger, the other lesse, we opened the greater and found in it a great quantitie of fine and perfect Red Powder, and in it the bones and skull of a man. The skull had fine yellow haire still on it, and some of the flesh unconsumed; there was bound up with a Knife, a Packneedle, and two or three old Iron things. It was bound up in a Saylers Canvas Casacke [cassock], and a payre of Cloth Breeches; the Red Powder was a kind of Embaulment [embalming substance], and yeelded a strong, but not offensive smell; It was as fine as any Flower.*

Most striking here is the reckless curiosity of the group, although it should be said that they had enough tact to replace the bones that they dug up. The only linguistic aspect that the reader may notice is the capitalization of many of the nouns, a habit that persisted in written English well into the 18th century, but which is now employed only for proper nouns.

There are some usages carried across by these early American settlers that persist in contemporary American English. The most familiar is *gotten*, which was already dying out in British English (Shakespeare uses it five times in his plays but more frequently writes *got*), even though this Middle English form still clings on in the old-fashioned *ill-gotten* and *begotten*. *Fall*, deriving from Old English, is universal in the United States but was long ago replaced in British English by *autumn*, from French. Other survivals include *mad*, primarily used in the sense of 'angry', *hog* for 'pig' and *rooster* for 'cock'. But these original expressions are few and far between, and it is a myth that some remote parts of America – the Appalachian region of Virginia and the Carolinas are often cited – preserve the speech of 16th-century England.

HOW THE COLONISTS GOT THEIR WORDS

The colonists required new words to describe features that were foreign to them: unfamiliar birds and trees, unknown plants and animals, even strange but man-made objects. The most obvious solution was to adapt the existing terms used by the native Americans who were already living on the eastern seaboard, the very tribes who were to be displaced by the settlers in the long run. The related languages spoken by these peoples, languages known collectively as Algonquian, were complicated for the new arrivals to grasp. Although some expressions like *wikiwam* or *tamahuk* made a fairly easy transition into English, others tended to get whittled away like twigs until they emerged in a form that could be comfortably handled. This applied to the tribal names themselves, with *Tsalaki* becoming *Cherokee*, for example, or *Mohowawog* turning to *Mohawk*.

John Smith (1580–1631), leader of the Jamestown settlement, noted down the animal name *raughroughouns* which turned into the *raccoon*. Other creatures Anglicized from the Indian include the skunk (*segonku*), woodchuck (*otchock*) and moose (in fact from the even simpler Narrangansett *moos*). An exception seems to have been those birds' names that were derived from their calls, such as *bobwhite* and *whip-poor-will*. The same John Smith mentioned above is supposed to have transcribed the Algonquian word for 'tribal adviser' as *Caw-cawaassough*, which eventually emerged as the distinctively US *caucus* (although there is an alternative etymology from 'caulkers' meetings', caulkers being workmen who made ships watertight). One contemporary Native American

C. Smith taketh the King of Pamavnkee prisoner. –1608.

Captain John Smith of the Jamestown settlement taking the Powhatan Confederacy chief Opechancanough prisoner. The natives of Virginia and the English colonists increasingly came into conflict as more settlers arrived.

NATIVE AMERICAN METAPHORS

As well as borrowing and simplifying Native American names for plants and animals, English also adopted various ideas and phrases for metaphorical purposes. Only a couple are literal. *Indian file* means 'one by one', while an *Indian summer* refers to a patch of good weather late in the year and derives from the fine Octobers in northeast America – although the phrase also carries the figurative sense of a period of happiness or achievement coming towards the end of a person's life.

Generally, terms deriving from Indian culture were adopted for their graphic quality, sometimes worn down through years of use, as with *burying the hatchet, going on the warpath, happy hunting ground* or *keeping one's ear to the ground*. Others have retained a certain sharpness: *speaking with forked tongue* or *scalp-hunting* (i.e., going after trophies in a single-minded fashion) and *scalper* (US slang for ticket-tout) or *sending out smoke signals*. Yet other terms, perhaps more familiar from old-style Westerns than real life, have distinctly disparaging or patronizing overtones: *squaw, papoose* (Native American baby), *putting on warpaint* (i.e., make-up), *paleface, fire-water* (for any strong alcoholic drink and supposedly a translation of an Algonquian word).

Some Native American-derived terms are current in US English but have never crossed the Atlantic. A *potlatch*, for instance, originally a winter festival, can be applied to any gift-giving occasion/feast. *Caucus* is a key concept in US politics but has almost no resonance in British English. *Mugwump* is even more unfamiliar: a Natick word connoting 'great chief', it came to mean a political independent or someone who is politically stand-offish. *Totem*, however, has acquired widespread metaphorical value in recent years, particularly in offshoots like *totemic* with the sense of 'emblematic', 'symbolic'. It appears too in the phrase 'low man on the totem pole', indicating someone at the bottom of the hierarchy, even though the lowest position on a real totem-pole was actually quite an important one.

commentator has observed that the adoption of 'caucus' shows that the European colonists had little experience with genuinely democratic institutions, and were required to look towards native forms of self-government when they wanted a term for a consultative body.

Even in the relatively early years of European settlement, a linguistic pattern was being set by the country's openness to new arrivals who were not of Anglo-Saxon stock. It should be remembered too that immigrants came not merely from particular Puritan enclaves of England like East Anglia but also from the descendants of the Scots who had been encouraged from 1609 to settle in Ulster by James I (as a method of destroying the indigenous Gaelic culture). Beginning a century later, what was eventually an estimated 2 million Scots-Irish made the longer voyage across the Atlantic. Supposedly, their aggressive and even anarchic streak of independence made them good frontiersmen.

OTHER LINGUISTIC INFLUENCES

The English spoken by the *Mayflower* pilgrims and their descendants, as well as the other 16th- and 17th-century colonists, was to be augmented by the languages of other European incomers. The Dutch settlers were fairly small in number but had a disproportionate effect on the language, probably because they were concentrated around the New York area. New York was called New Amsterdam before the British seized it in 1664 but, even though the city changed its title, the Dutch left their name-stamp on the boroughs of Harlem, Brooklyn and the Bronx. Quintessentially American terms such as *cookie, stoop* (for front-door step) and *waffle* all have Dutch origins. The innocuous-sounding and outmoded exclamation *Poppycock!* comes from the not-so-clean Dutch *pappekak* ('soft dung').

The French impact was less marked in what subsequently became the United States of America, although it was fundamental to the development of Canada, which is still officially bilingual. A few current US terms – such as *picayune* and *jambalaya*, both from Provençal roots – can be traced back to the French-dominated region around New Orleans, capital of Louisiana (named after King Louis XIV, just as the capital was named for Louis' brother, the duc d'Orléans).

The Cajun dialect, sometimes considered as a separate language, originated from the forced deportation by the British of the inhabitants of a French colony (Acadia) in the area around Nova Scotia in the 1750s. They settled in the bayous of Louisiana, the southern coastal area of creeks and marshes where there is still a sprinkling of French place names. The unromantic source of *bayou* may be the French for 'entrails' (*boyau*) and, if so, was presumably suggested by the winding waterways of the region. An alternative source is the Choctaw word *bayuk,* meaning 'little river'.

Similarly, the effect of German was fairly localized. Early German-speaking immigrants settled particularly in Pennsylvania and the dialect that developed as a result of interaction with English was confusingly known as Pennsylvania Dutch ('Dutch' being an Anglicization of *Deutsch* = German). Other pockets of German speakers established themselves in Indiana, Montana and the Dakotas. The survival, albeit

KEYWORD

POW-WOW

The earliest English-speaking settlers in the northeast of America adopted a number of words from the indigenous peoples, most obviously those that described animals which were unfamiliar to them such as the moose, skunk and raccoon. *Pow-wow*, from an Algonquian language, is first recorded in English in 1624. It derives from a word meaning 'sorcerer' or 'medicine man' and also applies to a ritual meeting, and hence to any kind of get-together involving a discussion between two or more parties. The word is enduringly popular, but it tends to be applied in a slightly facetious spirit, perhaps encouraged by the internal rhyme that makes a *pow-wow* sound less serious than, say, a summit meeting.

I have fallen in love with American names,
The sharp, gaunt names that never get fat,
The snakeskin-titles of mining-claims,
The plumed war-bonnet of Medicine Hat,
Tucson and Deadwood and Lost Mule Flat.

STEPHEN VINCENT BENÉT, 'AMERICAN NAMES' (1931)

Amish farmers harvesting wheat in rural Pennsylvania. These descendants of Anabaptist evangelical reformers, who fled religious persecution in their native Switzerland and southern Germany in the 18th century, speak Pennsylvania Dutch, a hybrid of German and English.

precarious, of Pennsylvania Dutch is explained by the still-closed nature of the Amish and Mennonite religious sects who use it and who have deliberately turned their backs on almost all aspects of the modern world.

More recently, the biggest linguistic donation to American English has come from Spanish speakers, far outstripping the contributions made by any European tongue other than English itself. This contribution dates from a later era, but some terms can be traced back to the early days of European imperial expansion. These words were either imported from Spain in the first place or were indigenous to the vast Caribbean region once known as the Spanish Main. The Carib peoples who populated parts of the area prompted the Spanish to come up with *canibales* or *cannibals*. (And that, in turn, probably gave Shakespeare the name Caliban for the 'savage and deformed slave' in his final play, *The Tempest*.) *Canoe* and *hammock* also come, via Spanish, from Caribbean words. Most visibly, the place-names of the southwestern USA are ample proof of the Spanish presence from San Francisco to the Rio Grande (literally, 'big river').

Perhaps most surprising of these early Spanish terms is *barbecue*, surprising because in its colloquial forms of *barbie* and *BAR-B-Q* it may strike us as such a

modern word. But the *barbecue* goes back a long way, to the Spanish *barbacoa*, which was taken in the 17th century from a Haitian word describing a framework of sticks. Moving to another product that involves smoke and toasting, *tobacco* derives from the Spanish *tabaco*, the name they gave to the dried leaves which were smoked by the Indians, although an alternative application is to the tube or pipe used for inhaling. Whatever its origins, *tobacco* was firmly enough established in early 17th century English for King James I to write a diatribe against its pernicious effects. From the same period, *tomato* and *chocolate* were Spanish adaptations of *tomatl* and *chocolatl*, both terms from Central America. From a slightly later period, *avocado* comes from the Aztec *ahuacatl*. Other expressions, such as *plaza* and *tornado*, were carried by the Spanish across the Atlantic.

An important strand in American English was the contribution of the Africans forcibly brought across in the slave trade, although it took some time for these words to enter the mainstream. For example, *banana* was the term originally used in Guinea, while the interjection *OK* may derive from one of the many regional languages in West Africa. Similarly, *bogus*, dating back to the late 18th century when it defined a counterfeit coin, may come from *boko*, a Hausa term meaning 'deceit'. But the real impact of African-derived terms comes with the arrival of jazz and juke-boxes and, later still, musical forms like hip-hop and rap.

An 18th-century print of a Carib hunter from the Antilles. The Carib were the first indigenous people encountered by the Spanish in their exploration of the Americas, but soon fell victim in their thousands to European diseases to which they had no immunity, such as measles and smallpox. Some Carib loan-words, like 'hurricane', 'maize' or 'manatee', survive in modern English.

WHY DOES AMERICA SPEAK ONE LANGUAGE?

America was – and is – a melting-pot of peoples and of languages. An interesting series of questions relates to why, given the astonishing diversity of the immigrant arrivals from almost the earliest days, the country did not become a botched linguistic jigsaw in which none of the pieces would comfortably fit together. Why didn't languages compete in those places where, for instance, German and English speakers rubbed up against each other? Or, if competition was not at issue, what about simple co-existence? And while it is understandable that ethnic and linguistic groups in large cities should slowly lose some of their defining features, how was it that the isolated groups from, for example, the Scandinavian countries who settled in remote Minnesota or Nebraska would eventually make the shift away from their own languages?

The simplest answer is probably the numerical one. By the end of the 18th century, when the first census took place, there were more than 2 million people of English and Welsh extraction recorded in 16 states. To this must be added a substantial quantity of Scots-Irish. The total of the other principal language speakers – German, Dutch and French, in the order of their numerical significance – hardly exceeded 200,000. All of these figures may seem almost absurdly small to us, given the size of the landmass of the USA and the current population of the country (over 300 million). But it was always the ratio of English speakers to the non-English that counted.

The new non-English-speaking immigrants contributed much to America, including (sometimes) hundreds of terms from their own languages. But they had to grasp the rudiments of the prevailing language, which happened to be English. At least they had to grasp those rudiments if they wanted to venture outside their own communities, since the millions already in place were not going to suddenly start learning German or Dutch in order to converse solely with *them*. The very variety of the immigrant tongues would actually have helped establish English as the lingua franca. Had there been a single substantial rival to English, a battle for supremacy might conceivably have resulted. But there was no single rival, rather a diverse group of (mostly) European languages arriving in piecemeal fashion, each of which brought something to the table but none of which had the desire or capacity to sit at the top place.

Of course, many ethnic and linguistic groups did maintain their identity for a long time after their arrival, as is shown by the existence of well over 100 German-language newspapers in mid-19th century America or the publication of up to a dozen Yiddish newspapers in 1930s New York. There were isolated groups who preserved their own tongue, as is still the case to an extent with the Amish. But the literal mobility of American society, from the earliest days of the pioneers trekking westward ('Manifest Destiny') to the age of the freeway, has been a powerful counterforce against the closed community and thus the long-term preservation of any language other than English.

More important than mobility, perhaps, was the aspirational nature of the new society, later to be formalized and glamourized in phrases like the 'American Dream'. As Leslie Savan suggests in her book on contemporary US language, *Slam Dunks and No-Brainers* (2005), the pressure was always on the outsider to make adjustments: 'The sweep of American history tilted towards the establishment of a single national popular language, in part to protect its mobile and often foreign-born speakers from the suspicion of being different.' Putting it more positively, one could say that success was achievable not so much as a prize for conformity but for adaptation to challenging new conditions, among which would be acquiring enough of the dominant language to get by – before getting ahead.

By the time of American Independence, there is no doubt about the status or the future of English. Writing in 1780, John Adams (1735–1826), one of the signatories to the Declaration and the second president, foresaw the situation with a confidence that might sound arrogant were it not also absolutely accurate:

> *English is destined to be in the next and succeeding centuries more generally the language of the world than Latin was in the last or French is in the present age. The reason for this is obvious, because the increasing population in America, and their universal connection and correspondence with all nations will, aided by the influence of England in the world, whether great or small, force their language into general use, in spite of all obstacles that may be thrown in their way . . .*

FURTHER NORTH

Engraving of Inuit people from Hudson Bay. The words 'kayak' and 'igloo' – from Inuit qayaq *and* iglu – *came into English in the late 1700s.*

Out of the modest number of Native American words that have entered the English language, such as *moccasin* or *tepee*, the majority have come from the indigenous peoples who lived in what is now the United States or southern Canada. There is a handful, however, which have been borrowed from the Eskimo or In(n)uit tongues, spoken by the original inhabitants of Greenland, northern Canada and Alaska. The word *Eskimo* itself, first recorded in English in 1744, may derive from a term signifying 'eaters of raw flesh'. The working dog of the region, the *husky*, may also be an adaptation – or, as language specialists would express it, a corruption – of *Eskimo*. The preferred current term, Innuit or Inuit, means no more than 'people' in the Inuit language.

Almost all of the few Inuit-derived expressions in English have come into the language quite recently. An exception is *kayak* which appears in the 18th century, about the same time as *Eskimo*. *Igloo* arrives in the next century. By contrast, two items of clothing – *anorak* and *parka* – have entered the dictionaries quite recently. More recent still is the colloquial British English sense of *anorak*, dating from the 1980s and meaning either a studious person or, more usually, an obsessive, the equivalent to the US 'nerd' or 'geek'.

One word that the Inuit languages have *not* provided is any of their terms for 'snow'. They are popularly – and mistakenly – believed to have hundreds of such terms, on the shaky logic that they live much of the time with the stuff. It is not true. The Inuit in fact have no more words for types of snow than we do.

MODERN ENGLISH

THE AGE OF DOCTOR JOHNSON
1700–1800

AMERICAN INDEPENDENCE
1787–1885

*The surrender of British commander Lord Cornwallis at the
siege of Yorktown in 1781 signalled the end of the American
War of Independence. The emergent United States was to
play a key role in the global dominance of English.*

The late 17th and early 18th centuries bring the first substantial concerns about 'correct' English, and a corresponding rise in complaints and protests among some educated people against what they see as the misuse of language, particularly in its written form. This was the beginning of a programme that continues to this day, that of 'policing' the language and its users. In historical terms, it is also one of the factors that allows us to identify the emergence of modern English at this time.

THE AGE OF DOCTOR JOHNSON

The consciousness of the 'need' for correctness and order in language may be attributed to several factors. It can be seen as a long-term reaction to the politicial and civil turmoil that marked much of the 17th century, in particular the Civil War. More immediately, a population boom went hand in hand with other demographic changes such as greater mobility and a growth in literacy, while from the cultural perspective a new focus on standards of politeness and good conduct naturally extended to speech and writing. Whatever the reasons, this period saw an increase in anxiety and uncertainty over the English language and the ways in which it was developing.

Paradoxically, debate and disagreement over language become possible only when the boundaries and rules are fairly clear. Orthography, or spelling, provides an obvious example. In the time of Geoffrey Chaucer (1345–1400) it was accepted, and quite acceptable, to spell the same word in different ways because spelling was not fixed. Even in Shakespeare's day, English spelling could be, in the words of his biographer Anthony Burgess (1917–93): 'gloriously impressionistic.' By the 18th century everything had changed. There were rules, and with the arrival of rules came the whiff of sanctions, even if it was only being mocked for one's ignorance. There were some benefits too, however. Perhaps the greatest benefit of all was the appearance in 1755 of Dr Samuel Johnson's *Dictionary of the English Language*.

In 1775 Dr Johnson's friend, the celebrated artist Sir Joshua Reynolds, painted his portrait, depicting him as near-sighted. Johnson hated this candid picture, accusing Reynolds of showing him as 'blinking Sam'.

JONATHAN SWIFT WRITES A LETTER

In 1712 Jonathan Swift (1667–1745), best remembered today as the author of *Gulliver's Travels* (1726), wrote an open letter to Robert Harley, the Earl of Oxford. Harley was the senior minister in the Tory government, in effect the prime minister of the country. Swift lards his letter with the usual – and necessary – compliments to this powerful man, although he is not afraid to hint at the consequences for Harley's future reputation if he does not follow his (Swift's) advice.

The subject of this long letter was the condition of the English language. After a gallop through the history of English, taking in the Romans, Saxons and Normans, Swift explains what he considers is wrong with it and what should be done to put it right. The nub of the writer's complaints is that:

> our Language is extremely imperfect; that its daily Improvements are by no means in proportion to its daily Corruptions; and the Pretenders to polish and refine it, have chiefly multiplied Abuses and Absurdities; and, that in many Instances, it offends against every Part of Grammar.

Swift cites only a few instances to back up his claims. He objects to the fad for new words. He objects to words being shortened, and he particularly blames poets for the:

> ...barbarous Custom of abbreviating Words, to fit them to the Measure of their Verses; and this they have frequently done, so very injudiciously, as to form such harsh unharmonious Sounds, that none but a Northern Ear could endure.

In the letter he singles out the jarring sounds of '*Drudg'd, Disturb'd, Rebuk't, Fledg'd*', words that might have been pronounced with what to us would sound like an extra syllable (drudg-ed, disturb-ed). Elsewhere Swift expressed his unhappiness at abbreviations such as *rep*(utation) or *incog*(nito).

Jonathan Swift was a satirist, but these were objections which he intended to be taken seriously. Before laughing at his fuddy-duddy comments we ought to remember that, although the specific points of criticism may have changed, the underlying attitude that there is a right and a wrong way to use English is still with us. Until recently, any formal use of English would have rejected abbreviations like *fridge* or *phone*, just as Swift would never have written 'rep' and 'incog'. In the same style as he dismissed *drudg'd* or *disturb'd*, so in some types of writing it is still unacceptable to use standard elisions (i.e. it's, isn't, couldn't). We are not so different from Swift as we might imagine.

> *Our Language is extremely imperfect; [...] its daily Improvements are by no means in proportion to its daily Corruptions; [...] in many Instances, it offends against every Part of Grammar.*

JONATHAN SWIFT, LETTER TO THE EARL OF OXFORD (1712)

In addition, Swift had some sensible things to say in the letter. For example, he rejected the idea that spelling should be reformed so that it reflected the way people actually sounded their words. He believed that the Authorised Version of the Bible and the *Book of Common Prayer* had established a standard of English, a view shared by later generations. But at bottom Swift seems to have found something ugly in the Anglo-Saxon roots of English – as well as the 'Northern Ear' remark in the letter quoted above he talks of 'the Barbarity of those Northern Nations from whom we are descended' – while being drawn to the more 'liquid' vowels of Italian.

So what was Swift's answer to this intolerable situation of the decline and fall of a language? It was to be a committee, following the example of the French who had set up the *Académie Française* in 1635 to oversee the development of their language (it still issues its pronouncements to this day). Swift was vague about numbers and qualifications, although he did suggest that the earl of Oxford himself might be willing to join them. His overall aim was not exactly vague, even if it was certainly unrealistic:

> *But what I have most at Heart is, that some Method should be thought on for ascertaining and fixing our Language for ever, after such Alterations are made in it as shall be thought requisite.*

Whether or not the earl of Oxford considered making a favourable response to Swift's ideas, they were never realized. It took Dr Johnson, more pragmatic than Swift, to recognize many years later that language could never be fixed.

SAMUEL JOHNSON WRITES A DICTIONARY

Doctor Samuel Johnson (1709–84) was one of the dominant figures in English life of the mid-18th century. A poet, critic and essayist, he also compiled the first English dictionary of real substance and authority. Johnson's reputation grew after the publication of the dictionary in 1755 but his posthumous fame is closely

Contemporary engraving of Jonathan Swift. His motives in proposing a standing committee on the English language were not without self-interest; Swift feared that his own immortality as a writer might be compromised if English were allowed to descend into 'barbarity'.

DICTIONARY

OF THE

ENGLISH LANGUAGE:

IN WHICH

The WORDS are deduced from their ORIGINALS,

AND

ILLUSTRATED in their DIFFERENT SIGNIFICATIONS

BY

EXAMPLES from the beſt WRITERS.

TO WHICH ARE PREFIXED,

A HISTORY of the LANGUAGE,

AND

An ENGLISH GRAMMAR.

By SAMUEL JOHNSON, A.M.

In TWO VOLUMES.

VOL. I.

Cum tabulis animum cenſoris ſumet honeſti :
Audebit quæcunque parum ſplendoris habebunt,
Et ſine pondere erunt, et honore indigna ferentur,
Verba movere loco ; quamvis invita recedant,
Et verſentur adhuc intra penetralia Veſtæ :
Obſcurata diu populo bonus eruet, atque
Proferet in lucem ſpecioſa vocabula rerum,
Quæ priſcis memorata Catonibus atque Cethegis,
Nunc ſitus informis premit et deſerta vetuſtas.   HOR.

LONDON,

Printed by W. STRAHAN,

For J. and P. KNAPTON ; T. and T. LONGMAN ; C. HITCH and L. HAWES ;
A. MILLAR ; and R. and J. DODSLEY.

MDCCLV.

Title page of the second edition of Johnson's Dictionary (1755). Johnson's patron, the earl of Chesterfield, clearly hoped Johnson's work would impose order and structure on the English language: 'We must have recourse to the old Roman expedient in times of confusion, and choose a dictator. Upon this principle, I give my vote for Mr Johnson to fill that great and arduous post.'

linked to James Boswell's *Life* (1791), which devotedly recorded Johnson's table-talk and wide-ranging opinions.

Johnson fought against idleness all his life but, in truth, he was a one-man academy. He rented a house (17 Gough Square) off Fleet Street in London and used the topmost floor, the garret, as the 'dictionary work-shop'.

He employed six assistants, five Scots and one English, to copy out the quotations illustrating the words to be defined. Given Johnson's frequent rudeness about the Scots – often as a way of getting under the skin of his great biographer Boswell, who was born in Ayrshire – it is ironic that he picked the majority of his helpers from that nation.

Johnson not only chose, from his own vast reading, quotations which numbered almost a quarter of a million (around 114,000 were actually used) but wrote the definitions to more than 40,000 words. The best known definitions now are the ones where Johnson let his prejudices or his sense of humour show through. *Lexicographer* is defined as 'A writer of dictionaries, a harmless drudge', while oats are 'A grain, which in England is generally given to horses, but in Scotland appears to support the people'. But Johnson's definitions were generally considered outstanding. He did his job so well that, for more than a century, his *Dictionary of the English Language* had no meaningful competitor.

Johnson had a difficult relationship with his patron, Lord Chesterfield, who had shown an interest in the Dictionary in its planning stages. But where Jonathan Swift depended on the earl of Oxford to further his plan for an English Academy, Johnson was eventually able to dispense with a patron altogether. As the work neared publication he felt that Chesterfield was trying to claim some of the glory. He wrote a letter in which he told Chesterfield with magnificent coldness: 'The notice which you have been pleased to take of my labours, had it been early, had been kind; but it has been delayed until I am indifferent, and cannot enjoy it; till I am solitary, and cannot impart it; till I am known, and do not want it.' Chesterfield seems not to have been too upset and left the letter where it might be seen by visitors, saying generously and rightly of Samuel Johnson: 'This man has great powers.'

SAMUEL JOHNSON, THE KING AND THE ROYAL LIBRARY

Dr Johnson was a deeply loyal subject of the British crown. In 1767 he frequently visited Buckingham House (on the site of which Buckingham Palace now stands) to use the library there, probably to consult books on law. King George III (1738–1820) was an active bibliophile and had recently appointed the youthful Frederick Barnard as librarian. Barnard went out of his way to make Johnson feel welcome. Aware that the king wanted to meet Johnson, Barnard saw his opportunity during one visit when the great lexicographer was settled and reading by the fire. Without saying anything to Johnson, he crept out of the room, fetched the king from his private apartment and escorted him by candlelight through a suite of rooms until they came to a private door into the library. Johnson was so deep in his reading that he started up when Barnard went across and whispered in his ear, 'Sir, here is the King'.

George III came forward and – in the words of Johnson's biographer James Boswell – 'at once was courteously easy'. The conversation went well. Johnson was respectful but not overawed, talking in his usual 'sonorous voice' and not dropping into the soft, deferential tones most people would have adopted when facing the monarch. They talked of books and writers, including Johnson himself:

Caricature (1786) by the satirist Thomas Rowlandson of James Boswell hawking his publications in the streets of London, including his forthcoming Life of Samuel Johnson.

His Majesty enquired if he was then writing any thing. He answered, he was not, for he had pretty well told the world what he knew, and must now read to acquire more knowledge. The King, as it should seem with a view to urge him to rely on his own stores as an original writer, and to continue his labours, then said 'I do not think you borrow much from any body.' Johnson said, he thought he had already done his part as a writer. 'I should have thought so too, (said the King) if you had not written so well.' – Johnson observed to me, upon this, that 'No man could have paid a handsomer compliment; and it was fit for a King to pay. It was decisive'. When asked by another friend, at Sir Joshua Reynolds's, whether he made any reply to this high compliment, he answered, 'No, Sir. When the King had said it, it was to be so. It was not for me to bandy civilities with my Sovereign.' Perhaps no man who had spent his whole life in courts could have shewn a more nice and dignified sense of true politeness, than Johnson did in this instance. (James Boswell, Life of Johnson)

SOME DEFINITIONS FROM DR JOHNSON'S DICTIONARY

Ambition The desire of something higher than is possessed at present.

Bookworm 1. A worm or mite that eats holes in books, chiefly when damp. 2. A student too closely given to books; a reader without judgement.

Candidate A competitor; one that solicites, or proposes himself for something of advancement.

Dull Not exhilaterating [sic]; not delightful; as *to make dictionaries is* dull *work*.

Excise A hateful tax levied upon commodities.

Melancholy A gloomy, pensive, discontented temper.

Patron One who countenances, supports or protects. Commonly a wretch who supports with insolence and is paid with flattery.

Pension An allowance made to anyone without an equivalent. In England it is generally understood to mean pay given to a state hireling for treason to his country.

Pleasure Delight; gratification of the mind or senses.

Tory One who adheres to the ancient constitution of the state, and the apostolical hierarchy of the church of England, opposed to a Whig.

Whig The name of a faction.

JOHNSON'S UNDERSTANDING

Dr Johnson explained some of the background to his Dictionary in the preface that he wrote for it. He outlines the principles he used for inclusion. The word *highwayman* needs to be in the Dictionary because its two parts ('highway'+'man') do not by themselves give the sense, but *coachman* is self-explanatory and so is not included. He comments on an aspect of English that has always been problematic for those trying to learn the language: the vast number of phrasal verbs. These are expressions formed by a verb and preposition or adverb, such as *fall in, fall out, fall back, fall to, fall on*, in which the distinct meanings are hard to work out if the words are taken one by one. Johnson says that he has noted these 'with great care', one of several comments that show he intended the Dictionary to be used by 'foreigners' as well as native speakers.

He is full of a common sense which reveals itself in honest awareness of the limitations of the task. He has not attempted an almost endless list of words beginning *re-* or *un-*, since these can be made up almost on the spot. He reflects on the inherent difficulty of the dictionary maker's task, of being under the necessity of explaining words by using other words. Some definitions, he says, are inevitably circular (*hind, the female of the stag; stag, the male of the hind*). He comments on how the greatest problems tend to lie in the commonest terms like 'cast', 'full', 'get', 'give', 'do', 'put'.

There is something heroic and touching about Johnson's description of the gap between the very high aims with which he began and the realization, as the magnitude of the task sank in and as the time for publication approached, of the compromises that he was compelled to make. In a famous and poetic passage he tells how he had to set boundaries to his quest:

> *To deliberate whenever I doubted, to enquire*
> *whenever I was ignorant, would have*
> *protracted the undertaking without end,*
> *and, perhaps, without much improvement;*
> *for I did not find by my first experiments,*
> *that what I had not of my own was easily to*
> *be obtained: I saw that one enquiry only*
> *gave occasion to another, that book referred*
> *to book, that to search was not always to*
> *find, and to find was not always to be*
> *informed; and that thus to persue perfection,*
> *was, like the first inhabitants of Arcadia,*
> *to chace the sun, which, when they had*
> *reached the hill where he seemed to rest, was*
> *still beheld at the same distance from them.*

KEYWORD
COFFEE-HOUSE

The word *coffee* is, like the drink itself, an import. It comes via Turkish from the Arabic *qahwah*. The first written reference to a *coffee-house* in England is to one in Oxford in 1650. A couple of years later there is a confirmed sighting in Cornhill in the City of London, the first of several in the area. In the course of the next century coffee-houses and chocolate-houses proliferated in the capital and some became the favourite meeting-places of the nation's literary, artistic and political élite. Figures such as John Dryden, Alexander Pope, Joseph Addison and Thomas Gainsborough frequented these male preserves, usually named for their proprietors (Slaughter's, Tom's, Will's). Lloyd's, the famous London insurance market, started in Edward Lloyd's coffee-house, a place frequented by shipping merchants. During the 19th century the term *cafe* gradually eased aside the *coffee-house*, and the whole concept went downmarket. It has taken the rise of various chains to revive the ghost – a very pale ghost perhaps – of the places that Dr Johnson would have recognized as hubs of gossip, newspaper-reading and idling.

But the most significant passage in Johnson's preface is the answer it gives to Swift's desire to 'fix' the language. Johnson plainly did not like some linguistic innovations, and as an instinctive conservative viewed most changes as being for the worse. But he also realized that change was inevitable, in language as in everything else. The passage justifies quoting at length:

> *Those who have been persuaded to think well of my design, require that it should*
> *fix our language, and put a stop to those alterations which time and chance have*
> *hitherto been suffered to make in it without opposition. With this consequence I will*
> *confess that I flattered myself for a while; but now begin to fear that I have indulged*
> *expectation which neither reason nor experience can justify. When we see men grow*
> *old and die at a certain time one after another, from century to century, we laugh at*
> *the elixir that promises to prolong life to a thousand years; and with equal justice*

may the lexicographer be derided, who being able to produce no example of a nation that has preserved their words and phrases from mutability, shall imagine that his dictionary can embalm his language, and secure it from corruption and decay, that it is in his power to change sublunary nature, or clear the world at once from folly, vanity, and affectation.

Johnson understood that any dictionary is always provisional. It must be provisional, because any living language is a work in progress, never fixed and never finished. However, while a language may never be fixed, there is a sense in which it can remain settled for a long period in its spelling, its punctuation and grammar, even in its pronunciation within fairly wide margins. And this was the stage which English had now reached.

> *I am not yet so lost in lexicography, as to forget that words are the daughters of earth, and that things are the sons of heaven.*
>
> Dr Johnson (1755)

NOVELS, NEWSPAPERS AND TATTOOS

By the early to middle parts of the 18th century the English language was recognizably modern. There are a few differences in spelling between the forms used then and those used now, but where they do exist – Jonathan Swift putting *enthusiastick*, for example, or the novelist Daniel Defoe (1660–1731) writing *cloaths* – the differences are negligible. There are contrasts in punctuation habits. Defoe in *Robinson Crusoe* (1719) employs the semi-colon where we would reach for the full stop. And as late as the period when Jane Austen (1775–1817) is writing, in the early 19th century, we find forms like *her's* (for *hers*), where the apostrophe is technically wrong by modern grammatical standards. But these are the exceptions that prove the rule.

It is no coincidence that this period of linguistic settlement is marked not only by Johnson's Dictionary and others but by a surge in books on grammar and pronunciation. Correct pronunciation, that is. Elocution lessons were popular with those striving to speak 'proper' English and perhaps to shed their regional or class accents. At the same time, grammar teachers and pundits were establishing some of the rules which, depending on your point of view, have shaped or plagued English ever since. Among them is the principle or fetish that you should not end a sentence with a preposition. Another is the taboo on double negatives (*I can't get no satisfaction*) although doubles and even triples had regularly been used in the past by great writers, for example Shakespeare, who has one of his characters in *Twelfth Night* say: ' ... nor your name is not Master Cesario; nor this is not my nose neither.'

Another factor that contributed to the standardizing of English, and which would have encouraged people to believe that there was some universal level of correctness, was the growth of literacy and the sheer increase in reading matter. The Elizabethan and early Jacobean ages were pre-eminent in drama and poetry.

The first of these is designed to be seen and heard in public places rather than read in private, while the second – apart from ballads – is likely to be the preserve of well-educated individuals with time on their hands. The era of Dr Johnson saw the rise of the novel, an inherently populist form, as well as other types of printed entertainment and information.

The situation was helped by the slackening of various laws which had for centuries governed the production of books and pamphlets. From the 1530s onwards the authorities had maintained oversight of what was published and had also limited the number of printers. In 1662 a new version of the Licensing Act banned the publication of any material that was hostile to church or state. By the turn of the century, however, parliament was refusing to renew the law, and a era of freedom began. This freedom was relative, of course, since publishers and others could still be prosecuted for libel and sedition.

Newspapers had been circulating from before the time of the English Civil War but the 18th century saw a startling increase in the numbers. There were 12 newspapers in London in 1712; a century later that number had grown more

Freedom of expression in early 18th-century England was still by no means absolute. In 1703, novelist and pamphleteer Daniel Defoe was sentenced to three days in the pillory for publishing an ironic tract, 'The Shortest Way With the Dissenters', which satirized those in the established Church who called for harsh measures against dissenting Protestants.

DRAMATIC WORDS

The 18th century was, like the Elizabethan period, one in which the theatre flourished. Even Dr Johnson, a lifelong friend of David Garrick, the greatest theatrical figure of the day, tried his hand at a tragedy. *Irene* ran for nine days, a quite respectable run for the time and one which brought Johnson a little (and much needed) cash. It was also the period in which certain terms relating to drama entered the English language. Boys had taken female roles in Shakespeare's Globe Theatre and women players appeared on stage only in the latter part of the 17th century after the arid Puritan period. In 1666 diarist Samuel Pepys could talk of a woman as an *excellent actor* and the expression *actress* for a woman taking a stage role is not found before 1700. It was an unrespectable profession, as the reference (from poet John Dryden) shows:

To stop the trade of love behind the scene,
Where actresses make bold with married men.

Riot during a performance of Thomas Arne's opera Artaxerxes *at the Covent Garden Theatre in 1763.*

At about the same time *behind the scenes* is first recorded in its metaphorical sense of *private*, with a suggestion of surreptitious activity. This might take place in the *green room*, the place where actors relaxed and entertained, and probably so called because of the colour of its walls. One of the characters in a 1701 play by the now largely forgotten dramatist Colley Cibber talks of being familiar with 'the Green-Room, and all the Girls and Women-Actresses there'.

Technical theatrical terms which came in English included *flat*, to describe a scene mounted on a wooden frame so that it could be rolled or lowered onto the stage, first found in a 1746 letter of David Garrick, and the later use of *wings* for the area invisible to the audience and each side of the stage, and *dress(ed) rehearsal* to describe the full-scale practice before a public performance.

than four-fold. There was a similar increase in the provincial press, coinciding with the growth of cities such as Bristol, Manchester and Glasgow. Periodicals like the *Spectator* or *Tatler* may have been short-lived at the time – although they have thriving modern incarnations – but they were evidence of the appetite for print and of the leisure to read it. Before the 18th century, a *magazine* was a place of storage, usually for arms and ammunition. By 1731 the word had acquired its principal modern definition: 'a publication containing articles by various writers intended chiefly for the *general reader*' [author's italics].

If the general reader in the 18th century wanted something more substantial than a newspaper or magazine then he or she could always pick up a novel. This new literary form was wide-ranging. *Gulliver's Travels* and *Robinson Crusoe* have already been mentioned. These were, respectively, satirical/absurd and realistic (although also exotic because of Crusoe's desert island). Novels could be romping and farcical on the surface, like the archetypal 18th-century work, *Tom Jones* (1749) by Henry Fielding. They might be sinister and rather silly – like Horace Walpole's proto-typical Gothic novel *The Castle of Otranto* (1764) – or sober and instructive. In this second category comes Dr Samuel Johnson's one and only novel, *Rasselas* (1759), a philosophical tale written in a single week to pay for his mother's funeral.

These, and countless others, were the books taken up by the expanding middle classes. The flourishing printing presses, which fed the appetite for reading by turning out not only novels but everything from grammar guides to gossipy gazettes, were a testament to the growing robustness and confidence of the English language.

This strength was on its way to becoming a universal phenomenon. English was, of course, the predominant language of America in the years before Independence. But it was spreading to other quarters of the globe too. Whereas English had, until this point and with the considerable exception of America, been largely confined to the British Isles, it was now starting on its long passage around the world. No longer at the mercy of invaders like the Anglo-Saxons and Normans, free to develop at its own pace, the language was turning into an exporter rather than an importer.

The trade in words is a two-way process, however. To take a single example: in the years between 1768 and 1776, Captain James Cook (1728–79) made three exploratory voyages to the southern hemisphere. On his arrival in Tahiti, he observed how the indigenous islanders painted their bodies and covered them with tattoos. The original Polynesian word is *tatau*, and in the 18th century it entered English as *tatt(a)ow* before settling to its current form. *Tattoo* is one of many terms to enrich English which now began to arrive from the far corners of the Earth.

The first page of the first edition of Joseph Addison and Richard Steele's daily newspaper The Spectator, *1 March 1711. The majority of* The Spectator*'s readers were not subscribers, but frequenters of subscribing coffee-houses.*

In the years leading up to the Declaration of Independence, there was little difference between the English used in America and in Britain. This did not stop many in the educated classes of England looking down on what they regarded as ugly new words emanating from America, and a sometimes apologetic tone from people such as Benjamin Franklin. But American confidence was growing, and by the middle of the 19th century there had evolved a distinctly transatlantic mode of expression, both in speech and in writing.

AMERICAN INDEPENDENCE

After the Declaration of Independence (1776) and the signing of the US Constitution (1787), America asserted its autonomy and selfhood in several ways, for example by the establishment of a federal government in the same year as the Constitution or by the creation of a navy in 1794. Linguistic independence was never seriously on the cards but there were ways in which the new nation would seek to proclaim its difference from the old country. One of them was to stop the constant over-the-shoulder glance for British approval. Another was to forge distinctive expressions and spellings.

THE MOTHER LANGUAGE?

The British had a proprietorial attitude towards English in the 18th century, by which period the language had evolved to the shape it still essentially has today. The attitude of some educated people towards the one-time colony on the other side of the Atlantic was a combination of snobbery and alarm, as if they were watching a giant playing with a valuable but fragile toy. Even in the 21st century it is not that unusual to hear complaints about the 'Americanization' of English. The danger of such prejudices – even their absurdity – is shown by the fact that people once objected to the words *belittle* and *lengthy* because they came from the USA. Interestingly, *belittle*

The Declaration of Independence, adopted by the US Congress on 4 July 1776, famously contains a rousing invocation of the people's rights to 'Life, Liberty and the Pursuit of Happiness'.

AMERICAN
INDEPENDENCE

1776 American Congress carries Declaration of Independence; following years see the defeat of the British in various battles

1787 Signing of the US Constitution

1803 US greatly expands territory through Louisiana Purchase from France

1806 Noah Webster publishes *A Compendious Dictionary of the English Language*

1828 Webster publishes two-volume *American Dictionary of the English Language*

1830 Beginning of one of the great 19th-century population shifts as an estimated 4 million Irish emigrate to the US in 1830s and 1840s; other national groups arriving in millions include Germans (1840s and 1860s), Italians (1860s) and Scandinavians (1870s)

1844 Samuel Morse's electric telegraph is used for the first time between Baltimore and Washington

1861 Beginning of American Civil War

1863 Abraham Lincoln delivers the Gettysburg Address

1865 End of the Civil War

1866 Transatlantic telegraph cable completed

1885 Publication of *The Adventures of Huckleberry Finn* by Mark Twain, pseudonym of Samuel Langhorne Clemens (1835–1910)

was reputed to be the invention of the third president Thomas Jefferson (1743–1826). If so, it fits his belief in the need for coinages (see below).

Where the British were only too eager to criticize, the Americans responded with a mixture of defensiveness and self-assertion. John Witherspoon, a signatory to the Declaration of Independence, wrote articles attacking the bad language habits of his countrymen, such as using *mad* in the sense of 'angry' (although it had medieval roots and appears in that sense in one of the psalms in the King James Bible). Benjamin Franklin, taken to task for using the words *colonize* and *unshakable*, was quick to back down.

Paradoxically, alongside the defensiveness there was also an innate confidence and certainty that the future of the language lay in *American* hands. John Adams, another of the Independence signatories and the president who followed George Washington, foresaw the global advance of English. Equally presciently, he attributed this to the growing population and power of his own country, relegating England to second place. In a letter written in 1813 Thomas Jefferson, the man behind *belittle*, explained why the American branch of English had no choice but to invent and expand:

> *Certainly so great growing a population, spread over such an extent of country, with such a variety of climates, of productions, of arts, must enlarge their language, to make it answer its purpose of expressing all ideas, the new as well as the old. The new circumstances under which we are placed, call for new words, new phrases, and for the transfer of old words to new objects. An American dialect will therefore be formed ...*

In the same letter he refers to 'judicious neology' (i.e., the sensible creation of new terms) and sums up the situation:

> *Here, where all is new, no innovation is feared which offers good [...] necessity obliges us to neologize.*

One of the earliest ways in which Jefferson's 'American dialect' might be traced and celebrated was in the creation of a specifically American dictionary, one that would reflect American culture rather than being simply a product of the old colonial regime.

NATIONALIZING THE LANGUAGE?

The challenge of compiling a dictionary that would fix the language to American tastes rather than to British ones was taken up by Noah Webster (1758–1843), the Yale-educated son of a Connecticut farmer.

Brought up as a Calvinist, Noah Webster was an instinctive educator and a highly moral one at that. Not content with producing a spelling book which was outsold only by the Bible, he also edited the *King James Bible* itself both to clear up textual obscurities and to clean up those dubious words 'such as cannot, with propriety, be uttered before a promiscuous [mixed] audience'. For the sake of clarity Webster made quite sensible changes in his version of the Bible, like substituting *know* or *knew* for *wist, wit* and *wot*, while to protect the sensibility of readers he altered *stones* (testicles) to *male organs* or turned a *whore* into a *harlot*.

The same evangelizing streak, the desire to clarify and correct, went into the compilation of the dictionary. Or rather dictionaries, since Webster produced two. The first, *A Compendious Dictionary of the English Language* (1806), was built on an earlier spelling dictionary by an Englishman, but contained – so Webster claimed – 5000 new words that were specifically American.

With a combination of flag-waving and common sense, Webster also asserted American individuality and the difference from Britain by introducing spelling reforms. Some of these, like the French-looking *medicin* for *medicine*, didn't catch on. But others did, and have been linguistic markers between the two countries ever since. Webster was responsible for such distinctively US forms as *theater* and *center* as well as *check* (instead of the British *cheque*), *tire* (*tyre*), *defense* (*defence*), and the dropping of the useless *u* in words like *colo(u)r* and *hono(u)r*. One of his motives was to encourage American printing and publishing businesses since, for both financial and cultural reasons, books with these spellings were not being produced in Britain.

More than 20 years passed between the *Compendious* and the reference work for which Webster is principally remembered, his two-volume *American Dictionary of the English Language* (published in 1828). The title is a declaration of national ownership. The English language is no longer the exclusive property of the British. Like any dictionary-maker, Webster had enormous confidence in himself. But he had an unbounded confidence too in the potential of American English and a belief, which turned out to be justified, that it would become the dominant form of the language across the globe.

The strength of Webster's 1828 dictionary is generally reckoned to lie in its definitions. Take a seemingly simple word like *net*. In his 1755 dictionary Dr Johnson had made one of his rare slips and given a definition of *net* which was comically complicated ('Anything reticulated or decussated at equal distances with interstices between the intersections.'). By contrast Webster's explanation of the word was straightforward: 'An instrument for catching fish and fowls, or wild beasts, formed with twine or thread interwoven with meshes.'

In his dictionary-making, Webster had a couple of axes to grind – and, incidentally, 'having an axe to grind' is an American expression which just

Noah Webster's American Spelling Book, *part of a three-volume compendium entitled* A Grammatical Institute of the English Language *(1783), was commonly known as the 'Blue-backed Speller' from the colour of its cover. It was hugely popular, selling a million copies annually by 1861.*

SENATE

The term and the institution *senate* go back to ancient Rome (Latin *senatus* meaning 'council of elders', deriving from *senex*, 'old man'). Though sometimes applied to the British parliament several centuries earlier, *senate* was officially adopted after the War of Independence as the name of the upper and smaller branch of the US legislature. The term is also used for the governments of the individual states as well as in countries such as France and Italy. The association between age (and presumably wisdom) is maintained in America, where the average age of the senators in Washington is at the time of writing over 60.

pre-dates him. Many of the definitions and examples reflect Webster's religious convictions, so that even the 'neutral' word *parallel* is illustrated with the example: 'When honor runs parallel with the laws of God and our country, it cannot be too much cherished.' But the other aspect of Webster's motivation is hinted at in the same example. It consisted of respect and admiration for his relatively new country and its institutions.

Webster was a patriot who was determined to plough (or, in the US spelling, plow) an American furrow. His championing of simplified forms of spelling and of uniquely American terms like *congress* and *caucus* struck a chord in an ambitious and expanding republic. However little may survive of Noah Webster's original work his name is synonymous with 'dictionary' in a way that Samuel Johnson's is not. And one can safely say that it is the only work of its kind to be referred to in a song, specifically the Johnny Mercer lyrics for the Frank Sinatra/Ella Fitzgerald classic 'Too Marvelous For Words' (*'You're much too much, and just too very, very/ To ever be in Webster's Dictionary'*). It's worth noting that *marvelous* is the spelling favoured by Webster in his reforms and the one used in his dictionary, while *marvellous* is standard in British English.

THE GETTYSBURG ADDRESS

Evidence for the self-confidence of American English by the later part of the 19th century can be found everywhere in the words of two of the most famous citizens of the period, a president and a Mississippi steamboat pilot who became a writer. It is significant that neither of these figures, Abraham Lincoln (1809–65)

I have contributed, in a small degree, to the instruction of at least four million of the rising generation; and it is not unreasonable to expect that a few seeds of improvement planted by my hand, may germinate and grow and ripen into valuable fruit, when my remains shall be mingled with the dust.

NOAH WEBSTER ON HIMSELF, IN A LETTER TO JOHN PICKERING (1817)

and Samuel Clemens (Mark Twain;1835–1910), was born on the long-settled and culturally established eastern seaboard but in Illinois and Florida, respectively.

The most famous speech in American history, Abraham Lincoln's address at the Gettysburg military cemetery in 1863, during the Civil War, contains little more than 250 words and took about two minutes to deliver. It followed another speech which lasted two hours, and the audience of thousands standing in the cold of a November day must have been grateful for the president's brevity. But the listeners may not have responded with the kind of admiration, even reverence, which the speech has received since. It was only slowly that the Gettysburg Address acquired the iconic status it has today in the US and other parts of the world (the French constitution contains a direct translation of Lincoln's closing words when it refers to its guiding principle as being 'gouvernement du peuple …').

The speech has been likened to poetry in its use of language and its rhythms. With a more objective eye, it has been criticized for its lack of logic.

The American Civil War was fought to prevent the Southern states achieving secession and self-determination, yet Lincoln is asserting the right and necessity of government by universal consent. For all that, its emotional appeal transcends the occasion and the Gettysburg Address comes to stand as a supreme statement of the validity of democratic rule and the honour which should be given to those who die in that cause:

Four score and seven years ago our fathers brought forth on this continent a new nation, conceived in Liberty, and dedicated to the proposition that all men are created equal.

Now we are engaged in a great civil war, testing whether that nation, or any nation, so conceived and so dedicated, can long endure. We are met on a great battle-field of that war. We have come to dedicate a portion of that field, as a final resting place for those who here gave their lives that that nation might live. It is altogether fitting and proper that we should do this.

But, in a larger sense, we can not dedicate – we can not consecrate – we can not hallow – this ground. The brave men, living and dead, who

Troops and dignitaries assembled at Gettysburg, Pennsylvania on 19 November, 1863, the occasion of Abraham Lincoln's famous address. At the time, the president thought the speech had missed its mark, confiding to an aide as he sat down: 'That speech won't scour. It is a flat failure.'

First draft of the Gettysburg Address, written by Lincoln well before he left Washington to attend the ceremony. A persistent myth claims that he jotted the speech down on the back of an envelope as he rode by train to Gettysburg.

struggled here, have consecrated it, far above our poor power to add or detract. The world will little note, nor long remember what we say here, but it can never forget what they did here. It is for us the living, rather, to be dedicated here to the unfinished work which they who fought here have thus far so nobly advanced.

It is rather for us to be here dedicated to the great task remaining before us – that from these honored dead we take increased devotion to that cause for which they gave the last full measure of devotion – that we here highly resolve that these dead shall not have died in vain – that this nation, under God, shall have a new birth of freedom – and that government of the people, by the people, for the people, shall not perish from the Earth.

How does the speech work? It has a biblical and religious resonance in expressions such as *Four score and seven years ago, our fathers, fitting and proper, consecrate* and *hallow*. It draws together various threads by verbal repetition: the lives of the fallen have been given so that the nation might live; the ceremonial dedication of the battlefield is less important than the moral dedication of those who fought and died there, which must be matched by the dedication of the living to continue the struggle. In the last paragraph dedication is transformed to *devotion*.

Lincoln employs the rhetorical device of varying and balancing weighty phrases: *will little note ... nor long remember ... can never forget ... of the people, by the people, for the people*. He repeatedly draws the distinction between 'we' and 'they', the living and the dead, stressing the nobility of the fallen soldiers compared to the *poor power* of the survivors to enhance this occasion. He does this not to dishearten his listeners but to give them fresh hope and encouragement to go on with the fight, following in the footsteps of the illustrious dead. In other words, Lincoln is forging links rather than creating boundaries. Finally, the language is extremely simple, the words mostly monosyllables.

MARK TWAIN AND DIALECT

Samuel Clemens was born in Florida but is forever associated not so much with the town or state where he grew up (Hannibal, Missouri) but with the Mississippi River which flowed through it. Clemens's early career was a kind of checklist of the opportunities available to an enterprising young man in a dynamic and expanding country. By his own account, he worked as a river-pilot on the Mississippi, a silver-miner in Nevada and a gold-miner in California, as well as a journalist in several places, before becoming an author. He adopted the name of Mark Twain from the cry of the riverboat crewman who took soundings with a lead plummet.

Twain's best-known books are *Tom Sawyer* (1876) and its sequel *The Adventures of Huckleberry Finn* (1885). While *Tom Sawyer* is, essentially, a children's book that can be read with great pleasure by adults, *Huckleberry Finn* is the reverse, a profound and mature work masquerading as an adventure story. The

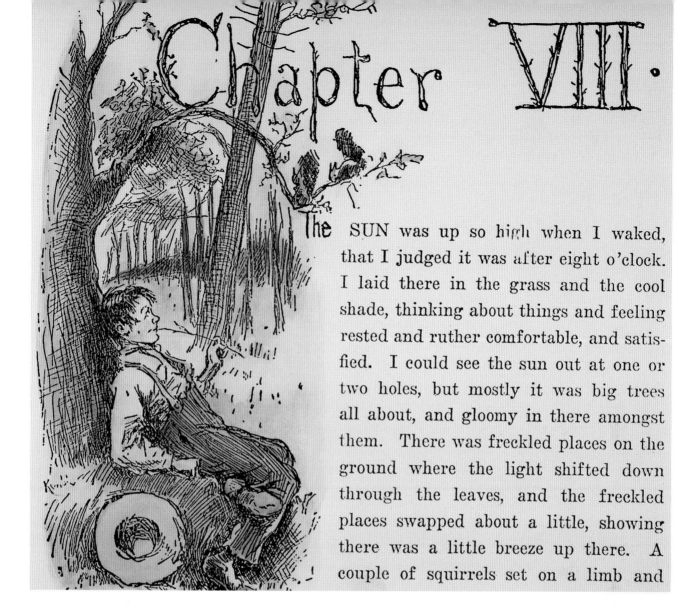

Chapter VIII.

The SUN was up so high when I waked, that I judged it was after eight o'clock. I laid there in the grass and the cool shade, thinking about things and feeling rested and ruther comfortable, and satisfied. I could see the sun out at one or two holes, but mostly it was big trees all about, and gloomy in there amongst them. There was freckled places on the ground where the light shifted down through the leaves, and the freckled places swapped about a little, showing there was a little breeze up there. A couple of squirrels set on a limb and

book, mostly occupied with Huck's escape on a raft down the Mississippi with the runaway black slave, Jim, is a eulogy to Twain's childhood. But it is also a panorama of the often rough frontier spirit of an American society far removed from the niceties of New England, and a subtle treatment of the racial issues which have dogged the USA from its earliest days.

From the language point of view, *Huckleberry Finn* represents the appearance of a vigorous, vernacular voice, as Twain puts himself inside Huck's head and heart. Huck has a button-holing, 'uneducated' style but one which tells an American story in a uniquely American style, as in this excerpt where Huck and Jim's raft is run down by a steamer:

> *We could hear her pounding along, but we didn't see her good till she was close. She aimed right for us. Often they do that and try to see how close they can come without touching; sometimes the wheel bites off a sweep, and then the pilot sticks his head out and laughs, and thinks he's mighty smart. Well, here she comes, and we said she was going to try and shave us; but she didn't seem to be sheering off a bit. She was a big one, and she was coming*

Page from a late 19th-century illustrated edition of The Adventures of Huckleberry Finn. *Twain prefaced his novel with a note on the various dialects used by his characters. With the rapid westward expansion of the United States from the 1860s onwards, Americans began to recognize and embrace the different forms of English spoken around the country.*

WILD WEST WORDS

The expansion westwards brought a small horde of fresh words to American English. *Cowboy* had first been recorded in British English in the early 18th century (simply to define a boy who tends cows). The word took a detour during the War of Independence when it was applied, disparagingly, to crown loyalists before assuming its glamorous Wild West sense in the 1880s and spawning a couple of slangy off-shoots like *cow-poke* and *cow-puncher*.

Two individuals who kept cattle on a grand scale bequeathed their names to posterity. Joseph McCoy was shipping up to half a million head of cattle from Kansas to Chicago every year during the 1870s, and may be the origin of 'the real McCoy'. If so, the phrase sounds like a slogan invented to distinguish his stock from his competitors'. Someone who didn't bother to distinguish his property at all was a Texan called Samuel Maverick. He deliberately chose not to brand his own livestock and, on the assumption that everyone else did their branding, he was thus able to claim any unmarked cattle as his own. Therefore a 'maverick' comes to describe a person who is a free spirit, a non-conformist – and sometimes a pain in the neck.

A large number of terms that we asssociate with the West and Southwest of the USA came via Spanish. Some are topographical: *canyon, mesa* (table-land), *sierra*. Some impart a flavour of the frontier life: *vigilante; bonanza* (in Spanish the equivalent of 'fair weather' and so 'prosperity'). But most are to do with animals and animal-handling: *mustang* (Spanish *mestengo*), *bronco* (*bronco* = rough/sturdy), *stampede* (*estampida*), *lariat; rodeo*. Curiously, *posse*, a word that has a faintly Spanish sound and inevitably conjures up images of the sheriff riding out with a party of gun-toting citizens, actually goes back to a much earlier period and another country. The *posse comitatus* was the body legally required to answer a sheriff's summons not in the still-undiscovered USA but in the England of the Middle Ages.

in a hurry, too, looking like a black cloud with rows of glow-worms around it; but all of a sudden she bulged out, big and scary, with a long row of wide-open furnace doors shining like red-hot teeth, and her monstrous bows and guards hanging right over us. There was a yell at us, and a jingling of bells to stop the engines, a pow-wow of cussing, and whistling of steam – and as Jim went overboard on one side and I on the other, she come smashing straight through the raft.

But Twain wasn't content simply with creating Huck's voice. He explained that he had used a number of different dialects in the books, including 'Missouri Negro ... backwoods Southwestern dialect [and] ordinary "Pike County" dialect'. Dialects, as reproduced in literature, are not likely to be accurate in the way that a verbatim oral recording would be. The author may work them up for effect or fall back on old usages. Nevertheless, the very fact that a dialect is enshrined in print gives it status, as well as providing useful material for linguistic specialists. Twain knew what he was talking about or, rather, what his characters were talking about. He had grown up among the kind of figures who populate *Huckleberry Finn*. In particular he gave to the runaway Jim a distinctive speech, as here when Huck is reunited with him after capsizing on the river (the raft has also been saved):

> *It was Jim's voice – nothing ever sounded so good before. I run along the bank a piece and got aboard, and Jim he grabbed me and hugged me, he was so glad to see me. He says: 'Laws bless you, chile, I 'uz right down sho' you's dead agin. Jack's been heah; he say he reck'n you's ben shot, kase you didn' come home no mo'; so I's jes' dis minute a startin' de raf' down towards de mouf er de crick, so's to be all ready for to shove out en leave soon as Jack comes agin en tells me for certain you IS dead. Lawsy, I's mighty glad to git you back again, honey.'*

Twain's was, of course, a white voice reproducing black dialect speech. He was not doing it from the inside, but he was doing it from a sympathetic standpoint. There were other white writers doing the same, notably Harriet Beecher Stowe (1811–96) in *Uncle Tom's Cabin* (1852) and Joel Chandler Harris (1848–1908), creator of Brer Rabbit.

And there were black writers, producing material both in dialect and in standard English. This was not a straightforward choice. The poet Paul Dunbar (1872–1906), who won early praise for his verse, complained: 'I am tired, so tired of dialect. I send out graceful little poems, suited for any of the magazines, but they are returned to me by editors who say, Dunbar, but we do not care for the language compositions.' Dunbar could write lines like:

> *Look hyeah! What you axing'?*
> *What meks me so merry?*
> *'Spect to see me sighin'*
> *W'en hit's wa'm in Febawary?*

Obviously his audience had grown used to such 'colourful' material. Dialect had become quaint. At other times, it could be a badge of identity and an assertion of difference from standard or conventional English.

The debate continued into the 20th century. The move northwards of large numbers of blacks who were looking for new opportunities in the cities as well as escaping from restrictive laws in the southern states led to a resurgence of black culture that became known as the Harlem Renaissance. One of the differences in the black linguistic debate of the 1920s was over the extent to which African Americans should be encouraged to discard their distinctive idiom and adopt the style of the white mainstream. An alternative view endorsed the black vernacular as perfectly valid.

All modern American literature comes from one book by Mark Twain called Huckleberry Finn.

ERNEST HEMINGWAY,
THE GREEN HILLS OF AFRICA (1935)

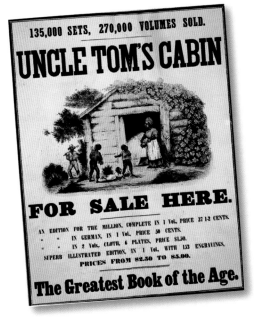

An 1859 advertising poster for Uncle Tom's Cabin. The eponymous hero of Harriet Beecher Stowe's anti-slavery novel was a martyr who gave his life to protect other slaves. However, later stage and screen adaptations debased him into a subservient figure loyal to his master at all costs. Hence the modern black use of 'Uncle Tom' as a term for an obsequious race-traitor.

THE FOOD TRAIL

Every immigrant community of any size brings its own style of food and cooking to its adoptive country. With the older, colonial countries, it is often a legacy of empire. Witness the popularity of Indian food in Britain or the plethora of Vietnamese restaurants in France. America has been the beneficiary of waves of immigration, and the result is a hotch-potch of ethnic and national eating places, particularly in cities like New York.

During the 19th century, people arrived in far greater numbers than before and the cooking lexicon expanded. Some terms, such as the Spanish/Mexican *tortilla* (first recorded in English in 1699), had been around for centuries. Other meaty foods, like the *frankfurter*, *hamburger* and *wiener/weeny* (from *Wienerwurst* = 'sausage from Vienna') did not emerge until the later 19th century, reflecting the sheer size of the German-speaking community.

The Italians, who came later, brought their varieties of pasta (literally 'paste') from *cannelloni* to *lasagne* to *spaghetti*, and the ubiquitous *pizza*.

It is ironic that black usages and slang terms – many of them dating from the 1920s and some from earlier (*jive, chick, hype, jam, mellow, pad*) – were eagerly taken up during the 1930s and the following decades by white speakers who wanted to appear 'cool', another quintessential black expression. Of course, the adoption of such terms could be seen as (another) act of appropriation, while the flattery implied by these early users' imitation of black speech is double-edged. White speakers might have occasionally wanted to sound like blacks, but very few would have wanted to share their social and political disadvantages.

YIDDISH

Another very significant component in the increasingly complex culture of the United States was European Jewish immigration. There were several waves, the largest of which took place in the decades before the First World War, when an estimated 3 million Jews from eastern and central Europe came to New York's immigration centre on Ellis Island, escaping persecution or looking for a better life. Although among the poorest and least educated of new arrivals, this wave was to be the one that helped create the film and popular music businesses.

Along with energy and creativity, the immigrants brought with them their own language, Yiddish. Yiddish derives from the form of German that Jewish settlers picked up in the Rhineland a thousand years ago. Leo Rosten points out in *The New Joys of Yiddish* (2001) that since 'Jewish women were not taught Hebrew, the "sacred tongue", they spoke Yiddish to their children [...] So Yiddish became known as *mameloshn*, "mother tongue".' The heyday of Yiddish in America was probably in the first part of the 20th century when the culture of the immigrants was required to be at its most cohesive in a new country. As late as 1935 New Yorkers could choose between a dozen Yiddish newspapers.

Quite a few Yiddish expressions have found a place in mainstream English. Phrases like *Don't ask, Go figure* or *Enough already* derive from Yiddish. While a handful of individual words are familiar – *glitch, bagel* – some retain a slightly exotic tinge and are not always easy to 'translate'. *Chutzpah*, for example, is usually defined as 'cheek' or 'impudence' but carries overtones of brazenness with a hint of stylishness that leaves the onlooker gaping. *Shtick* has several definitions in Yiddish but is used in English only in the sense of 'special routine' or 'gimmick', and relates particularly to comics. Yet the true Yiddish *shtick* carries a predominant sense of disappointment, almost of dismissal on the part of the speaker.

Indeed, Yiddish is rich in terms combining amusement and disdain. The sound alone is enough to convey the meaning of *schmuck, klutz* and *putz*, although *nebbish* (hapless person), *schlemiel* (fool) or *schnorrer* (whingeing beggar) may need a word or two of explanation.

The impact of Yiddish on English outstrips the limited number of words it has brought. Many still sound 'foreign', at least to British ears, but they fill niches not occupied by 'native' words. A very small selection might include:

> *maven* – an expert (but with the merest suggestion of 'self-proclaimed')
> *schlepp* – move slowly, drag (almost onomatopoeic, surely)
> *schmaltz* – sentimental stuff (to the point of being sickly; derives from German word for cooking fat)
> *schmooze* – chatter (with networking implications)
> *shtum* – silent, dumb (but you keep shtum only about things that it would be compromising or risky to reveal)

Poor European emigrants (in this case, Italians) arriving at Ellis Island in New York Harbour in the early 20th century. In the former immigration centre on the island, now a museum, a standing exhibit entitled 'The Peopling of America' contains a 'language tree' showing foreign words that have become naturalized into English.

GLOBAL ENGLISH

THE SPREAD OF ENGLISH
1600–1900

THE NINETEENTH CENTURY
1800–1928

Members of an Indian Army polo team in the late 19th century. During the British Raj in India, English was the language of the ruling élite, though it imported many loan-words from Hindi.

For most of its history, the English language has imported words, usually as the result of invasion and settlement (the Anglo-Saxons, Vikings and Normans). But from the 17th century onwards, as the country's colonial and commercial ambitions grew, Britain turned into a linguistic exporter. America is the prime example, but many other territories around the world were claimed and colonized. Wherever the Union flag went, the language followed. But it was a two-way process, with the cultures of newly acquired lands supplying new loan-words to English.

THE SPREAD OF ENGLISH

The foundations of the British empire were laid in the space of around 100 years, beginning in *c.*1750. During this imperial heyday Britain acquired, by military conquest or annexation or by diplomatic settlement, vast territories in every continent except Europe. Extending from British Guyana and British Honduras (now Belize) in central America to India, Australia and New Zealand, British authority also reigned supreme over colonies of a few square miles such as Gibraltar on the tip of Spain or Ascension Island in the South Atlantic, a volcanic outcrop that now serves as a naval staging-post. Given this global spread, Britain's claim that her empire was one on which the sun never set was less a piece of imperial boasting than a bald statement of fact. By the time of Queen Victoria's death in 1901, the British empire covered more than a fifth of the Earth's land surface.

Within any particular territory the question of whether English became the official language or the most widely spoken language – the two are not necessarily the same – depended on the circumstances under which it had fallen into British hands, the history of its settlement and so on. Where substantial Anglophone colonies had been established from the earliest days, as in America and Australia, and where there was only a scattered indigenous population, English acquired pre-eminent status

Detail from the painting Allegory of the British Empire *(1901) by Arthur Drummond (1871–1951). Queen Victoria sits serenely on her throne while loyal subjects from around the globe pay her homage.*

THE SPREAD OF ENGLISH

1600 Founding of East India Company

1756 – 63 Seven Years' War sees British troops fighting against French and Indian forces; British power slowly extended across India

1770 James Cook charts New Zealand and east coast of Australia

1784 India Act makes Board of Control responsible for tax and government; East India Company diminishes in importance

1786 William Jones gives speech in Calcutta outlining belief that almost all European languages derive from a common Indo-European root

1787 Transportation of convicts to Australia begins

1835 Thomas Macaulay proposes English as official language of higher education in India, and Anglicization of selected Indians

1857 – 8 Indian Mutiny; East India Company disbanded; India under direct British government rule

1868 Last convicts to be transported arrive in western Australia

1900 Australian Commonwealth Act creates federal parliament in Canberra

1901 Death of Queen Victoria, empress of India

1947 India achieves independence after partition into two states, India and Pakistan (East Pakistan now Bangladesh)

without, in a sense, having to strive for it. Where there was already a highly organized social structure and written culture (or cultures) as in India and elsewhere in Asia, then English was able to achieve pre-eminence only through a mixture of education and official decree. To these factors should be added the desire of at least some of the indigenous population to align their own ambitions to those of their new rulers by learning the language. After independence, English tended to lose its 'official' status but to remain quite widely used.

In other colonies or protectorates, the status of English either was, or subsequently became, less clear-cut. The Mediterranean island of Malta was acquired by the British in 1799 and was a lynchpin of Allied strategy in the Second World War but Italian was its official language until 1934. In Malta today English is widely spoken and understood, and will continue to be so since it is the preferred medium for higher education, but the visitor is more likely to hear Maltese spoken. Similarly in Egypt, which became a protectorate in 1914 after long-standing British involvement, English (and sometimes French) may be found in business or educated circles but otherwise the language tends to be confined to the usual tourist contexts.

Officially bilingual, Canada is tugged in two directions (between English and French) although English is the majority language. But Canadian English has also felt the impact of its US neighbour and imports some usages including spellings, although at an official level it conforms to British English (colour, flavour, etc.).

In the complicated history of South Africa, a country made up of British colonies and the Boer Republics of Transvaal and Orange Free State, the English language took on the unlikely role of the liberators' speech during the long years of *apartheid* which kept the black and white races separate from each other. Since the language of the ruling white élite was Afrikaans, a tongue descended from the Dutch of the first white settlers in South Africa, the use of English by black leaders could be seen as an implicit act of protest. Not only were they communicating with their followers, they were also

The great breeding people had gone out and multiplied; colonies in every clime attest our success; French is the patois of Europe; English is the language of the world.

WALTER BAGEHOT, *EDWARD GIBBON* (1856)

talking directly to the outside world, something that they would never have achieved by using Afrikaans, from which language the word *apartheid* (meaning 'apartness') comes.

An Indian painting from the late 18th century shows a grandee of the British East India Company (his status emphasized by his disproportionate size) riding in a procession with local rulers and their retinues.

INDIA

The East India Company was established by London merchants in 1600 to foster trade with India, and later China. British involvement with India at a governmental level really began in the 18th century. What had been a commercial project slowly turned into an imperial one, with a booming trade in the English language as well as in more tangible goods.

In 1786 the philologist William Jones gave a speech at the Asiatick Society in Calcutta, in which he outlined his belief that Sanskrit, an Indian language surviving only in ancient texts, was a source for many other Indo-European languages (see A Universal Language?). Jones was convinced of the superiority of this *ur*-language: 'The Sanscrit language, whatever be its antiquity, is of a wonderful structure; more perfect than the Greek, more copious than the Latin.'

Within 50 years, though, it was the superiority of English that was being asserted against the indigenous languages by Thomas Macaulay (1800–59), author of a best-selling *History of England.* Indeed, Macaulay was in no doubt about the superiority of all things English, once declaring that an 'acre in Middlesex is worth a principality in Utopia'. Before writing the *History,* which made him rich and helped him to gain a place in the House of Lords, Macaulay had served on the Governor-General's Council in India. There he had seen the impossibility of the small number of British administrators having a direct effect on the mass of the population or even having any line of communication with them. What was needed was a class of 'interpreters between us and the millions whom we govern'. In a document written in 1835, Macaulay proposed the education of a group of Indians so that they became 'English in taste, in opinions, in morals, and in intellect'.

So it was that English became the official language of instruction in higher education when universities were set up in cities such as Bombay and Madras. Perhaps more significantly, English became the language of aspiration. Those who wanted success or, simply, esteem took the trouble to master it and ensured that their children did so too. The effect of Macaulay's original proposal was long-lasting. Even after the declaration of Indian Independence in 1947, English was recognized as an 'associate' official language of the subcontinent. Today, there are probably more speakers of English in India than there are in Britain.

English adopted several hundred expressions from the Indian languages. Some of them came into the language early, like *curry* (first recorded 1598) from Tamil, or *juggernaut* (1638) from an incarnation of the Hindu deity Vishnu – Jagannatha – whose devotees were said to throw themselves under the wheels of a great chariot bearing his image. The succeeding centuries brought a miscellany of useful terms, ranging from *pariah* (Tamil) to *pundit* (Hindi) to *pyjamas* (US *pajamas;* from Persian/Urdu).

The 19th century was the high-point of the British love affair with India. From 1877 until her death in 1901, Queen Victoria was empress of India, the 'jewel in the crown' of British possessions. The title of empress, bestowed upon her by Prime Minister Benjamin Disraeli, proclaimed her status in a country that she never visited. Nevertheless the impact of India on England and English was marked. In Osborne House, Victoria's grand summer villa on the Isle of Wight, there is a Durbar Room, a vast audience chamber modelled on those in Indian palaces. Meanwhile, those who worked in the country itself, soldiers or civil servants or engineers, might at the end of a long day sit on their *verandahs,* sipping their hot *toddys,* sucking their *cheroots* and reflecting on the white man's burden as the sun went down, while indoors one of the household *wallahs* folded the *mem-sahib's jodhpurs.*

KEYWORD
BUNGALOW

The spread and influence of English was not all one way. Expressions from other countries and cultures found a home in the English-speaking world. Literally so in the case of *bungalow.* Coming from the Hindi *bangla,* 'belonging to Bengal', and applying to a single-storey dwelling, the word is found as early as the late 17th century in English but achieved real popularity in the age of suburban mass housing and ribbon development. It also spawned the slightly disparaging term *bungaloid.*

HOME FROM HOME

An intriguing sidelight on the spread of English around the globe from the 16th century onwards is provided by the distribution of place names deriving from Britain. When colonists arrived in uncharted territory, their instinct was to use names already familiar from home, occasionally with the prefix 'New'. The northeastern region of the United States is dotted with town and city names familiar to English ears: within a few miles of Boston are to be found Worcester, Northampton, Marlborough, Norwich, Portsmouth and Manchester. In at least one case, not only the name but also its associations have been transplanted. Like the city of Cambridge in England, the Cambridge in Massachusetts is renowned for its world-famous university – in fact, two of them (Harvard and MIT, the Massachusetts Institute of Technology).

The most popular British place name around the world, occurring 55 times, is Richmond. In second, third and fourth places are London (46), Oxford (41) and Manchester (35). Among the Richmonds is the capital of Virginia. This name supposedly occurred to its founder, William Byrd (1674–1744), because the view

Early 19th-century view of Richmond, Virginia. This important industrial centre became the capital of the Confederacy during the American Civil War (1861–5).

across the James River was like that across the Thames from Richmond in Middlesex.

Not all such acts of naming derive from picturesque views or a taste for nostalgia. Just as it was respectful or shrewd to name your settlement after a king or queen (Jamestown, Elizabethville), so it paid to do homage to potential patrons. The fashion for Richmonds owes something to a succession of dukes of Richmond who were active in other early US colonies. A similar aristocratic connection is with the duke of Wellington. There are only two Wellingtons in England – it was from the small Somerset town that Arthur Wellesley (1769–1852), the first duke, took his title – but more than 30 of them around the world, including the capital of New Zealand.

The impact of Scottish explorers and settlers can also be seen worldwide, from Livingstone in Zimbabwe to the Falkland Islands, from New Glasgow in Nova Scotia (Latin for 'New Scotland') to the Murray River in Australia.

AUSTRALIA

Rottnest Island, off the port of Fremantle in Western Australia, was established in 1838 as an Aboriginal penal colony. Indigenous people who defied British rule by continuing to pursue their traditional life style were imprisoned there. The island's 'English' name is a corruption of Rattenest, *coined by a Dutch sea captain who mistook native marsupials called quokkas for rats. Its name in the language of the Noongar people of Western Australia is Wadjemup ('place across the water').*

There is a story, almost certainly (and unfortunately) untrue, that the kangaroo got its name from a question put by a crew member of HMS *Endeavour*, after Captain James Cook made land at Botany Bay, on the east coast of Australia, in April 1770. Pointing at one of these peculiar, two-legged, bounding animals, the sailor asked a native what it was called. 'Kangaroo,' was the reply, or 'I can't understand you'.

In all likelihood, *kangaroo* was simply an indigenous name for the beast. It would probably have been one of several terms; contrary to popular belief among the first explorers, the original inhabitants of Australia did not speak a single language, but many. As with the early European colonizers of America, there was a constant tendency to simplify and underestimate indigenous culture. Even so, the contribution of the Aboriginal languages to English is both small and largely restricted to those animals and plants that were unfamiliar to the first arrivals, like the *koala* and *wallaby*. Out of all Aboriginal-derived terms, *boomerang* is probably the most widely used. In a broader cultural context, the term *walkabout* was coined to denote an Aboriginal rite of passage that involved young men spending time alone in the bush; in modern English usage, its sense has shifted to describe politicians and royals 'meeting the people'.

The Australian treatment of the English language is distinctive, but it has rarely prompted the same snobbish attitude that the British occasionally direct at America and Americanisms (not that Australians would care if it did). Australians have often played up to British perceptions and turned their pronunciation, in particular, into a kind of assertive national joke. In the mid-1960s there appeared a cod-dictionary entitled *Let Stalk Strine*, which both celebrated and sent up the accent. The joke started with the pseudonymous author, Afferbeck Lauder (alphabetical order), real name Alastair Morrison. His examples included *Ebb Tide* meaning 'hunger' (as in: 'I jess dono watser matter, Norm, I jess got no ebb tide these dyes.') and *Sly Drool* defined as 'An instrument used by engineers for discovering Kew brutes'.

It has been suggested that the vigorous, colourful style of Australian English is attributable to the forced transport of a convict population and to voluntary immigration by those desperate or daring enough to journey to the far side of the world in search of a new start. These were natural rebels, malcontents, people who didn't know their place. Perhaps so. Certainly, Australian English preserves some traces of its origins. *Swag* was underworld slang in the 17th and 18th centuries for thieves' loot and was transmuted in Australia to the bag carried by the itinerant worker ('jolly swagman') of the national song, 'Waltzing Matilda'. Another term that has been going almost as long as Australia itself is *sheila* for a woman. This Irish-derived name is a reminder of the significance of Irish settlement, both forced and voluntary, in the early days.

Australians have always been very tolerant of what they call 'larrikins' – otherwise known as villains, bohemians, unconventional people. *Larrikin*, which may derive from a defunct English Midlands dialect word, is widespread enough to give rise to *larrikinism*, a style of behaviour and speech in which colourful abuse rates highly. A former Australian prime minister once described a political opponent as a 'painted, perfumed gigolo' and another as a 'mangy maggot'. By contrast, the British should count themselves lucky to be characterized merely as 'poms' or 'pommys' (apparently derived from pomegranate, rhyming slang at two removes for immigrant).

Yet aside from such high-spirited colloquialisms, in its fundamentals Australian English is indistinguishable from British English. Only very few usages are shared with US English (e.g., 'cookie' for 'biscuit', 'teller' for 'cashier').

PIDGIN ENGLISH

Pidgin – or Pidjin – English is a very simplified form of the language. The word itself is supposedly a Chinese rendering of the word 'business', and indicates the link between pidgin and trade. Pidgin English has its origins in the slave trade, specifically in the transport of tens of thousands of West Africans across the Atlantic from the early 17th century onwards. The victims of this traffic were drawn from many different tribes speaking different languages. Before the crossings, the European traffickers frequently broke up the tribal groupings. If the captives could not speak the same language they would be less capable of plotting together to cause 'trouble' en route. Pidgin English probably developed from two requirements: the need for the sailors to communicate with the slaves, and the need for the slaves to communicate with each other. Once the survivors of the crossings had arrived and been set to work, pidgin would also have been a means of communication between the slaves and slave-owners.

Pidgin English then spread round the world, following sailors and trade-routes. A distinctive branch of it is found in Papua New Guinea and its nearby

LEGHORN — OR LIVORNO?

The names of foreign cities and countries have until recently been known in English only in their Anglicized form. This still applies to major European cities, which tend not to be spelled or pronounced in the way that their own citizens would use (Florence rather than Firenze, Cologne not Köln). For an English speaker to use the 'foreign' designation is usually seen as an affectation. But changes occurring in place names in countries that were once under Western colonial rule are increasingly found in the English-speaking media. In India, Calcutta is now Kolkata and Madras is Chennai while Bombay, named by the British from the Portuguese for 'good bay' (*bom bahia*), is Mumbai, deriving from the goddess *Mumba* together with *ai* ('mother' in the regional Marathi language). Ceylon long ago became Sri Lanka. An exception is Burma; the ruling military junta renamed it Myanmar in 1989, but international condemnation of the regime means the old name is still preferred (a similar instance occurred when the Khmer Rouge renamed Cambodia 'Kampuchea').

islands. Pidgin language is not unique to English. There is also Pidgin French, Pidgin Portuguese, and so on. *Savv(e)y*, a useful and almost global word which can be verb, noun or adjective, derives from the Portuguese *sabe* or 'know'.

Unsurprisingly, pidgin tongues tend to be associated with European colonizing nations. A significant exception is Swahili, which developed from a pidgin language based on a Zanzibar dialect and which was spread by Arab slave traders.

A pidgin language will be simplified by comparison with its source language. It may dispense with word endings or drop certain words altogether, such as pronouns or the definite and indefinite articles. It will be simple, therefore, but it is not the equivalent of baby-talk or of a tourist raising his voice and speaking very slowly to make himself understood by the locals. Pidgin can be defined, rather, as a language pared to the bone. 'Long time, no see' and 'no can do' are examples of the compressed way in which pidgin English works. If used by enough people for long enough, pidgin will develop into *creole*, a more elaborate form of language with an expanded vocabulary and a more complicated syntax.

GAELIC AND THE SPREAD OF ENGLISH

English has not always been received with enthusiasm. Where it is seen to displace an existing language, there may be resistance to its encroachments. Even when English is the tongue used by almost everybody, there will still be attempts to restore the original language. This is the case in Wales and also in Ireland.

The proportion of native Irish speakers of Gaelic is small. This, the descendant of the original tongue used by the Celtic settlers of the island, is spoken natively by scarcely 1 in 70 of the population (though, as a compulsory subject in Irish schools, many more speak it as a second language). Despite the fact that Gaelic is the first official language of the Republic of Ireland, English is used in 99 percent of the debates conducted in the *Dáil Éirann*, or Irish parliament.

The relationship between the indigenous people of Ireland and the English across the water has always been problematic, to put it mildly, and Irish sensitivity towards the language of those who were regarded as occupiers continues to this day. In 2005 a law was passed that took away legal status from English place names in the west of Ireland, the area with the highest concentration of Gaelic speakers. For example, two villages with the English names of Dunquinn and Ventry were changed to Dun Chaoin and Ceann Tra on road signs and Ordnance Survey maps. In other parts of the country outside the officially designated *Gaeltacht* (Gaelic-speaking areas), English place names remain legal as long as the Gaelic version is displayed alongside.

There is no language like the Irish for soothing and quieting.

JOHN MILLINGTON SYNGE, THE ARAN ISLANDS (1921)

The first thorough mapping of Ireland by the British was an Ordnance Survey project beginning in 1825, intended to cover the island from top to bottom at a scale of six inches to the mile. Its ostensible purpose was to provide a basis for the reform of Ireland's local taxation system and, in the course of the project, place names were to be checked and 'standardized'. It is not hard to imagine how this would have been received by many of the locals on the ground. So it could be argued that the law of 2005 was simply an attempt to restore the status quo.

If Irish eloquence (or, less respectfully, 'blarney') is an attribute that the English half admire and half resent, the attitude of the Irish towards the English language has also been ambivalent. In previous centuries, those Irish who were ambitious to get on would naturally have turned to English. In the early 19th century the Anglo-Irish aristocracy sent their children to be educated in England. Ireland has produced a disproportionate number of writers of international renown, including Oscar Wilde, Bernard Shaw, James Joyce and Samuel Beckett. They would be largely unknown to most people if they had chosen to write in Gaelic. Different as they are from each other, there is a linguistic resilience and resourcefulness to these writers and others such as Jonathan Swift and Oliver Goldsmith from an earlier period. It is significant that they all had to escape from Ireland to achieve recognition, and that their 'exile' (James Joyce's word) from their native country was also a way of coming to terms with it.

County Clare (Gaelic: Contae an Chláir) in the west of Ireland has no areas officially within the Gaeltacht. As a result, road signs are in both Gaelic and English.

protrusive manner. **promi-**
thrusting protruded or in-
being protruded or
-ran), n. a swelling.

having excessive self-
ostentatious; haughty;
mien; pleased; grand;

adj. capable of
to ascertain or try by
or test; establish or as-
ment or other evidence;
genuineness of; experience;
suffering; show or demon-
racy of (a calculation).
adj. proved.

-ov'en-der), n. dry food for
etc; v.t. to feed, as a horse.
n. a short, familiar, pithy
essing some well-known truth
fact of experience); adage.
pro-ver'bi-al), adj. pertaining
mentioned, in, or like, a
widely spoken of, or well known.

-ro-vid?), v.t. to make ready; be-
furnish; v.i. to procure supplies
condition (with for or against).
rations (on condition.

provocation
which calls
act of provoking.
to provoke.
tends to provoke.
provoke (-vōk), v.t.
action; enrage or
passion; vexatious.
provoking (-ing), p.adj.
provost (prov'ust
head of a college;
president; chief dig-
chief magistrate of
provost marshal
the head of a
prow (prou), n.
prowess ('es)
prowl (proul
as for pre-
prey or
proxima
proximate
point
proxi-
ne
pro-
pru
pru
adj.

timely
condition. n.
economy; his creat

The 19th century was the heyday of British imperial power. While English consolidated its progress around the globe, the language was being researched and codified as never before. There was a great expansion in reading matter for a print-hungry audience on both sides of the Atlantic. Towards the end of the Victorian era, new inventions and technologies gave rise to new words.

THE NINETEENTH CENTURY

In Britain in 1842, a year before the death of US lexicographer Noah Webster, the first moves were being made in a process that would lead eventually – a very long eventually – to what is arguably the most influential dictionary in the English-speaking world: the *Oxford English Dictionary,* or *OED* for short. In that year the Philological Society was founded in London to research the 'Structure [...] and the History of Languages'. (London had actually been beaten to the punch by New York, which had established its own Philological Society as early as 1788, although it had not lasted long.)

Those involved in the London Society and in the early discussions about compiling a new dictionary are a roll-call of the great and the good in mid-Victorian England. They included Thomas Arnold, headmaster of Rugby School and author of *Tom Brown's Schooldays*; Richard Chenevix Trench, a churchman who later became archbishop of Dublin; Herbert Coleridge, grandson of the poet Samuel Taylor Coleridge; and Hensleigh Wedgwood, grandson of the famous pottery manufacturer Josiah Wedgwood. These men and others were high-minded, enthusiastic scholars with a strong commitment to public service.

According to these Victorian worthies, the existing dictionaries, including Dr Johnson's, were just not good enough. As Chenevix Trench pointed out to a meeting of the Philological Society held in November 1857, no dictionary yet published was truly comprehensive or thorough. Not one included a full account of words that had fallen out of use, not one gave a properly reliable history or etymology of a word, not

The clear format of modern dictionary definitions, showing parts of speech, giving guidance on pronunciation and stress, and providing etymologies and examples of usage, is the fruit of 19th-century scholars' labour.

one paid enough attention to distinguishing between similar-seeming words – and so on. What Chenevix Trench proposed was extraordinary. It was to produce a dictionary that would start from scratch and cover everything. Each word would be traced back to its roots and its meanings explained through all its changes and developments. Examples of how words were used would be sought not only in great literature (or any kind of 'literature', for that matter) but in all manner of printed resources, including magazines and newspapers. There would be no distinction made between sources. No discrimination, no claims that there was a 'right' or a 'wrong' way to use a word.

This was a long way from Samuel Johnson, whose own voluminous research included no books written before 1586 and who would certainly have rejected any newspaper as his word-source. A long way too from Noah Webster, who made no secret of his religious beliefs in his dictionary. This new English dictionary was to be a monument to a great language and a reflection of a country which in the mid-19th century was the most powerful, ambitious and confident nation on Earth.

Engraving of Richard Chenevix Trench (1807–86) from c.1860. A keen philologist, Trench was fascinated by words and their etymologies, seeing them as 'boundless stores of moral and historic truth, and no less of passion and imagination'.

It was also an attractively democratic plan, since the general public was to be asked to read for the dictionary, to track down words and their earliest usages, and so on. As Simon Winchester points out in his history of the *Oxford English Dictionary*, *The Meaning of Everything* (2003), the project was on a par with other great Victorian enterprises. In contrast to the building of roads or railways or the physical apparatus of empire, the dictionary was a purely intellectual edifice, but one conceived on a heroic scale. It needed money, manpower and mental application, and called for immense reserves of stamina and industry from those involved.

THE GREAT ENTERPRISE BEGINS

Just how much those reserves would be required was to be demonstrated time and again over the following years. As with most great projects, there were unrealistic expectations about costs and time. But the English dictionary didn't overrun its schedule by a year or two. Rather, it took more than seven decades for Chenevix Trench's radical proposals of 1857 to bear fruit. Partly in an effort to recoup costs, the dictionary was published in instalments covering individual letters or segments of them (the first, *A–Ant*, appearing in 1884), but the full glory of the *Oxford English Dictionary* was not available in its completed form until 1928. Begun when Queen Victoria was some way from the midpoint of her long reign, it would not be completed until her grandson, King George V, was nearing the end of his.

Not surprisingly, the project came close to collapse several times. Problems arose over finding a publisher and then, once the Oxford University Press was contracted to the project, over keeping the publishers happy or at least not dissatisfied to the point where they would pull out. Costs spiralled. Intensive research generated yet more research in its turn. The first editor, Herbert Coleridge, died prematurely at the age of 31. The second, an eccentric called Frederick Furnivall, had many virtues but organization was not one of them. Fortunately the third editor, James Murray (1837–1915), possessed both longevity and a high degree of organization.

If anyone deserves to be called the founding father of the *OED*, it is the remarkable Murray. Like Noah Webster, he came from a relatively humble background and, also like Webster, there was a knotty strand of Calvinism in his make-up. Brought up in Roxburghshire in lowland Scotland, he seems to have been interested in almost everything from astronomy and botany to zoology, in a manner that was typical of Victorian intellectuals. To this polymathic tendency was added a wide-ranging facility for languages. He knew a dozen European tongues, living and dead, as well as sufficient 'Hebrew [...] to read at sight the Old Testament'.

MURRAY'S METHOD

Murray's appointment as the principal *OED* editor came about almost by accident after he dropped a casual remark to Frederick Furnivall, but once settled into the post he remained there from 1879 until his death in 1915. Despite Murray's dominance of the dictionary compilation, it was no longer the one-man-band operation it had been in Dr Johnson's day or in Webster's. Many, many books remained unread in the quest for quotations to illustrate early or unusual word usages. Murray systematized the business of appealing to readers. He issued a pamphlet that was distributed to newspapers, bookshops and libraries not only in Britain but overseas. Its title is self-explanatory: 'An Appeal to the English-Speaking and English-Reading Public in Great Britain, America and the British Colonies [i.e., Australia and Canada] to read books and make extracts for the Philological Society's New English Dictionary'. (It did not become the *Oxford English Dictionary* until later.) Murray issued slips on which the readers, soon amounting to hundreds of men and women, could enter their replies in a standardized way.

It sounds like a demonstration of the old saying about many hands making light work, except that the work never did become light. Some of the hundreds of readers returned hundreds, even thousands, of replies in which they provided key words, quotations, sources and dates. These had to be checked and sorted by Murray's assistants before they were examined by the editor-in-chief. Slowly, an order could be imposed on each word by seeing how its use had developed over the centuries. Finally it was up to James Murray to perform the most difficult and delicate task of all, that of writing the definitions. In this he was doing what Johnson and

THE NINETEENTH CENTURY

1830 Opening of Liverpool–Manchester railway line

1837 Victoria succeeds to the throne; Samuel Morse exhibits electric telegraph in New York

1842 Founding of Philological Society in London to research the 'Structure and the History of Languages'

1857 At meeting of Philological Society, Richard Chenevix Trench proposes creation of new, comprehensive English dictionary

1859 Charles Darwin publishes *On the Origin of Species by Means of Natural Selection*

1869 Completion of America's first transcontinental railway

1879 James Murray appointed principal editor of *Oxford English Dictionary*

1884 First instalment of *Oxford English Dictionary* (covering *A–Ant*) appears

1895 Invention of radio telegraphy by Guglielmo Marconi

1901 Death of Queen Victoria, the longest reigning monarch in British history to date; Marconi sends radio message from Cornwall to Newfoundland

1928 Completion of the *Oxford English Dictionary*

Webster had done before him but he was doing it with a greatly expanded base
of knowledge and many more examples to work from.

At first Murray worked from a purpose-built structure that he called the
'scriptorium' (originally denoting the writing room in a monastery) in the garden
of his house in north London, where he had been a schoolmaster. But in 1884
he and his family moved to Oxford. If anything, the work grew increasingly
complex and laborious as it went on. Entries under the letter B, for instance,
were far more complicated than the compilers had anticipated. One of Murray's
assistants, a clergyman, spent no less than three months on the simple monosyllable
black because of all the other terms associated with it. Even in today's *Shorter
OED*, black-derived terms occupy more than a page. Two centuries before, Dr
Johnson had observed that the more simple and commonplace a word – *put, get,
nice* – the more complex and multifarious are its meanings and applications.

Bearing all this in mind, it is perhaps surprising not that the first edition of
the *OED* took so long to finish but that it was finished so soon. The first Supplement
to the *Oxford English Dictionary* was published in 1933. But a dictionary, of course,
is never a finite undertaking, since new words are being added to the language
literally by the day. Further supplementary volumes that appeared in the 1970s
and 1980s were assimilated into a 20-volume second edition in 1989. And the
work goes on, as it must not just for the *OED* but for all dictionaries of all
languages that are not dead and buried. The biggest leap forward – a quantum
leap, to use an expression that has only recently entered the English lexicon –
came with the application of IT to do the work that would once have been done

DICTIONARY, n. A malevolent literary device for cramping the growth of a language and making it hard and inelastic. This dictionary, however, is a most useful work.

AMERICAN SATIRIST AMBROSE BIERCE *THE DEVIL'S DICTIONARY* (1911)

by the thousands of volunteers who combed texts and sent examples to the dictionary editors. Most texts are now available electronically. Indeed, some writing (like blogs) is only available in that form. No team of humans could hope to process all the material that is out there, but specific software programs are able to read, compare and collate usages. They can show which words and groups of words are gaining real traction in everyday English, which ones are fading away, which countries or regions favour particular formulations, and so on.

LEVELS OF LANGUAGE

The appetite for reading and information grew in the 19th century, and it was met in a variety of ways, from the 'three-decker' (i.e., three-volume) novel to the 'penny dreadful', a general term for cheap and sensational publications. Novelists such as Charles Dickens, Elizabeth Gaskell and Wilkie Collins issued their work as serials in magazines in advance of publication in book form. Before the public library service became established, Mudie's and W.H.Smith and other circulating libraries, so called because their books were 'circulated' among paying subscribers, flourished from the 1840s onwards.

There was a growth in genre fiction, from mystery to romance to science fiction to (in the United States) Wild West stories. The century was bracketed by two novels that made household names of their monstrous central figures, Mary Shelley's *Frankenstein* (1818) and Bram Stoker's *Dracula* (1897). Shelley's book encapsulated suspicions of scientific experimentation going 'too far' and bequeathed an alarmist shorthand prefix to the English language – as in 'Frankenfoods' to describe genetically modified products.

KEYWORD

DINOSAUR

The word *dinosaur* was coined in 1842 by palaeontologist Richard Owen to describe long-extinct creatures whose appearance could be reconstructed only from fragmentary remains. The early 19th century was a great age of fossil- and bone-hunting, as people came to realize that the Earth was immeasurably older than religious teaching claimed. *Dinosaur* was formed from two Greek words meaning 'terrible lizard' (*deinos+sauros*), and the more specific terms that came later such as *pterosaur* and *stegosaur* were, like many scientific expressions, also Greek-derived. Today, *dinosaur* is occasionally used metaphorically to describe a company or institution that is slow and lumbering, destined for extinction. But recent research has shown that the *dinosaurs* were more complex and intelligent creatures than their image in the popular imagination.

Writers like H.G.Wells (1866–1946) and Arthur Conan Doyle (1859–1930) were not only immensely popular but also familiarized their audience with authentic scientific terminology, whether it was applied to time travel or to cracking a criminal case. This did not operate just at the fictional level. In 1859 Charles Darwin published his seminal work *On the Origin of Species by Means of Natural Selection*. Within a few years, terms such as *evolution* and *natural selection* had become firmly established in the public mind and accepted as a logical way of interpreting the world. Shadowing genuine science was pseudo-science, as in the fad for *phrenology* (literally, 'mental science'), whose proponents believed that a person's character could be divined from the shape of the cranium. This was facetiously known as 'bumpology', because its practitioners drew conclusions from one's head 'bumps'.

The spread of literacy and all kinds of reading was not welcomed by everyone. As before and since in the history of language, English – or rather the right and proper use of it – was seen as the preserve of the few. An editorial in the short-lived but influential *Yellow Book* magazine in 1895 put the blame on education. It was not that there had been too little education but too much of it, and that it was the wrong sort:

The hugely popular Sherlock Holmes *stories by Sir Arthur Conan Doyle, which appeared in* The Strand *magazine from 1891 to 1927, introduced readers to new crime detection methods, including finger-printing and cryptanalysis (code-breaking).*

> *What is obvious is this: that with the dissemination of ignorance through the length and breadth of our island, by means of the Board School* [i.e., locally funded schools for the poor], *a mighty and terrible change has been wrought in the characters both of the majority of readers and of the majority of writers. The 'gentleman scholar'* […] *has sunken into unimportance both as reader and writer. The bagman* [commercial traveller, salesman] *and the stockbroker's clerk (and their lady wives and daughters) 'ave usurped his plyce and his influence as readers; and the pressman has picked up his fallen pen, – the pressman, sir, or the presswoman!*

This is the familiar 'dumbing-down' argument, citing the inadequacies of public education and the failings of the press (today the scapegoats would be the tabloid press and television). It is shot through with snobbery and nostalgia. Of particular interest is the writer's patronizing imitation of a Cockney or supposedly common style of speech when, referring to the 'gentleman scholar', he describes how members of the newly literate class and their 'lady' wives and daughters ''ave usurped his plyce'.

VICTORIAN LOW-LIFE

Victorian London was the largest city in the most powerful country on Earth. But hand-in-hand with prosperity, industry and national pride came poverty, disease and crime, much of it unseen or at least easy to ignore. One of the earliest investigators of the predicament of the urban poor was Henry Mayhew (1812–87), who visited London slums and talked to their inhabitants. He wrote a series of articles for the *Morning Chronicle*, describing everything from the sales patter of market traders to 'ratting' (a sport in which dogs were set to kill rats in a small arena). Mayhew is a great resource for documentary evidence on the Victorian underclasses, including styles of speech.

There was a fascination with crime, exploited by writers such as Charles Dickens (1812–70), while the detective story had its origins in works by Edgar Allan Poe such as 'The Murders in the Rue Morgue' (1841). As in every period, the criminal underworld created its own jargon. The Victorian variety was especially colourful, with a stress on trickery and burglary. The brief sample below also gives an idea of the nature of 19th-century crime:

flying the blue pigeon stealing roof lead
fine wirer skilled pickpocket
gull a choker fool a clergyman
mutcher thief who steals from drunks
prater bogus travelling preacher
shake lurk begging under pretence of being a shipwrecked sailor
toffken house with well-off occupants

TRAINS, CARS, CABLES AND TELEPHONES

It would take a long time for variants of 'correct' English like the Cockney style lampooned above to be accepted as perfectly valid ways of speaking. There was little or no snobbery, however, about the addition of new words to describe the new processes and artefacts that arrived with new technologies.

Sometimes it was easier to update old terms than create new ones. The coming of the steam age meant that various words that had existed in English for hundreds of years acquired a new lease of life: *train, engine, carriage, station, porter* are found during the late Middle Ages. But from now on they would be associated with the railway, which for the Victorians was not just a mode of transport but a world every bit as exciting as air travel was to mid-20th century travellers. It was also a rapidly developing world. Within little more than 20 years of the opening of the first railway between Liverpool and Manchester in 1830, around 7000 miles (11,265 km) of track had been constructed throughout the country. The term *railway* had been used from the 1750s to describe a track laid with rails (of wood, and later of iron or steel) on which heavy wagons could be shifted more easily. Now railways were found not only in mines and quarries but threaded across the land, carrying both goods and passengers. *Locomotive* is also found earlier, although no one quite seems to have known what to do with

THE PECULIARITY OF TELEPHONE CONVERSATIONS

Although the telephone did not have a direct impact on the English language, other than by the specialist application of terms like *operator* and *exchange*, it did bring about changes in the context in which English is spoken. No doubt early telephone conversations were rather stilted and formal – Alexander Graham Bell's first words over the phone to his assistant were: 'Mr Watson, come here, I want to see you' – but the invention gave people something quite new in human history, the ability to talk and listen across vast distances.

It hardly needs saying that a telephone conversation is not quite the same as a face-to-face encounter. There are no facial expressions or gestures to help the listener interpret

Alexander Graham Bell inaugurating the long-distance telephone line between New York and Chicago in 1892.

meaning, although most people still smile and grimace and even gesture in minor ways when they are on the 'phone. Nuances have to be conveyed through the pitch and the tone of voice. As a result, telephone calls tend to be slightly more structured than, for example, a conversation between two people meeting in the street. There is a clear beginning, signalled by the bell/ring-tone, although (unusually) the dialogue is initiated not by the person who wants to speak but by the one who answers. There is also an established formula for finishing, which should leave no doubt the conversation is over but avoid the rudeness of simply hanging up.

a word that was generally applied in a humorous sense to the act of walking. It took the puffing arrival of the train in the early 19th century to give *locomotive* its due weight.

The univeral *car* has a curious history. The word may go back thousands of years to Old Celtic *karros*, meaning a two-wheeled war chariot. It was used poetically by the Elizabethans to describe the chariot of Phoebus, the classical sun-god. Its application to motor vehicles seems to have been almost a chance affair. In Britain a name was needed as an alternative to the awkward 'horseless carriage', and *car* entered the language just before the end of the 19th century as a shortened form of 'motor-car' or 'autocar'.

In the US, *automobile* (from the French) was already the preferred usage. Appropriately, the American word was assembled from different parts, even if there were only two of them (Greek *autos* = *self* + French/Latin *mobile*). The French, who were at the forefront in developing automobile technology, also provided a tool-kit of other driving words, from *chauffeur* to *garage, limousine* to *coupé*. When *automobile* entered English usage, linguistic purists were up in arms at what they saw as a 'near indecent' hybrid, half-Greek, half-Latin. Similar objections were later made to *television*, also a combination of Greek and Latin – a salutary reminder that, when it comes to the English language, apparently no protest is considered too silly.

It wasn't only people but also words that went faster in the later 19th century. In 1815 news of the outcome of the Battle of Waterloo took four days to travel the 240 miles (384 km) or so between the Belgian battlefield and London. Within less than 70 years, an event of international interest like the volcanic eruption of Krakatoa in the Pacific (1883) could be 'seen' on the other side of world almost as soon as it occurred, either through the cabled testimony of witnesses or through the evidence provided by scientific instruments. The new science of telecommunications had replaced the exhausted human messenger or the string of horses or the signal waved from hilltop to hilltop.

Telegraph had been used as early as the 1790s to describe a primitive signalling system involving flags – now called semaphore – but, like *locomotive*, the word really came into its own after a world-changing invention, specifically that of the electromagnetic telegraph by Samuel Morse in 1836. This ushered in the era of telegrams and cables (so called because messages were sent between countries by underwater cable) and of the clipped style of language known as *telegraphese*. The next stage dispensed with cables altogether and, following Guglielmo Marconi's experiments, 'wire-less' messages could fly over oceans instead of beneath the waves. Hence the *wireless*, which persisted for years in Britain as a rather dated term for the radio and which now has a new lease of life in the age of *Wi-Fi* (a play on words with the old audio-recording term 'Hi-Fi'). The telephone was invented in 1876 by Alexander Graham Bell, although the word itself had already existed for several decades as a description of instruments that carried sound over a distance, including such primitive devices as a foghorn. It did not take long for this new method of communication to catch on. By the end of the 19th century there were more than six million telephones in the US.

A Morse code telegraph machine. The telegraph quickly became a key tool in news gathering, and was incorporated into the title of newspapers founded after its introduction, such as The Daily Telegraph *(1855) and the Dutch* De Telegraaf *(1893).*

ENGLISH IN TODAY'S WORLD

ENGLISH NOW
20th and 21st Centuries

THE FUTURE OF ENGLISH
21st Century On

*Newspaper and magazine headlines, incorporating a welter of
modern English buzz-words. Unsurprisingly, many of these
new coinages come from the world of Information Technology.*

English is thriving. It is spoken by hundreds of millions of people as their first language. Yet even this imposing number pales in comparison to the growing global total of those who employ English as a lingua franca in trade, travel and tourism. The language is growing in another sense too, as new words and expressions are added daily.

ENGLISH NOW

Three or four new words and phrases make their début in English every day. This phenomenon will only be intensified by modern modes of communication like blogging, texting and tweeting, all of which have greatly accelerated and broadened the spread of information. It is impossible to keep up with this profusion of new words. Indeed, some terms are so specialized that they will never appear in regular dictionaries. Every branch of science and technology, every area of human activity involving processes that are unfamiliar to most people (from aromatherapy to UFOlogy), generates its own language and develops its own variations on existing terms. One chemical dictionary, for example, contains the names of almost half a million compounds.

Non-specialist terms may never make the dictionary for a quite different reason: they are too ephemeral, the linguistic equivalent of those insects that live for a few days. By contrast, a few terms – a very few – might stick around for a century or two. It may be almost impossible to work out why certain words are successful and others are not. It is less difficult to work out their origins, although not always straightforward. And it is relatively easy to answer the question: what makes a word dictionary-worthy?

DEDICATED FOLLOWERS OF FASHION

For a new word, getting into a mainstream dictionary is a badge of respectability, like being given the keys to the house. This is because dictionaries tend to be regarded as the repositories of everything that is official and approved about language. As far as definitions are concerned, dictionaries ought to have the last word, if only because

Coined in 1925, 'motel' was formed by blending 'motor' and 'hotel'. It is an example of what Humpty Dumpty, in Lewis Carroll's Through the Looking-Glass *(1871) calls a 'portmanteau' word ('two meanings packed up into one word').*

ENGLISH NOW

there is no one and nothing else to turn to. But no dictionary – or rather no dictionary editor – passes judgement on a new word, in the sense of giving it some sort of moral green light. What he or she has to decide is whether a word justifies inclusion because it is widely used and/or has staying power. Once the decision has been made, the job is not finished because the word has to be defined and its history accounted for.

As examples of the problems of origin and definition which make the lexicographer's job so tricky, take the British term *chav* and the worldwide phrase *credit crunch*. These expressions from the early 21st century have staying power and already figure in dictionaries. The sources of *chav*, a highly derogatory term for an uncouth person, are disputed. It may be a dialect term akin to the Liverpudlian/Mancunian usage 'scally', or it may be related to a Romany (gypsy) expression. Its use is contentious, the snobbish equivalent of the US 'white trash' according to one commentator. Whatever its origins or its acceptability, *chav* is a word with a life of its own, as can be seen in tabloid headlines (*From chip-shop chav to catwalk queen*) or upmarket spin-offs like *uber-chav*, a bizarre combination of a German prefix and English slang.

Credit crunch may appear relatively straightforward by contrast. It fits at least one rule for the formation of new expressions, that of memorability (because of its alliteration, like *baby boomer* or *free fall*). Yet is it really all new? The colloquial use of *crunch* to signify a 'crisis', as in *when it comes to the crunch* or *crunch time*, long pre-dates the late 20th century. It is attributed to Winston Churchill in a newspaper article written shortly before the outbreak of the Second World War and may come from a decade earlier. One of the dictionary editor's main tasks is to pin down the first recorded use as precisely as possible.

Even when a word seems to qualify for dictionary inclusion, editors may differ. For instance, the American term *yadda yadda yadda*, equating roughly to *yackety-yak* or *blah blah blah*, was considered to have enough durability by one lexicographer to make it into his edition of a mid-1990s US dictionary but was rejected by another on the grounds that it was disappearing from use. Incidentally, the roots of *yadda yadda yadda* are also in dispute, with some attributing it to a 1960s routine by the comedian Lenny Bruce and others placing it much earlier, in the 1930s.

In these circumstances, being enshrined in the cold white pages of a dictionary looks both like an accolade and the final stages of a process. Yet the fortunes of a word may change even after it has received the dictionary's blessing. More than a few entries will turn curious or dated or even laughable as the years pass. *Funky, groovy, far out* and *with it* all appear in contemporary dictionaries but it is hard to imagine anyone using them now without a touch of irony.

Other expressions are here to stay. As an example of a newish piece of phrase-making, take *quantum leap*. Deriving from the highly specialized realm of quantum mechanics, it did not surface in everyday English until the later part of the 20th century when it tended at first to be used in business-speak rather than routine conversation. Like *seismic shift* and the more recent *step-change* (deriving from electronics), *quantum leap* suggests an abrupt departure from a previously established pattern, a change that is revolutionary rather than evolutionary.

It is not easy to say why such scientific terms establish themselves in everyday English and so become eligible for inclusion in standard dictionaries. Presumably, part of the answer is that people use them because they like the sound of them. To refer to a change as *seismic* or *quantum* has a more dramatic or authoritative ring than talking about a 'great' change, or a 'revolutionary' one. Scientific accuracy certainly isn't involved, since a quantum leap may actually be very small. However, the job of a dictionary is not to judge the appropriateness of particular terms nor to answer the (probably unanswerable) question of why some words and expressions carve themselves a niche in English. It is to record the meaning, and secondarily to provide other pieces of information like the etymology and pronunciation of the word.

Finally, it should be remembered that, when it comes to new words, dictionaries are followers of fashion and not makers of usage. Even though the latest editions will highlight their 'new' words and phrases to show how up-to-date they are, mainstream dictionaries are conservative by nature. Even so, they may not please all linguistic conservatives. For instance, some people object to the use of *disinterested* to mean 'bored by' and want it to keep its older sense of 'impartial'. But many more people are happy to use *disinterested* in the 'bored by' sense, and so that now appears in dictionaries too. The word *minuscule* is now more frequently found incorrectly spelled as 'miniscule' than in its right form, probably because of the 'mini-' association. If this variant spelling persists and becomes the established preference of the great majority, then that too will eventually end up in the dictionary as a variant spelling.

From business-speak to everyday usage: the alliterative 'credit crunch' caught on instantly as a term describing the crisis that hit the world's financial markets in 2008. 'Business-speak' has an interesting derivation in its own right, being formed by analogy with 'Newspeak' in George Orwell's novel 1984. *All such compounds now denote the impenetrable jargon of an élite group, which is designed both to intimidate and to obfuscate.*

A definition is the enclosing a wilderness of idea within a wall of words.

SAMUEL BUTLER, *NOTEBOOKS* (1912)

WHERE DO NEW WORDS COME FROM?

There are several ways in which words may be created but they are not likely to be made up from scratch. A 'new' word will only be part-new. Some component of it will be recognizable to its users. If it were not, then it would not be understood.

The simplest way to create a new term is by affixation, in which a modification is added to the beginning or end of a word. Prefixes such as *un-*, *dis-*, *re-* and *bi-*, and suffixes like *-ful*, *-less*, *-headed* and *-like* have been part of English for centuries. The process continues. The prefix *super-* can be attached to almost anything that needs a boost, from *supermarket* to *super-fast* to *superspy*. The suffix *-lite* started out as an advertisers' version of 'light' to refer to calories or alcohol content. Now it is used about anything that is either easy to absorb or is a (probably unsatisfactory) imitation of an original. A free newspaper is called *London Lite*. The attachment of *Lite* to a politician's name is a shorthand way not of disparaging him but a rival or successor (Blair Lite, Bush Lite). Even more popular, the suffix *-gate*, from the 1970s Watergate scandal, has shown extraordinary staying power.

Slightly more complex is the creation of a compound term in which each part is capable of standing alone (unlike re- or -less) but whose combination produces something new. These compounds number in the tens of thousands and usually operate as nouns or adjectives: *barcode, draft-dodger, blue-sky thinking, punch line, policy wonk, fixed-penalty, free-range, user-friendly, hit-and-miss*. Verb examples include: *air-freight, jump start, panic buy, second-guess, skydive*. English is particularly suited to this compound formation, and it is one of the principal ways in which the language grows.

Portmanteau terms are created when two existing words are not so much decorously joined together, as in the examples above, but forcibly pushed into partnership. In the process, some part of each term will be lost: *brunch* (breakfast +lunch), *gazunder* (gazump+under), *infomercial* (information+ commercial), *motel* (motor+hotel), *Spanglish* (Spanish+English), *staycation* (staying put+holiday).

'New' words may also be formed by simply chopping bits off old ones and turning them into new parts of speech. By a process known as back-formation, nouns and

KEYWORD
WATERGATE

Watergate is a Middle English word describing a gate opening onto water or a place through which water traffic passes, but it is much more familiar as a shorthand term for the US political scandal which resulted in the resignation of President Richard Nixon in 1974. An attempted burglary at the Democratic Party headquarters in the riverside Watergate building in Washington DC was linked to the 1972 campaign to re-elect Nixon, although it was the subsequent cover-up rather than the break-in itself that caused his downfall. The Watergate effect was so dramatic and far-reaching that the suffix *-gate* has been added ever since to any scandal, particularly if it threatens the reputation of a public figure, and use of the term has even spread to non-English-speaking countries like Germany and Greece. *The Oxford Dictionary of American Political Slang* (2004) lists over a hundred '-gate' expressions. Most are quickly forgotten and some are absurd. The Hoagie-gate 'scandal' in Philadelphia, for example, resulted from fans' displeasure at not being able to bring food into a sports stadium (hoagie = filled baguette).

occasionally adjectives are the usual sources for a fresh verb: *burgle* is a back-formation from *burglar*, *enthuse* from *enthusiasm*, *escalate* from *escalator*, *laze* from *lazy*. Sometimes a word that was one part of speech will be used as another without any change at all: so nouns such as *handbag, impact, message, progress* and *task* have all been given the job of verbs. Even the noun *verb* has been used as a verb ('I see you're verbing again') to describe the process.

Words join the ranks of English by other routes, however. In particular there are three areas where it could be claimed that a word is genuinely new rather than being cobbled together out of pre-existing components. These are borrowings from other languages, abbreviations and acronyms, and the use of eponyms.

An American stock car sponsored by Miller Lite. The first mainstream light beer sold in the United States ('Great Taste…Less Filling!'), Miller Lite was a runaway success when it was first marketed in 1975. The linguistic impact of the brand was long-lasting, with '-lite' later being appended to all sorts of terms to suggest that they are glib or 'dumbed-down' versions of the original.

FOREIGN WORDS AND BORROWINGS

English has always been enriched by 'foreign' words and phrases. The language was created and enlarged by outsiders, from the Romans to the Angles and the Saxons to the Normans. When the invasions ceased, and Britain began to be first a trading and then an imperial power, it imported thousands of terms from around the globe whether they were originally French or Hindi, Spanish or American Indian. These are now so thoroughly embedded in English that it would take a specialist to say where they came from. How many people are aware that *bungalow* comes from Hindi while *patio* is Spanish and *veranda* ultimately from Portuguese? But there are other words and phrases that still wear their foreignness like a badge, not yet at home but growing in popularity.

The German term *Schadenfreude* ('pleasure in the misfortunes of others') is a good example of a word that expresses a concept for which there is no direct equivalent in English. On the other hand, *tsunami* is needlessly supplanting 'tidal wave'. At the slangy end of the scale, there is the Italian-by-origin and genuinely useful *bimbo*. Once such a term feels at home, it spawns spin-offs like *bimbette* and *himbo*, a process that is a sure sign of the vitality of the original expression and a demonstration of our real need for it.

English even imports prefixes and suffixes from outside. For example, the German *-fest* (= gathering, celebration) can be tacked onto a variety of terms: *filmfest, talkfest, campfest*. Also popular are the Spanish-sounding *-ista* (*fashionista, recessionista*), and *-thon*, deriving from the Greek marathon but in itself meaningless (*talkathon, readathon*). More rarefied are three little German nouns/adjectives that function as prefixes and denote respectively something authentic, fake or very old: *echt, ersatz* and *ur*. If an actor is said to have *echt* (genuine) star quality, she is on her way to success and is unlikely to be content with *ersatz* (substitute) designer products. She may even be an *ur*-feminist (*ur* = original, archetypal).

There is also a humorous application of terms from other languages. The French *moi?* is used in this way. There is a range of no- or nothing-words from other languages which may be spoken either humorously or for emphasis: *nix* from the German *nicht, nada* from Spanish, *nyet* from Russian, as well as the slangy *zip* and *zilch*, whose origins are unknown. The odd colloquial expression may be employed in imitation of another language: *cheapo, no problemo* (even though the Spanish for 'problem' is actually *problema*).

Different languages are deployed in different fields. French was historically the language of diplomacy, of *détente* and *démarche*, but it is just as traditionally the language of sex and romance as in *billet doux* or *cinq à sept*, the time between afternoon and evening for lovers' rendezvous. Latin, functional and precise, provides us with many of the abbreviations we still use (*e.g., i.e., etc.*). From Spanish comes a handful of self-assertively 'masculine' terms like *macho* and *cojones* (= 'testicles' = 'balls' = 'courage'). German gives us complicated concepts like *Weltschmerz* ('sadness at the state of the world') while Italy offers up *dolce far niente* (literally 'sweet doing nothing' and so the 'pleasure of idleness').

ABBREVIATIONS AND ACRONYMS

Abbreviations exist partly to speed up writing and occasionally speech. They are multiplying so fast that a recent dictionary of all forms of abbreviation contains over half a million entries but the great majority are for specialist use. Anyone in an organization is likely to be familiar with abbreviations to do with work procedures, job titles, even the parts of a building, that would not be understood by outsiders. This illustrates another key function of specialist abbreviations – to create a sense of 'insider' familiarity.

Abbreviations in general use are shortened forms of a word (Dr, Mrs, St, Rd) which is not always meant to be said aloud, while an acronym is a combination of letters each of which stands for something and which are then run together to make a pronounceable word. Again, they can be general: AIDS (Acquired Immune Deficiency Syndrome); specialist: CAD (computer-aided design); or somewhere in between: POTUS (President of the United States). Some acronyms are so established as words that most people are unaware that they are abbreviations: radar (radio detection and ranging), scuba (self-contained underwater breathing apparatus).

Other sorts of abbreviation take part of a word or words and become so routine that it would be odd to refer to them in full except in the most formal circumstances: fridge, phone, pram, bus. Texting and e-mails are responsible for a plethora of abbreviations designed to be read rather than said aloud, like LOL (laughs out loud), IMHO (in my humble opinion), FAQ (frequently asked questions). Some English abbreviations achieve worldwide currency even among those who have little or no knowledge of the language. AIDS is one example while the BBC is another, and among the British the latter is often shortened further to the 'Beeb'. The abbreviation *E.T.* was good enough for a film title and so was the less familiar *S.W.A.T.*, at least in the US (it stands for Special Weapons and Tactics).

Other abbreviations do double or triple duty and only the context will make clear which is meant: ETA is 'estimated time of arrival' but also the Basque separatist organization in northern Spain. Upper-case PC stands for Police Constable or Political Correctness while its lower-case form (pc) means personal computer. The terms making up acronyms in particular may be chosen to create a word that fits their function. In Britain, the police information database is known as HOLMES (Home Office Large and Major Enquiry System). The pop artist Andy Warhol (1928–87) was shot and seriously wounded in 1968 by a woman who wrote a manifesto for an organization calling itself SCUM or the Society for Cutting up Men.

EPONYMOUS WORDS

Eponyms form a category of words that are authentically fresh to the English language from the moment they are coined. This is because they are expressions that derive from people (and occasionally places) and describe a process or an object, a quality or an attitude. Since the expression is wholly dependent on the fame or inventiveness of the person responsible for it, the word would not exist without its originator. Occasionally, such a term may become so familiar that we forget there really was a Braille (Louis Braille, 1809–52) who invented the reading-by-touch method for the blind or a Biro (Lászlo Biró, 1899–1985) who created the ballpoint pen.

Eponyms go beyond physical inventions. The 40th US president Ronald Reagan (1911–2004) had an entire economic system named after him in *Reaganomics*, as did the genuine economist John Maynard Keynes (1883–1946),

Poster in Ho Chi Minh City, Vietnam, warning against the spread of AIDS. The English acronym for a condition first diagnosed in the United States, caught on worldwide. Except, of course, in Francophone countries, which insist on retaining Gallic word order, which requires a post-positioned adjective – hence, SIDA.

Prime Minister Winston Churchill delivering one of the rousing wartime speeches that won him a reputation for pugnacious defiance. The adjective 'Churchillian' is synonymous with 'dogged' or 'determined'. Churchill himself is often credited with inventing the term 'Iron Curtain' (in a speech in March 1946), but in fact he was merely Anglicizing a term first used the year before by Nazi Propaganda Minister Joseph Goebbels ('Eiserner Vorhang').

who gave us *Keynesianism*. Eponyms can also be drawn from places. *Oxbridge*, describing the type of education provided by Oxford and Cambridge Universities, is sometimes used as shorthand for 'privileged', or 'élitist'. *Ruritanian* derives from the imaginary mid-European country created by Anthony Hope (1863–1933) in the novel *The Prisoner of Zenda* (1894) and means 'colourful and intriguing' or simply 'make-believe'.

Eponyms, whether nouns or adjectives, are often selective. Politicians are pleased to be called *Churchillian* and may go out of their way to court the comparison, as the term alludes only to Churchill's inspirational leadership, not to his hobby of brick-laying or his notorious bouts of depression. Eponymous descriptions can also be contradictory or ambiguous. Writers are called *Dickensian* if they throw a grotesque character or two into the mix, but the expression is just as frequently used to describe a grimy, real-life scene (one of '*Dickensian* squalor') while, paradoxically, it may also mean 'sentimental' or conjure up an image of a cosy, old-fashioned Christmas. Political epithets such as *Thatcherite* or *Blairite* or *Bushite* taken from world statesmen (interesting that these distinctive figures all have that snappy '-ite' suffix) are common, at least while the leader is in power, but only the tone or context will indicate approval and disapproval.

Eponyms therefore qualify as genuine additions to the language. Sometimes they apply to something which is authentically new, like braille or the biro. Most of the time, though, eponymous terms are applied to things already in existence. There would be jealousy within families if Sigmund Freud had never come up with the Oedipus Complex, just as there would be suspense films if Alfred Hitchcock had never been born, but the eponym pins down the subject in ways that expressions like 'jealousy' or 'suspense' don't quite manage.

SLANG AND JARGON

Of all the sources of fresh words into English – whether borrowings from other languages or abbreviations, and so on – the most vigorous and unfailing are slang and jargon. These two related linguistic forms are vital and inescapable parts of language. On the linguistic spectrum, slang lies on the far side of language termed 'colloquial' or 'conversational'. On the same spectrum, colloquial English is itself beyond the band known as 'formal'. But language is never fixed. Yesterday's slang may be welcomed with open arms into the standard language of today. *Mob* was once objected to as a slang or vulgar usage because it was a shortened version of the Latin *mobile vulgus* (roughly, an 'excitable crowd'), rather as *ad* for *advertisement* would be rejected in today's formal English use.

Jargon is more upmarket than slang. It describes the language used by a particular group, often one associated with a trade or profession. Jargon is related to slang in that it cannot naturally be used in many situations, unlike standard English, and also in that it will frequently be baffling to outsiders. In general, jargon isn't as vigorous or attractive as slang and it lacks slang's potential to cause offence, but these two forms of English have enough similarities to be treated under the same heading here.

RHYMING SLANG

Rhyming slang is most commonly associated with Cockneys and London's East End. It is formed by taking a phrase which rhymes with the word that is being given the slang treatment, and then using that phrase instead. Almost everyone recognizes that *trouble and strife* means *wife*, that *apples and pears* are *stairs* and *whistle and flute* a *suit* or that to *have a butcher's* is to have a *look* (butcher's hook = look) while *porkies* (pork pies) are *lies*. This is colourful, tourist-friendly slang. One of the distinctive features of rhyming slang is the use of proper names so that *Adam and Eve* equals *believe* while a *Mars Bar* is a *scar*.

There's a cheekiness and irreverence about the use of some names which fits the traditional Cockney image and which is part of the point of the expression. *Doris Day* stands for 'gay' while British DJ Pete Tong figures in *It's all gone Pete Tong* meaning *It's all gone a bit wrong*. The phrase was sufficiently familiar to be used as the title of a 2004 British film about a DJ in Ibiza. Celebrity couple David and Victoria Beckham reputedly do double duty in rhyming slang with *Posh and Becks* standing for *sex* while the reverse *Becks and Posh* equals *nosh* (itself a slang term for food, from Yiddish). Colourful as they are, it seems unlikely that all or many of these recent coinages come from the East End, just as it's unlikely that very many people use them regularly in everyday speech. Even so, they make for linguistic variety.

The slang that consists of routine and familiar words is widely accessible although its use will be governed by people's preferences and the context for speaking or writing it. An illustration from British English: *nick* has a formal dictionary definition as a *small notch* but is widely understood – and much more widely used – in at least three different slang senses, as a noun (*prison*) and as a verb with two definitions (*to arrest, to steal*). But nick in these latter senses would never be written or spoken in a formal situation, for example by a policeman giving evidence in court, and there are quite a few people who would avoid using nick in any slang sense at all. In the same way, the many slang terms for money whether in general or in specific amounts – *bread, dosh, dough, moolah, quid, fiver, tenner, buck, greenback* – would usually be avoided in formal contexts.

What one might call general or popular slang is in this respect like swear-words (themselves a form of slang, being unofficial, not respectable and so on). Everybody is familiar with the standard swear-words but many people either avoid using them at all or use them in specific company or situations.

The other type of slang is more private, almost privileged, and shades into jargon. It marks out its users as members of a group, whether by age, ethnic grouping, profession, interests and so on. It has a function other than simple communication. Since it can be fully understood only by those who fall into the same group, it marks out the boundaries of that group and effectively deters others from entering. No one over a certain age would be likely to follow a conversation among teenagers with the same degree of understanding, not to say enjoyment, as those taking part in it. Similarly, if an outsider was allowed to wander into a circle of chattering lawyers or soldiers or surfers who were talking about their specialism (law, war, surfing), then that person would probably be at a loss to understand. The gist of the conversation might be clear but the details would remain elusive because of the slang or jargon involved.

TALKING SHOP AND SOUNDING COOL

Slang and jargon derive from several sources and come in different styles, from technical to casual. The most significant from the linguistic point of view are those that filter into general usage. Three can be highlighted.

1 Slang deriving from criminal or quasi-legal activity has always been popular. Films and books glamourize criminal-related slang today just as Elizabethan guides to thieves' cant did 400 years ago. Crime buffs will know from Raymond Chandler's private-eye novels that *gat* is US slang for *gun* and also that its heyday was the 1940s, since when it has been replaced by terms such as *piece* or *heat*. Of all forms of slang, 'thieves' jargon' is arguably the most exciting because it seems to provide a glimpse of a closed and dangerous world. Drug-dealing and drug-taking have also spawned hundreds of expressions, a few of which like *pot* or *crack* or *shoot up* have entered mainstream English.

2 Almost every trade, job, profession or vocation has an armoury of specialist terms employed by those working on the inside but baffling, even incomprehensible, to those who aren't in the know. For example, in Royal Navy submarine jargon, it might be simple enough for the outsider to deduce that a *fish* is a *torpedo* but the same outsider would be thrown by the expression *lose the bubble*, meaning *to lose track* either literally or metaphorically (because when the bubble on the inclinometer in a submarine disappears control of the vessel has been lost).

The world of those who work with computers, or more specifically those who make, sell and repair them, is full of jargon. As is that of doctors or politicians. Or, to a lesser extent, teachers and bus drivers. The quantity of jargon will obviously be related to the number of special processes and procedures, the pieces of equipment and even the gadgets employed in any specialist area as well as to less obvious things like the the hierarchy of an organization or even the lay-out of a building – think of the terms used to describe different parts of a hospital. Sometimes the words of a particular specialism will break free and get into general English. You can be totally ignorant of how computers work and still talk about software, surfing and firewalls.

There is also a type of professional jargon which, while not closed to the outsider, remains quite hard to understand. The terms found in sports reporting can be tricky if you don't know the rules of the game. More markedly, the language deployed in business or financial journalism often comes near to a kind of coded speech which is only to be readily understood by initiates. Such language, formal and enclosed, may seem a very long way from slang but – like slang conversation – it employs shorthand expressions (*dead-cat bounce, leveraging, white knight*) and abbreviations (FSA, RPI, NASDAQ) which are familiar to insiders but would need a few sentences of explanation to the financial innocent.

3 The most influential slang, whether in the United States, Britain or other English-speaking countries, consists in terms either coined or made popular in African-American usage. From *bling bling* to the *blues*, from *chill* to *cool* to *hot*, from the *nitty gritty* to *rock'n'roll* to *tell it like it is*, these are words and phrases that have made themselves at home in English, and even infiltrated other languages such as French. They give their users – which is to say, most of us – 'street cred', another slang term. Although these expressions may sound contemporary, some go back a long way. Terms such as *hip, square* and *groovy* are defined in the *Hepster's Dictionary* of 1938 while a piece with the title 'Memphis Blues' was written in 1910. The origins of other terms are disputed or lost in time. This is not surprising, given the obscured and neglected history of the black forced settlement in America.

'Hoods' brandishing a 'gat' pull a 'heist' – all US gangster slang words that originated between the beginning of the 20th century and 1930. Still from the film Little Caesar *(1931), starring Edward G. Robinson.*

Popular or 'hip' as black slang is, it is not standard English, and so is much more likely to be used in speech rather than written down, at least in a formal context. It preserves a touch of its 'outsider' status, one reason why it is popular with young white speakers. These are *wannabes*, a term that as recently as the 1980s applied to black people who wanted to be white, but now operates in reverse in addition to describing those who want to be just about anything or anybody glamorous.

Advertisers and others were quick enough to catch on, when it became safe to do so. *Whassup?* from black English was an inescapable catchphrase for promoting a beer brand in the early 2000s. Irregular 'hip-hop' spellings have become almost standard if a youthful audience is targeted, as in films like *Antz* or *Boyz N the Hood* or any *X-treme* sport on television. Slang goes mainstream.

THE ALLURE OF AMERICA

The engine of global English is the United States. The fact that the language is still widely used in countries such as India and Malaysia is a legacy of Britain's colonial past. But the reason that citizens of other, expanding nations such as China and Brazil wish to learn English is a testament to the power of the United States, whether industrial, commercial or cultural. Relations between British

WORD GAMES

Word games are an inseparable part of many languages but it is probably the case that the English language is particularly suited to them – or, more accurately, that many English speakers have a passionate attachment to crosswords, puns, riddles, palindromes and the like. Riddles were popular in Anglo-Saxon times although they were more like little poems than the limp one-liners inside Christmas crackers. A popular image has these early English speakers sitting around and exchanging puzzles while they quaffed mead. Certainly the riddles show ingenuity as well as a taste for the *double entendre*. A well-known one talks about a 'wonderful thing hanging by a man's thigh' which is 'stiff and hard'. It goes on in this vein for some time leading the listener to an almost inevitable conclusion (in fact, the answer is 'key').

A giant Scrabble game at Wembley Stadium in 1998. Scrabble's inventor worked out the point values of letters according to a frequency analysis of various sources. These naturally change in other languages – in English Scrabble, Z is worth 10, but in Polish only 1.

Two great 20th-century inventions that have spread round the world testify to the continuing fascination of messing about with English words. Scrabble was created by an American architect called Alfred Butts in 1938 although it wasn't marketed as a board game until the 1950s. And the craze for crosswords began after the First World War. An interesting distinction between the United States and the United Kingdom is that the latter has a definite preference for cryptic puzzles, while the US leans more towards grids filled with straight definitions or synonyms.

English and the American variety have often been strained and sometimes close to abusive, at least on the British side. Now a kind of truce exists.

The linguistic influence is largely one-way. The days when American writers and politicians would look uneasily towards the mother country for linguistic approval died out around the time of Independence. The dominance of America in world culture today means that its form of English is likely to be the one that prevails. There is little that is conscious or deliberate about this, whether on the part of the linguistic exporters (the US) or from the importers' side. It is a process that is gradual, small-scale, undramatic. When someone says they are meeting a friend at the train station (rather than the railway station) they are using an American formula, just as when they say 'We're running out of gas'. President Truman famously had a sign on his desk in the 1940s announcing 'The buck stops here', referring to the 'buck' used to mark the dealer in a card-game and indicating that responsibility for everything ultimately lay with the occupant of the White House. Yet the phrase has been used for years in British English.

There used to be hostility towards the Americanization of British English. Indeed, in the 19th century and earlier there was a distinct disdain in Britain for all things American. In his novel *Martin Chuzzlewit* (1844), Charles Dickens drew on his own experience of visiting the country to produce a satirical portrait of a rowdy, bombastic culture in which lofty rhetoric was often at odds with reality. He has one of his characters remark: 'They've such a passion for Liberty, that they can't help taking liberties with her.' Describing the violence that follows an election Dickens comments: '[T]he friends of the disappointed candidate had found it necessary to assert the great principles of the Purity of Election and Freedom of Opinion by breaking a few legs and arms, and furthermore pursuing one obnoxious gentleman through the streets with the design of slitting his nose.'

But at the same time Dickens noted the almost boundless self-confidence of the country ('What are the Great United States for, sir,' pursued the General, 'if not for the regeneration of man?'). Nevertheless, Martin Chuzzlewit does not have a very happy time in the United States and almost dies of fever in a god-forsaken spot that goes by the ironic name of Eden. The novel caused considerable offence on its publication in America.

The same mixture of snobbery, condemnation and envy continued through the 19th century and even into the late 20th century. In *Mother Tongue* (1990), Bill Bryson quotes a member of the House of Lords saying in a 1978 debate: 'If there is a more hideous language on the face of the Earth than the American form of English, I should like to know what it is.'

This hidebound attitude hasn't entirely disappeared but it is far less prevalent than it used to be. The truth is that the vigour, inventiveness and reach of American English have been enormously enriching factors in the health of the language on both sides of the Atlantic and around the world. There is an old story that German was proposed as the official language of the United States at the time of its Independence. The story is apocryphal and, in any case, America

Slang is a language that rolls up its sleeves, spits on its hands and goes to work.

CARL SANDBURG,
THE NEW YORK TIMES (1959)

has no official language laid down by law. But had the German legend been true or had the dominant earlier settlers of the country not been of English-speaking stock – in others words if, through some historical circumstance, North Americans were today speaking some other language – then this story of English would be a very different one in its later chapters.

Of all the western European countries that held extensive imperial possessions in their heyday – Spain, Portugal, France, Britain, even Germany – there is only one that has gone on to find its language willingly employed right around the globe long after their respective empires crumbled or were dismantled. That this should be so is not on account of the intrinsic convenience or ease of speaking English and only partly because of the very wide extent of the British Empire but largely because of the pre-eminence of the US.

'TWO NATIONS DIVIDED BY A COMMON LANGUAGE'

Is it possible to discuss the difference between British and American English without introducing the famous remark about 'two nations divided by a common language'? Obviously not. The paradoxical comment has been attributed to a range of wits but it embodies a truth. Although speaking the same language, a British visitor to the United States could be struck by hundreds of linguistic differences. The same goes for an American visitor to Britain.

These differences of diction, spelling and punctuation are, individually, small. To take a random sample: in Britain, you write (a letter) to your sister, in America you write your sister. On New York's Broadway you would go to the *theater*, possibly making your journey by *subway* and completing it with a short stroll on the *sidewalk*, while on London's Shaftesbury Avenue it's the *theatre* you would be visiting after a *tube* trip and a walk on the *pavement*. In US written English it is correct practice to follow a colon with as capital letter, in British English with a lower-case one, as in the second sentence of this paragraph.

In the US, the 's' in verbs like *civilise* is replaced by 'z' – pronounced 'zed' by the British and 'zee' by Americans (the 'z' form of verbs is also used by some British publishers, such as Oxford University Press and the publisher of this book). Standard American pronunciation of *fertile* rhymes with *turtle*, while for the British the stress falls on the last syllable, to rhyme with *isle*. In Britain *faggot* was once a bundle of sticks and is still a type of meatball while in the US it's a piece of abusive and homophobic slang. A *hooker* for a British sports fan is a player in rugby football (someone whose job it is to 'hook' the ball) while for an American the word indicates a prostitute (deriving either from the name of a Civil War general or, more probably, from a district of Manhattan). And so on ...

Yes, these differences are slight, sometimes detectable only by the geeks (US slang) and anoraks (British slang) of language, but collectively they suggest the considerable gap that exists in the two countries either side of the 'pond'. And, incidentally the 'pond' description of the Atlantic, sometimes the 'big pond' or the 'herring pond', is a definitively American term.

Characters from Dickens's Martin Chuzzlewit (1844). The author's bitterly satirical attitude towards America in this novel was prompted by his unsuccessful attempts to lobby for an international copyright law while touring the country in 1842. Unscrupulous US publishers had made a fortune by pirating his works.

DIFFERENCES BETWEEN BRITISH AND AMERICAN ENGLISH

Spelling

Suffixes: the tendency is for simplification, with the US form of word-endings sometimes discarding redundant letters and in general having a spelling which is closer to the way the word is sounded.

Examples, with the British usage first, include:
- -ce/-se: *defence/defense; *licence/license; offence/offense; *practice/practise*

    (*British noun spelling, verb is spelled with an 's'; US spelling is 's' for both noun and verb)
- -ise/-ize: *civilise/civilize; colonise/colonize; harmonise/harmonize; organise/organize; realise/realize; recognise/recognize*
- -our/-or: *behaviour/behavior; colour/color; harbour/harbor; honour/honor; humour/humor; labour/labor; neighbour/neighbor; odour/odor*
- -re/-er: *accoutrements/accouterments; calibre/caliber; centre/center; fibre/fiber; litre/liter; sabre/saber; spectre/specter; sombre/somber*

Simplification of diphthongs (ae, oe) by removal of first letter
anaemic/anemic; anaesthetic/anesthetic; encyclopaedia/encyclopedia; foetus/fetus; leukaemia/leukemia; mediaeval/medieval; oesophagus/esophagus; paediatrics/pediatrics

Double or single 'l'

British English frequently doubles an 'l' where US English sticks to the single consonant:
counsellor/counselor; dialling/dialing; initialling/initialing; marvellous/marvelous; modelling/modeling; signalled/signaled; travelled/traveled

But the reverse also applies, with US English doubling the 'l':
distil/distill; enrol/enroll; skilful/skillful; wilful/willful

Omission of hyphens

American English tends to use fewer hyphens in compound words, particularly when those words are of US coinage:
anti-tax/antitax; long-time/longtime; non-violent/nonviolent; one-time/onetime; pre-teen/preteen

General spelling variants

aluminium/aluminum; axe/ax; cheque/check; grey/gray; sceptic/skeptic; storey/story (in building); *vice/vise* (workshop tool)

Word and phrase differences

A very small selection of the well-known and the more curious includes:
autumn/fall; braces/suspenders; car park/parking lot; condom/rubber; curtains/drapes; estate agent/realtor; tap/faucet; ground floor/first floor; full stop/period; mobile/cell (phone); nappy/diaper; prostitute/hooker; public school/private school; trousers/pants

The future of the English language is assured in the sense that it will continue to be used around the world by increasing numbers of people for spoken and written communication. For the foreseeable future, English is set to be the dominant global tongue. But the development of the language may not lie entirely in the hands of native speakers – people, that is, who learned to speak it before they were aware they were speaking English …

THE FUTURE OF ENGLISH

It is estimated that by 2020 the native speakers of English will be a small minority compared to the total numbers who will be using or learning the language. At the moment there may be as many as 350 million Chinese learning English, a higher number than the entire population of the United States. Such statistics suggest that already most English conversations are conducted between people who are not native speakers but are employing English as a lingua franca. Imagine a business meeting between individuals from China, Brazil, Singapore and Australia. Which language will they naturally turn to?

SINGLISH, CHINGLISH AND PANGLISH

The English that is used around the globe is often far removed from the regular (and easily recognizable) English employed by the BBC or *The New York Times*. Forms of pidgin or creole have appeared in countries such as Singapore, Malaysia and China, where they are known as Singlish and Chinglish respectively.

The historical reasons for the emergence of these different 'Englishes' are themselves distinct. In regions that were once under British control, like the Malay Peninsula, a knowledge of English would have been valuable for the indigenous population, in exactly the same way that the ability to speak some Latin would have been useful for the Britons living under Roman rule. After independence (1957 in the

Text messaging is deplored by traditionalists, but it is here to stay. It has given rise to a new, clipped mode of communication in English composed of (sometimes highly inventive) contractions, acronyms and rebuses.

The uppermost of these two signs, in the city of Zhouzheng in China, is an example of Chinglish: the Chinese characters mean 'This Way', but have been rendered as 'Moving Forward' (overuse of the gerund is very common in Chinglish).

case of Malaya), the language of the invaders or colonizers becomes something of a mixed blessing to its native users. On the one hand, it is the language of government and bureaucracy, and probably of business too. On the other, it is not 'their' language but the tongue of another nation, one with which relations will never have been equal or completely harmonious, even at their best. The emergence of a pidgin form of English can therefore be interpreted symbolically as a rejection of the 'pure' linguistic standards of the past. More practically, it may simply reflect a decline in the numbers of teachers capable of passing on standard English.

The situation is different in the case of China. British influence here was never very great, except in the enclave of Hong Kong, and the emergence of English variants such as Chinglish has more to do with China's growing status as a world power, particularly in trade and commerce, than anything in history. The importance of the United States here cannot be overestimated. Whereas in, say, Malaya and India the persistence of English as a significant language is largely because of their colonial inheritance, the current popularity of English in China and elsewhere is a reflection of the linguistic dominance of the US. The requirement for any country wishing to do business – in any sense – on the world stage is to acknowledge that fact and to encourage many of its citizens to master English. As it happens, people do not seem to need that much encouragement. They turn to English by choice, even if they make it their own through dialect variation like Singlish.

In Singapore English, or Singlish, terms from English, Malay and a Chinese dialect are mingled. Sometimes the result is to give an English term a slight twist. For example, *havoc* is used as an adjective to mean 'wild' while *horrigible* is a vivid blending of 'horrible' and 'incorrigible' to describe something or someone really dreadful. Some English words may be more thoroughly adapted and altered. *Sabo* is a shortened form of 'sabotage' and can imply anything from serious damage to a practical joke ('You don'ch sabo me, I warn you, ah!'), and a *sabo king* is a person who makes a habit of such behaviour. *Using eye power* describes the person who stands by and watches others do the work.

As there was until quite recently in Britain a disdain for non-standard forms of English, so too there is official suspicion of these new forms of the language emerging from Asia. As far back as 1978, the then prime minister of Singapore, Lee Kuan Yew, commented on the 'strange Singapore pidgin' which he considered to be damaging his country's image. It was a dialect he did his best to 'improve' through media campaigns and education reforms.

A similar concern with image prompted the Chinese authorities during the months leading up to the 2008 Beijing Olympics to try to eradicate clumsy or obscure public signs. Examples included *IF YOU ARE STOLEN, CALL THE POLICE AT ONCE* and *ENVIRONMENTAL SANITATION NEEDS YOUR CONSERVE*. In fact, almost all English speakers would be able to grasp the general meaning of such notices if they were aware of the context.

Whatever the attitude of the authorities, it is unlikely to make much difference in the long run to the development of these alternative Englishes.

If there is one conclusion to be drawn from a study of linguistic history, it is that language goes its own way. In the future a standard English will persist around the globe but it is likely that local variations will flourish too. An emerging term for this mass of regional tongues is Panglish, a combination of the Greek *pan* (= 'all') and English. The English language, or small portions of it, may be thought of as the essential component in a range of dishes to which local flavours and ingredients have been added.

> *Words are the leaves of the tree of language, of which, if some fall away, a new succession takes their place.*
>
> FIELD-MARSHAL SIR JOHN FRENCH (1852–1925)

FRANGLAIS AND SPANGLISH

One place where the widening impact of English is not welcomed, at least at the official level, is France. There is a certain irony in this, given that much of the English of the last thousand years has been shaped by Norman French, ever since the Conquest of 1066. The use by the French of English words, either because no equivalents exist in their language or because the English forms are preferred, is known as *Franglais*. This is a so-called 'portmanteau' term (see caption, page 161; in passing, it is worth noting that *portmanteau* is itself a French word!) combining *français* and *anglais*.

Familiar examples include *le weekend, le parking* and *le fast-food*. In each case the French have an equivalent expression but it evidently does not quite do the job required. For example, the French for *weekend* is *fin de semaine* or 'end of the week', which conveys a different sense. *Fast food* is more elegantly rendered as (food which is) *prêt-à-manger* or 'ready to eat', and the term sounds sufficiently stylish to English ears to have been used as a brand name to which no one in Britain has objected. Protests against Franglais, however, are longstanding on the other side of the Channel. As far back as 1964 there appeared a book called *Parlez-vous franglais?* It was critical of English imports but even the French referred to it as *un bestseller* rather than using their own more elaborate phrase, *livre à succès.*

Spanglish is another portmanteau term, combining Spanish and English, and describes the mixture of the two languages used by the sizeable Hispanic communities in the USA, particularly in the southern states. Sometimes an English word or phrase is inserted into an otherwise Spanish sentence: *'Tú tienes las keys ... I left mine adentro.'* ('You have the keys ... I left mine inside.'). Sometimes an English-sounding term is favoured over a Spanish one, like *marketa* for 'market' instead of *mercado*, or *troca* (truck) in place of *camioneta*. Spanglish does not cause the same anguish as Franglais partly because it is the preserve of immigrant communities rather than indigenous speakers, although there are concerns that it will eventually have an impact on Spanish itself.

From the opposite angle, there have been concerns expressed in the US about the linguistic impact of the sheer numbers of Hispanic speakers, with predictions of an emerging 'bifurcated America' that uses two languages, Spanish and English. Whatever may be occurring in some areas this seems unlikely to

Formed by analogy with 'prêt-à-porter' ('ready-to-wear', from the world of haute couture), the French term 'prêt-à-manger' was adopted by a British sandwich chain that was founded in 1986. It cleverly gave a new spin to fast food as being something modish and (stylishly) French. But not so French that the accents were retained.

MONDEGREENS

A bizarre category of new phrases related to mishearings is called *mondegreens*, although the origin is arguably the most interesting aspect of the term. The American writer Sylvia Wright used the expression 'mondegreen' in a 1954 magazine article to describe how, when young, she heard the final line of a verse from an old ballad as:

Ye Highlands and ye Lowlands,
Oh, where hae ye been?
They hae slain the Earl Amurry,
And Lady Mondegreen.

The poignant picture of a romantically named lady lying beside her dead lover is a mishearing of the actual fourth line, which runs 'And laid him on the green' (and it's also the Earl of Murray, not Amurry).

One of the most familiar mondegreens – 'Gladly, the Cross-eyed Bear', a creative mishearing of the hymn line 'Gladly the cross I'd bear' – is the title of a detective novel by Ed McBain. Many famous mondegreens come from pop songs, including 'I'm courting a tramp' ('I'm caught in a trap', from Elvis Presley's 'Suspicious Minds').

---

happen nationwide in any meaningful sense. For hundreds of years the USA has shown a unique capacity to absorb immigrants, the overwhelming majority of whom have mastered English if it was not already their first language.

NEOLOGISMS

The future of a language lies partly in its ability to recruit new words from a variety of sources. Some will be made up out of existing stock, some will be imported from other languages, and a few may be created almost from new or emerge as the result of misunderstanding.

Leaving aside eponyms such as *hoover* or *boycott*, in which an invention or process is named after someone (see pages 167–8), it is highly unusual to be able to trace the source of a word to a single person. *Chortle* was coined in the 19th century by *Alice in Wonderland* author Lewis Carroll, as was *galumph*. Both are so-called portmanteau words, formed by welding together two existing terms (*chortle* = chuckle+snort, *galumph* = gallop+triumph) along the lines of *brunch* or *motel*. James Joyce used *quark* in his last novel *Finnegans Wake* (1939) and it was taken up by grateful scientists and applied to a subatomic particle. The term *blurb*, describing the material on a book jacket, is attributed to the American humorous author Gelett Burgess in 1907.

Of course, anybody can create a new word or neologism, but the chances of its catching on are minimal. Media exposure is the surest way to implant a new coinage, although successes are likely to be catchphrases rather than genuinely fresh expressions (*bovvered* for *bothered*, for example, popularized by

ACRONYMS AND OTHER PUZZLES

Although there has been plenty of protest from language traditionalists about the deleterious effects of texting and the use of abbreviations or creative misspellings or the other devices (like repeated exclamation marks!!!!!), these are not unique to the age of text. During the Second World War love-letters between separated couples might feature ITALY on the flap of the envelope not as part of the address but as an acronym of I Trust And Love You. (There are other, more explicit acronyms, such as BURMA and NORWICH.) During the long era of telegrams, when each word came at an additional cost, brevity was vital. Novelist Evelyn Waugh, working as a foreign correspondent in the 1930s, was telegraphed about a supposed victim of an Italian air raid in Ethiopia: 'Send two hundred words upblown nurse.' Waugh, unable to find out whether the story was true, replied: 'Nurse unupblown.' As for the misspellings and manglings of language: a long-running advertising campaign claimed that BEANZ MEANZ HEINZ. You could once see a sign in some British pubs, asking 'RU18 or 1/8?' – meaning 'Are you over 18 or one over the eight?' Such puzzles, involving letters, numbers and symbols, are known as rebuses.

the BBC's *The Catherine Tate Show*). New 'literary' words tend to stay confined to the page where they first appeared. As well as creating the *quark*, James Joyce described the sea as *snotgreen* and *scrotumtightening* in the first pages of his novel *Ulysses* (1922) but, however vivid these adjectives, they were never likely to be part of everyday speech. The really successful neologisms have no father or mother. They just appear. The origins of terms like *blog, chav, bling* and *podcast* can generally be explained – although the derivation of 'chav' is as mysterious and contested as the much older *OK* (see page 14)– but they are not the invention of any specific individual.

Some new expressions arise by mistake. *A damp squib*, to describe something that doesn't go off with the expected bang, is frequently rendered as a *damp squid*, presumably through some association between wetness and undersea creatures and because more people can visualize a squid than they can a squib (a 16th-century term for a firework). Similarly, *fell swoop* emerges as *fowl swoop, foul swoop* and other variations. *To the manner born* is often written as *to the manor born*, while *praying mantis* may come out as *preying mantis*. But the mistaken version can not only preserve the sense of the original, sometimes it even strengthens the older form. A *fell swoop* describes the deadly descent of a hawk-like bird on its prey, so both *fowl* and *foul* fit the meaning. Someone who behaves as *to the manner born* probably carries the sense of entitlement that comes with being born in a manor, and the 'wrong' version of the phrase was the punning title of a BBC 1970s sitcom. And, finally, although the mantis is described as *praying* because it carries its forelegs in an attitude of prayer, it is also a very predatory insect.

TEXTING AND E-MAILS

People are always on the look-out for developments in English, usually so that they can pick holes in them. The advent of the internet and the mobile phone provoked some dire predictions about the future of English.

There was an outcry when texting and e-mail became really popular. Some language pundits claimed that these new forms of communication encouraged laziness, that the English language was being wrecked, that a generation of schoolchildren would never learn to spell words or to punctuate properly because they were hopelessly addicted to the abbreviations and short-cuts of text language. For such people, CUL8R was the message which signalled the end of the world.

As language expert David Crystal points out, many texters probably enjoy breaking the linguistic rules but, in order to do so, they first have to know what those rules are. The essential aspect of a message is that it is understood by the recipient and, if the sender disregards too many rules, then it becomes incomprehensible and fails in its primary purpose. One could argue that texting and e-mails have led to an increase in writing at all ages, at all levels and at all times. People text on the way to work, at work, on the way home and during every waking hour not covered by those times. And when they are not texting, they may well be firing off e-mails. It is sometimes said that this has been at the expense of traditional letter-writing, but the decline of the hand-written epistle long pre-dated the arrival of the computer and the mobile phone.

One newish feature which e-mails and texting have introduced is the 'emoticon', a combination of *emotion* and *icon*. The best known are the smiley face :-) and the sad face :-(added to a message and produced with bits of punctuation. With their instantaneous and casual back-and-forth style, e-mails and texting are closer to telephone conversations than they are to old-style letter-writing. But a phone conversation allows each speaker to convey meaning through vocal intonation. This is not possible on the internet so the emoticon is a substitute, clumsy but better than nothing, for the non-verbal ways which everybody uses to make themselves understood, whether by gesture, intonation or facial expression.

The 'smiley face' icon goes back to the 1970s, when it was emblazoned on novelty items like mugs and T-shirts, along with the slogan 'Have a happy day'. It was later taken up by the dance-club subculture as a symbol for drug-induced euphoria. With the advent of texting, the smiley :-) has reappeared – with or without a hyphen 'nose' – as a way of conveying pleasure or amusement.

ENGLISH EVOLVES

This book is the history of English as the language has changed over more than 1500 years. Indeed, the roots of English go back even further to the original Celtic inhabitants of the British Isles and to the Latin-speaking invaders and settlers of the first century AD. Celts and Romans have a distant common ancestry in the peoples who spread outwards from western Asia thousands of years before that and who brought with them that shared Indo-European tongue

BLOGOSPHERE

Blog is a 21st-century expression – literally so, since you will not find it in any 20th-century dictionary. It started out as a portmanteau term, combining *web* and *log*, and describes a website, usually produced by one person, that posts news, photos and the like on a fairly regular basis. It is satisfying to realize that such a contemporary concept has been built up from such old words. *Web* goes back to Old English and, as part of the phrase 'World Wide Web', was reputedly chosen in preference to 'Mine of Information' to describe the beginnings of the internet in the early 1990s. *Log* is a shortening of log-book, the 17th century term for a ship's journal (and the seemingly odd use of *log* comes from the block of wood that was attached to a line on a reel and then thrown overboard as a means of determining the ship's progress). *Weblog* swiftly became *blog*, and the word – with its suggestion of 'blurt' or 'blare' and its no-nonsense -og ending – is just right for the often rather blurry mix of fact, opinion, rant and rubbish which characterizes many *blogs*. The addition of 'sphere', a word whose roots are Greek, created the *blogosphere*, the virtual world in which so many of us spend so much time.

which was hinted at by William Jones in his seminal speech in Calcutta in 1786 (see A Universal Language?).

After undergoing many changes at the hands of the Angles and Saxons, the Norman French, and a host of other important but lesser influences, English itself has now spread to become the world's first super-language. While this is a process that may be gratifying to native speakers in Britain, North America, Australia and elsewhere, it is also one that raises certain anxieties. The language is no longer 'ours' but everybody's. The centre of gravity has shifted. Until well into the 19th century it was firmly in Britain. Then, as foreseen by the second US president John Adams ('English is destined to be in the next and succeeding centuries [...] the language of the world'), the centre shifted to America. Now there is no centre, or at least not one that is readily acknowledged as such.

English is emerging in pidgin forms such as Singlish which may be scarcely recognizable to non-users. Even the abbreviated, technical and idiosyncratic forms of the language employed in, say, air-traffic control (see page 15) or texting may be perceived as a threat to some idea of linguistic purity.

If these new forms of non-standard English are a threat, then they are merely the latest in a centuries-long line of threats to linguistic integrity. What were the feelings of the successive inhabitants of the British Isles as armies, marauders and settlers arrived in the thousand years that followed the first landing by Julius Caesar? History does not always record them, although we know that, say, the Anglo-Saxons were deeply troubled by the Viking incursions which began in the north towards the end of the eighth century. Among their responses would surely have been a fear of 'foreign' tongues, and a later resistance to having to learn the vocabulary and constructions of outsiders. Yet many new words and structures were absorbed, just as the outsiders, whether Viking or Norman French, assimilated much of the language already used by the occupants of the country they had overrun or settled.

With hindsight we can see what those who lived through each upheaval could not see, that each fresh wave of arrivals has helped to develop the English language as it is today. Similarly, the language will develop in the future in ways that cannot be foreseen, let alone controlled. It will change both internally, as it were, among native speakers, and externally at the hands of the millions in Asia and elsewhere who are already adopting it for their own use.

Britons from diverse ethnic backgrounds in the Wood Green district of North London. Britain continues to be a melting-pot of different cultures and languages.

Ye knowe eek, that in forme of speche is chaunge
With-inne a thousand yeer, and wordes tho
That hadden prys, now wonder nyce and straunge
Us thinketh hem; and yet they spake hem so.

['You know also that forms of speech change inside a thousand years and that words which had value at the time now seem very odd to us – yet that is how they spoke them.']

GEOFFREY CHAUCER, *TROILUS AND CRISEYDE* (C.1385)

ENGLISH MATTERS

ENGLISH: RIGHT AND WRONG

ENGLISH: TAKING SIDES

Unpunctuated and paratactic: this sign might raise the dander of grammar purists but conveys its meaning effectively all the same.

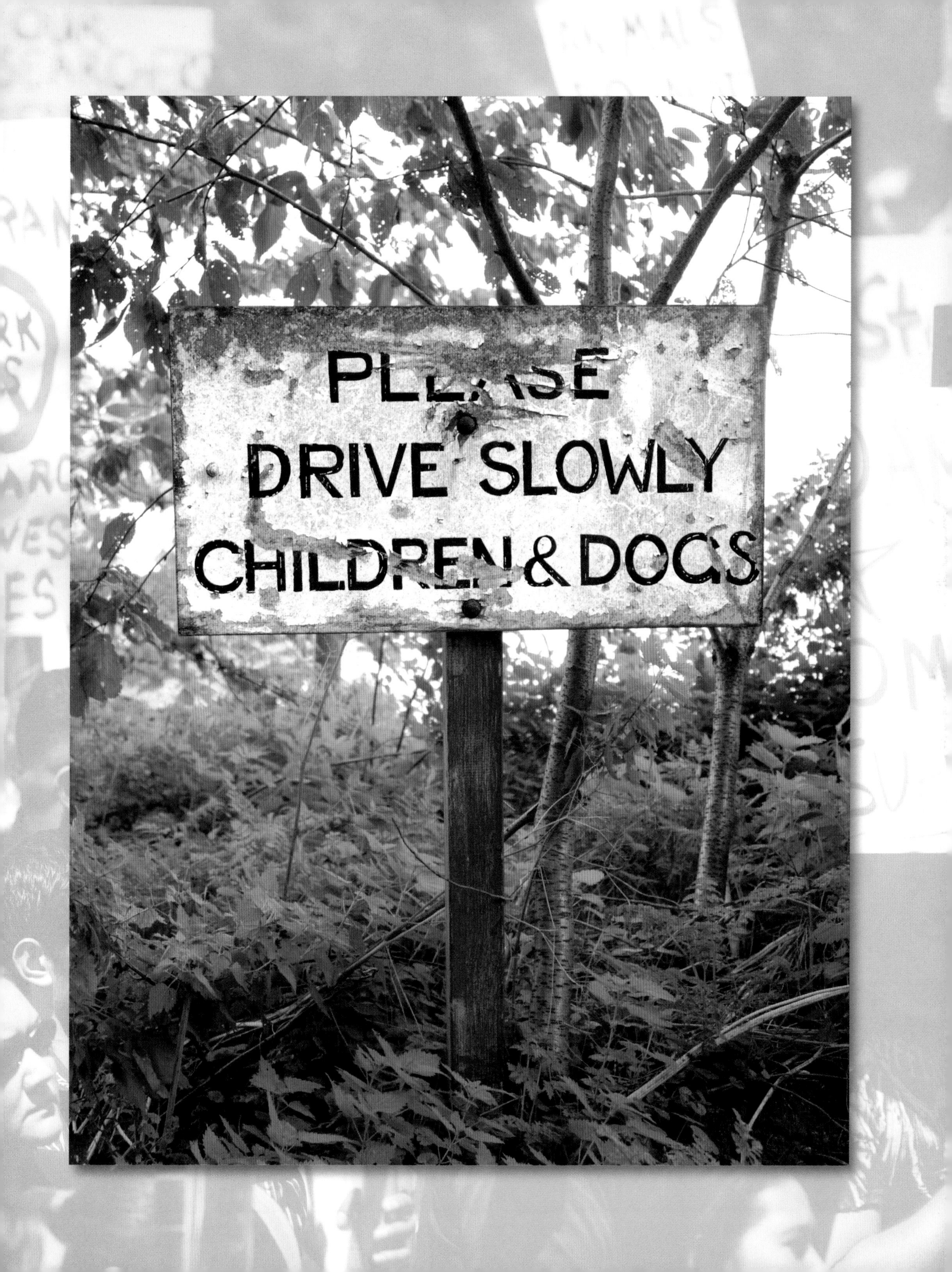
PLEASE
DRIVE SLOWLY
CHILDREN & DOGS

Ever since English became established as a national language, there have been arguments over every aspect of it, from vocabulary to spelling, from punctuation to pronunciation. The debate is as lively today as it was in the age of Dr Johnson (1709–84).

ENGLISH: RIGHT AND WRONG

A Facebook site numbering members in the hundreds of thousands is entitled 'I Judge You When You Use Poor Grammar' and encourages its members to 'seek out the infidels (grammar offenders) and ... document their acts of terror'. Other people are indifferent or even hostile to notions of correct English. The majority may just be confused. The battle can be described as one between the prescriptivists, who believe in rules, and the descriptivists, who believe language goes its own way, regardless of attempts to regulate it. What exactly are the areas of disagreement between these two sides?

THE PRESCRIPTIVISTS

Jeff Deck and Benjamin Herson are two young Americans who committed themselves to an unusual mission. Having established the Typo Eradication Advancement League (TEAL), these two graduates of Dartmouth College toured the United States at the beginning of 2008, equipped with permanent markers and ink-erasers and a determination to do their bit for the nation's errant grammar. If they saw a misspelled shop sign or a public notice with a misplaced or an absent apostrophe (for example, a warning that any vehicle parked without authorization would be removed 'at owners expense'), Deck and Herson set about correcting it.

Usually the grammarians obtained approval from the shop-keeper or other appropriate authority but sometimes they acted guerilla-style and without permission. They went an apostrophe too far when they decided to amend a handwritten sign at a historic watchtower in the Grand Canyon. After shifting an apostrophe and adding a

Man on a mission: Jeff Deck of TEAL uses a bottle of typewriter correction fluid to add an apostrophe to the word 'mens' in the window of a clothing store in Chicago.

comma, they were found guilty of vandalizing government property, fined and put on probation for a year. Unfortunately for Deck and Herson, the sign had been penned by the architect of the watchtower and so, regardless of any grammatical flaws, was itself a historic artefact.

Those who are not bothered or simply don't know about such things – and the not-bothered together with the don't-knows make up the great majority of any English-speaking population – might be surprised at the intensity and passion of the would-be regulators of the language. Such people are sometimes called 'prescriptive' because they think that rules for the right use of language can not only be laid down or prescribed but also enforced (or encouraged) through education and example. The term 'prescriptive' describes not only those who pounce on mistakes in the newspapers or on radio and TV, and write, phone or e-mail to complain, but also those who feel anxiety about 'falling standards'.

THE DESCRIPTIVISTS

The prescriptive label does not apply much to the professionals who compile dictionaries and usage guides, and who tend these days not so much towards prescription as description. These descriptivists, when professionally involved with language as lexicographers or commentators, see it as their job to observe and describe changes in language rather than to pass judgement on them. The descriptive group shades into the *laissez-faire* group, which believes, in effect, that any attempt to enforce linguistic regulation is self-defeating or absurd. There is animosity on both sides, with the descriptive or *laissez-faire* group referring to those trying to impose rules as 'language police', and the prescriptive group putting all the blame on lax education or the mass media or a general dumbing-down.

But this is a somewhat lop-sided battle, since the descriptive school, believing that language development is an almost impersonal process, rarely trouble to fight back other than by pointing out that attempts to regulate language are doomed. One might imagine them as two distinct camps on opposing sides of the river of English. On the 'purist' bank are those who want to protect the language and put down irregular behaviour (absent or misused apostrophes, for example). On the opposite bank is the 'anything goes' battalion, whose argument can be summarized as follows: language is a living organism, shaped daily and almost unawares by users who pay little attention to the minutiae of what they say and, in many cases, what they write. General usage is, by definition, the right usage. Go with the flow, they say, pointing to the river of language as it runs on, carving out its own course, steady and unperturbed.

WHO'S RIGHT?

But the analogy that compares English or any language to an unstoppable river doesn't quite fit the bill. Whatever the scientific and philosophical discussions about the sources of language, it is not a natural feature of the landscape like a

GEORGE BERNARD SHAW AND THE NEW ALPHABET

Writer and dramatist George Bernard Shaw (1856–1950) produced more than 50 plays as well as volumes of music criticism and varieties of political writing. He enjoyed setting the cat among the pigeons, being controversial and sometimes playfully perverse in his views. But when he launched the attempt to create a new alphabet, he was all seriousness.

Shaw was impatient with the inconsistencies and absurdities of English spelling. He is supposed to have come up with a well-known example to prove his point by claiming that the invented word *ghoti* should be pronounced as 'fish', using the following parallels: 'gh-' often has an 'f' sound as in 'rough'; '-o-' can be pronounced like an '-i-' as in 'women'; while '-ti' is frequently given a 'sh' sound ('nation'). Therefore *ghoti* = 'fish'. There's some doubt about whether *ghoti* was actually Shaw's idea, but it fits with his comments about language generally and the need for simplicity and harmonization. He made two key proposals: to discard useless grammar and to spell phonetically. According to his prescription, one could say 'I thinked' instead of 'I thought', or spell *tough* and *cough* as *tuf* and *cof*.

Shaw sat on the BBC's Spoken English Advisory Committee from 1926 to 1939, where he came to realize the advantages of phonetic spelling.

Shaw suggested a new alphabet and a new orthography (way of spelling). The purpose was to save time and trouble, although he admitted that initially it would be costly and unpopular – something of an understatement. However, the benefits were clear: 'With a new English alphabet replacing the old Semitic one with its added Latin vowels I should be able to spell t-h-o-u-g-h with two letters, s-h-o-u-l-d with three, and e-n-o-u-g-h with four: nine letters instead of eighteen: a saving of a hundred per cent of my time and my typist's time and the printer's time, to say nothing of the saving in paper and wear and tear of machinery.'

Shaw left money in his will for the advance of spelling reform and during the 1950s Kingsley Read, a typographer, was the winner of a competition to come up with a new orthography. The result has the appearance of a cross between shorthand and runic symbols. Like the attempts to create new languages, it never caught on. In fact, the only book ever to be produced using the Shavian alphabet was Shaw's own play, *Androcles and the Lion* (1912) with the standard script and the new one on facing pages.

river or a mountain range shaped by the elements. Although a propensity for language seems to be an in-built feature of the human brain, and to that extent something that could be described as natural, any spoken language is an artificial construct, unique to mankind.

The power of speech is acquired soon after birth by processes that are still not fully understood, and then shaped by years of learning whether at a subconscious level from parents and others or more deliberately through education. Nor does the process stop with the end of any formal learning. We go through life experimenting with language. We modify our vocabularies, picking up new words and discarding others. We say and write things differently according to the varying company we keep. We make choices.

So, although the arguments of the *laissez-faire*, anything-goes group have a certain appeal, they also have limitations. Anything doesn't go. If it did, if we felt free to use any words we wanted – even invented ones – in any order we wanted, it's an open question as to who would be more quickly exhausted, we or our listeners. It's tough talking gibberish. In reality, the choice of words and the word-arrangement (or syntax) of even the most 'uneducated' speaker conform to certain tacit, cultural rules about linguistic selection and construction.

'When I use a word,' Humpty Dumpty said, in rather a scornful tone, 'it means just what I choose it to mean – neither more nor less.'

LEWIS CARROLL, *THROUGH THE LOOKING-GLASS* (1871)

This can easily be seen through a couple of examples. In standard English, and in contrast to several other languages such as French, the adjective is placed before the noun that it qualifies. A more general in-built rule of language is that the subject of a sentence goes before the verb, the object coming afterwards. *The man bit the dog* means something quite different from *The dog bit the man,* but the two sentences employ exactly the same five words. It is only their order that specifies meaning. These rules are familiar at an instinctive level to even the most uneducated speaker. Knowledge also comes at an early stage. Quite a young child, looking at a photo of itself, knows the pronoun difference between saying 'That's me!' and, pointing to a toy in the same picture, 'That's mine'.

So rules exist. On the other hand, those who want to uphold very rigorous standards of English and protest against minor infringements are bound to be frustrated and disappointed. Indeed, one can't help feeling sometimes that the frustration and disappointment are themselves part of the pleasure of the protest. Those two young Americans who went hunting for typos and correcting signs with their markers might have been acting out of a high-minded determination to improve literacy standards in the US but it's a fair bet that they were also having their own kind of fun.

The great bulk of rules controlling the spoken language are, like the iceberg, hidden from sight. They are also acquired before we begin to be formally

fell off the wall in doing so) and offered Alice his hand. She watched him a little anxiously as she took it. " If he smiled much more, the ends of his mouth might meet behind," she thought : " and then I don't know what would happen to his head ! I'm afraid it would come off ! "

Ilustration by Sir John Tenniel for the first edition of Lewis Carroll's Through the Looking-Glass, *showing Alice conversing with Humpty Dumpty. This character's solipsistic use of language effectively subverts communication.*

taught and they are largely unchanging. The visible bits, which (some) people get so exercized about, can change. Not so much as a result of individual action as by a collective shift at a moment impossible to pinpoint. When did 'disinterested' stop meaning 'impartial' – its original sense – and switch its meaning to 'bored by'. Come to that, when and why was that little phrase 'bored by' replaced by 'bored of'?

For more than five centuries attempts have been made to regularize the language, both spoken and written. Spelling, grammar, punctuation, choice of words, pronunciation, all have been the subjects of innumerable dictionaries, guides and primers. Yet the continuing tension between the different camps, the purists and the anything-goers, is actually very healthy. It is one of the signs of a living and developing language. A brief outline of the various battlegrounds is given below.

NEW WORDS

The emergence of new words into English or, more usually the adaptation of old ones for new uses is one of the minor battlegrounds between the prescriptive and descriptive groups. Objections tend to centre on the transformation of nouns into verbs or vice-versa, on the ugliness of new formations, or the belief that the new words aren't necessary because there are perfectly good ones already in place.

Nouns such as *progress, transition, impact* are frequently used as verbs ('How are we going to progress this?'), especially in a business context. Other verbs such as *commentate* and *enthuse* have been created via the process called back-formation from pre-existing nouns (*commentator, enthusiasm*). Language purists argue that it is better to keep the word in its 'proper' part of speech with expressions such as 'make progress', 'have an impact on'. Related objections are to 'ugly' verbal creations like *prioritize* or *incentivize*. From the other direction, there is a tendency to turn verbs into nouns, as with *spend* or *ask* ('It's a big ask') where more traditional English would use *expenditure* or *demand*.

Like all linguistic debates, this is an old one. And it is more a matter of preference than correctness. Back in the 1940s, the distinguished language expert Eric Partridge made a mild objection to the verb-use of *contact*, calling it an 'American synonym for "to establish contact with"'. In his famous guide *Usage and Abusage*, which was being issued with revisions until the 1970s, Partridge also took exception to the use of *productivity* ('a horrible word; use output'). Elsewhere he commented that educated speakers would regard a phrase like 'It's us' as 'vulgar or dialectal' although he accepted it was 'justifiable when its use is exclamatory'. Highlighting these objections is not to run Partridge down. Rather, it is to show how fashions in language change. Who thinks twice about saying *to contact* now, or pauses to wonder whether 'It's us' is truly exclamatory?

Regardless of the objections to new words, whether on the grounds of redundancy or ugliness, history will sort out which are entitled to survive and which are not.

'Tire' is in fact an older spelling than 'tyre', but the latter became common usage for the pneumatic tyre in Britain during the 19th century (possibly because of its use in some patent documents).

SPELLING

Of all the areas of dispute over correct English, spelling is the most contentious although not the most sensitive (see Pronunciation page 199). The spelling issue is a high-profile one for straightforward reasons. Mistakes tend to stand out since, almost invariably, only one way of spelling a word is regarded as correct. There have been different approaches to the teaching of spelling over the years but, underlying any approach is the belief that it can (and should) be taught in schools. Another, and not so minor, point is that spelling is a favourite media topic, particularly in newspapers, whenever the question of the 'decline of standards' emerges.

English is notorious for being a language that employs illogical, even perverse, forms of spelling. Those arguing for simplification point to inconsistencies. For example, why should the British English spelling of the noun *humour* (*humor*, in the US) become humorous as an adjective? There is not even consistency in the inconsistency: *colour* has an identical suffix and sound to *humour* yet its adjectival form is *colourful* in British English.

A more powerful weapon in the simplifiers' armoury is the gap between the way a word looks and the way it is sounded. The long 'ee' sound can be represented not only by the obvious doubled 'e', as in *seem* or *teem*, but by combinations that contain quite different vowels, as in *quay, ski, debris, people*. A phonetic system, one which spells according to sound, would adjust the last four to 'kee', 'skee', 'debree' and 'peepul'. This would be more rational, so the argument goes, and it would also make it easier for those mastering the language not just as students but also as native speakers. English-speaking adults come near the bottom of the table in international studies of literacy and this is often ascribed to the vagaries of the way in which words are spelled (or spelt).

This is not a new campaign. Agitation to straighten out spelling goes back many decades (see George Bernard Shaw and the New Alphabet, page 191). What gives it current force is the support of some academics and experts who, either out of despair at the scripts they have to read or impatience with the illogicalities of English, believe we should waste less time on teaching spelling. The rise of texting, with abbreviations like TLK2UL8R, and the increasing influence of Americanized spellings (*program, thru, center*) have also had a minor effect.

But the campaign will not succeed. A few minor changes may occur but there can be no root-and-branch revolution in English spelling. There are several highly practical reasons for this. People who already know how to spell the words they use everyday (give or take the occasional error) are not going to sit down and learn how to spell their language all over again. This would be the case even if spelling could be organized along simpler lines as the result of some diktat from an imagined Ministry of English.

The most substantial flaw in the phonetic argument is that, although spelling is regularized, pronunciation is not. To take a couple of examples: *think* is spelled in only one way but it is pronounced as 'fink' by plenty of English speakers and as 'tink' by Irish ones. The same th-f-t variation applies to *three*. In these cases, instead of one uniform spelling, we would end up with three regional ones. The point was made forcefully by Jonathan Swift 300 years ago:

> *Another Cause [...] which hath contributed not a little to the maiming of our Language is a foolish Opinion, advanced of late Years, that we ought to spell exactly as we speak; which beside the obvious Inconvenience of utterly destroying our Etymology, would be a thing we should never see an End of. Not only the several Towns and Countries of England, have a different way of Pronouncing, but even here in London, they clip their Words after one Manner about the Court, another in*

the City, and a third in the Suburbs; and in a few Years, it is probable, will all differ from themselves, as Fancy or Fashion shall direct: All which reduced to Writing would entirely confound Orthography.

Finally, the attempt to simplify spelling would actually make things much more complicated. Any half-way experienced user of English recognizes the difference between *quay* and *key* when he or she sees it on the page; similarly with *bow/bough, caught/court, towed/toad/toed*, and countless other groups of homophones. Adopting a simplified single form would make the language much the poorer as well as causing confusion. We recognize words not syllable by syllable but as a 'whole'. Under a simplified system we might have difficulty distinguishing at a glance between *whole* and *hole*. The latter is the more logical spelling for both concepts but it does not convey the idea of 'wholeness' straightaway.

There is also a plausible cultural argument against phonetic simplification. The often odd forms of English spelling are a testament to the historical sources of the language. The 'b' in *doubt* is not sounded but it harks back to the word's Latin origins (*dubitare*). The silent 'k' in *knowledge* refers to the roots of the word in Old English and Norse. Many words are thus little parcels of history, their origins of interest mostly to specialists perhaps, but arguably worth preserving in the form in which we have them. One could also claim that the erratic, peculiar byways of English spelling are a fitting reflection of a language which, whatever else it may be, is not homogenous or orderly, and is never going to be either of those things. Yes, spelling changes over time but the changes come from the bottom up and they are piecemeal and small-scale.

GRAMMAR AND OTHER MATTERS

Several newspapers employ a readers' editor, someone whose job it is to respond to complaints about the content of the paper. Many complaints address such topics as biased coverage, intrusive interviews, sensational photographs and so on, but a substantial minority are to do with the use of language and with what are perceived as common, and therefore inexcusable, linguistic slips. Typical comments will query the habit of beginning sentences with a conjunction (usually *And* or *But*), turning nouns into verbs (to *impact*), the misuse of words (*crescendo* to mean a 'climax' rather than, correctly, a 'steady rise', *reign* instead of *rein*), and so on. Some newspapers actually make a feature of such queries and

GRAMMAR, n. A system of pitfalls thoughtfully prepared for the feet of the self-made man, along the path by which he advances to distinction.

<small>AMBROSE BIERCE, *THE DEVIL'S DICTIONARY* (1911)</small>

complaints, showing that they are responsive and open-minded – and also, no doubt, as a means of filling space at no great cost.

Complaints are less frequent in the broadcast media, given the more ephemeral nature of radio and TV, but a glance at on-line message-boards shows that, here again, plenty of listeners and viewers are ready to air their opinions on what constitutes correct usage.

Almost invariably, the protestors are on the 'conservative' side. They fear that language is changing, which it is, and object to the details of that process. The impression may be given that everything is going to the dogs, that a misplaced apostrophe is a herald of the end of civilization, and that nobody apart from them cares about it. This is to overlook the attention given by the British and American mainstream media, especially newspapers, to getting things right.

The reader may not like a particular usage but the odds are that various alternatives will have been considered and rejected, especially where any usage is likely to cause protest. Even in an age of faster-paced news, the writing of journalists is checked and sub-edited. Newspapers, like publishers, have in-house style guides and preferred ways of expressing things. The *Guardian* newspaper style guide, for example, tells us that the approved way of spelling the name of the queen of the rebellious Iceni in Roman Britain is Boudicca, not Boadicea, or that the writer should 'use Ms for women on second mention unless they have expressed a preference for Miss or Mrs', or that the word 'terrorist' needs to be used with care.

History is not on the side of the protestors. Sometimes the complaints will be justified. It is incorrect to write of a person being given *free reign* rather than *free rein*. But, more often, the complaints are wrong-headed. There is no reason

The most famous example of the split infinitive in English occurs in the introductory voice-over to the popular television science-fiction series, Star Trek: '*To boldly go where no man has gone before.' George Bernard Shaw had no time for crusaders against split infinitives, once writing to the* Times: 'There is a busybody on your staff who devotes a lot of time to chasing split infinitives: I call for the immediate dismissal of this pedant. It is of no consequence whether he decides to go quickly or to quickly go or quickly to go. The important thing is that he should go at once.'

not to begin a sentence by putting *And* or *But*, just as there is no reason not to split an infinitive or to go to great lengths to avoid putting a preposition at the end of a sentence. No reason as long as the meaning is clear and the sentence reads well. And even when the complaints are somewhere between right and wrong, as in the misuse of *crescendo* or putting *few* instead of *less*, there is little chance of reversing majority usage although it is technically wrong. No chance at all, in fact. But there is something valiant – and valuable – about the protest because it keeps the subject alive.

PUNCTUATION

There was a time when punctuation might literally be a matter of life-and-death. According to a *Times* report of 1837 two law professors from Paris University fought a duel with swords in a dispute over the *point-virgule* or the semicolon. The paper claimed: 'The one who contended that the passage in question ought to be concluded by a semicolon was wounded in the arm. His adversary maintained that it should be a colon.'

High-priestess of prescriptivism: the British author Lynne Truss enjoyed great success with her book Eats, Shoots and Leaves *in 2003, which announced 'the zero tolerance approach to punctuation'. Shouldn't that be 'zero-tolerance'?*

Punctuation, whether by its mere presence, its absence or its misuse, still raises strong feelings in a large minority. For all that, it is an area of written English in which there has been a definite trend towards simplification over the last century or so. The result is that the majority of people use only the basic bits of punctuation: the comma and the full stop, the question and exclamation marks, and perhaps the dash. The more rarefied punctation marks are notable either by their timid application or their complete absence.

The traditional use of brackets (to indicate a considered, parenthetical remark) is less common than what might be called their rhetorical use to show surprise (!) or to suggest confusion or doubt (??). There is widespread confusion over the apostrophe, with a 2008 survey showing almost half the UK population unable to use it correctly, a figure that may strike some as being on the modest side. Few individuals, apart from professional writers and journalists, have any need to use speech/quotation marks other than for ironic effect, as in *He asked me for a 'loan'*. Colons and semicolons have always excited anxiety and sometimes irritation. Professors may no longer fight duels over them but others find them fiddly and pretentious. The US writer Kurt Vonnegut once told a university audience that 'All [semicolons] do is show that you've been to college'.

When it comes to what one could call mainstream punctuation, there is widespread uncertainty over where to insert commas or what constitutes a sentence, and hence when to put a full stop. Language purists would and do claim that the exclamation mark is overused, particularly in the era of texting and e-mailing, while the question mark takes on a random life of its own.

It could be argued that punctutation is a more significant area of English compared to other forms of correct usage. Misspelling doesn't usually lead to misunderstanding, only annoyance among those who are likely to get annoyed. Formulations that are perceived as grammatical errors, like using *who* for *whom* or putting a preposition at the end of a sentence, are either not errors at all or have little or no effect on the overall clarity of a sentence. Pronunciation is quite a complex issue, involving class, education, aspiration and fashion, and not easily reducible to a right or wrong way of doing it.

By contrast, poor or casual punctuation can cause problems. At best, it may mean that the reader has to go back and work out what the writer is trying to say. In the worst cases, it may subvert meaning altogether. In 1991 an American court case for defamation in a magazine article turned on the extent to which speech marks indicated that the words inside them were actually said or whether they were an acceptable approximation (by the journalist) of what was said. In 2007 the US Circuit Court of Appeals for the District of Columbia ruled that locals could keep guns ready to shoot in their homes. They were interpreting the second amendment to the US Constitution, which reads: 'A well regulated Militia, being necessary to the security of a free State, the right of the people to keep and bear Arms, shall not be infringed'. By a majority of two to one, the judges decided that the meaning hinges on the second comma, which 'divides the Amendment into two clauses; the first is prefatory, and the second operative'.

Leaving aside legal questions arising from the commas in the US Constitution, there is a more humble but genuine ambiguity in a written phrase such as *the wearers clothes*. Here the absence of the apostrophe leaves it unclear whether the writer is referring to a single owner (wearer's) or to more than one (wearers'). The context will probably make it obvious but, even if it does, using the correct punctuation is a quicker and neater way of accomplishing the task.

Many teachers of English would claim that punctuation is the hardest aspect of formal English to teach, yet it is arguably the most important. Anyone doubting this should try to make sense of a completely unpunctuated piece of prose.

> *Do not be afraid of the semi-colon; it can be most useful.*
>
> ERNEST GOWERS,
> *COMPLETE PLAIN WORDS* (1954)

PRONUNCIATION

Pronunciation is another area in which there has been a shift towards diversity and a greater tolerance of variation. Anybody watching a British film or television programme dating back several decades is likely to be struck by the clear diction and cut-glass pronunciation of the actors. A clip from a film like *Brief Encounter* (1945) or an excerpt from an old BBC radio broadcast shows the participants speaking in tones that now seem almost comically refined and plummy. There was even an official term for this style of speech, particularly as it was employed by the BBC: Received Pronunciation or RP. This was the style of speaking and pronunciation used by educated people in the south of England, the most affluent part of the country and the home of most of its powerful institutions, including the BBC. From the Corporation's foundation in 1922 and

In My Fair Lady, *the musical adapted from George Bernard Shaw's play* Pygmalion, *Professor of Phonetics Henry Higgins famously laments: 'Why Can't the English Learn to Speak?' The central figure in Shaw's satire on the English class system is Eliza Doolittle, a Cockney flower-seller whom the professor teaches to speak like a 'lady'. In the 1964 film of the musical (above), Rex Harrison played Higgins, while Audrey Hepburn was Eliza.*

for many years afterwards, only newscasters who spoke RP were given jobs.

As significant as the idea that there was a gold standard of speech was the corollary that any other way of speaking was not just a deviation from Received Pronunciation but probably inferior to it. To an extent, exceptions were made for educated speakers who had Welsh, Scots or Irish accents but there is no doubt that RP was seen as the king of all other ways of speaking English – or the Queen's English as it became after the accession of Elizabeth II.

Regional accents could be heard on the stage, screen or radio, but they tended to be confined to comic or minor characters. Received Pronunciation, if you didn't already use it and wanted to get on in some public forum, was generally seen as a desirable aspiration. It took the arrival of 'kitchen-sink' drama and the neo-realist films of the late 1950s and 1960s, like *Room at the Top* (1958) and *Saturday Night and Sunday Morning* (1960), to make regional accents widely acceptable. And it took a lot longer for the major UK broadcasters, the BBC and ITV, to employ newscasters and reporters with markedly regional accents on the national networks. A claim in 2008 by a senior BBC figure that he wanted 'an increase in the range of regional accents on BBC shows as part of a drive to end the domination of the Standard English accent' indicated a continued bias in broadcasting in favour of RP. Even so, there is some justification in the claims made for RP that it is clear and easily understood.

In Britain in the early 1980s a kind of reverse process occurred whereby those people, particularly the young, who would once have naturally employed RP began to use less 'refined' pronunciation. This is easily heard by listening to the difference between Prince Charles (born 1948) and his two sons, William (born 1982) and Harry (1984). Although all three are distinctly upper-class in their speech, the voices of William and Harry are closer to their contemporaries both in pronunciation and diction. A similar process has happened with some British politicians, who are afraid of being seen as 'posh' – a likely vote-loser – and so drop 'T's at the end of words or insert a glottal stop (e.g., 'le'ah' for 'letter').

When people deliberately adopt the accent and vocabulary of a different (lower) class than their own they are trying to gain what sociolinguists call 'covert prestige'. Because working-class or ethnic minority speech may be seen as more authentic or 'tougher', the speaker hopes that those qualities may be perceived in him or her too. Whether in the USA, Britain or elsewhere, the adoption by white speakers of black terms and speech patterns is a clear sign of the attractions of a style of English that was once the property of 'outsiders'.

PRONUNCIATION AND THE 'H' QUESTION

A not so minor generational distinction in UK pronunciation is over the sound of the letter 'h' when pronounced by itself, whether as part of an abbreviation or spelled out as part of a name. Received Pronunciation is to say 'aitch' as in the NHS (enn-aitch-ess), but this is being pushed aside by the preference for 'haitch' (as in 'Haitch-Pee Sauce'), especially among those under 40. The 'haitch' version is usual in Ireland and parts of the north but has traditionally been seen as 'uneducated' in the south of England. This might seem insignificant – although not in Northern Ireland where saying 'aitch' marks you as a Protestant and saying 'haitch' as a Catholic – but it generates real irritation in newspaper columns and callers to radio programmes dealing with language.

Yet a wider look at the 'H' question suggests that pronunciation is a minefield of class and prejudice. Whatever the current status of 'aitch' versus 'haitch', sounding the 'h' at the beginning of a word has long been taken as an indicator of education or, England being England, an indicator of class and status. The educated say Hackney and Henry, not 'ackney and 'enry. But to sound the 'h' at the start of a small minority of words would, confusingly, be regarded as ignorant: so in Received Pronunciation honour has to lose its first letter (onour) as does hour (our). Still heard occasionally are pronunciations of hotel or historian also without their opening h's ('an otel', 'an istorian') although these forms now sound slightly affected. In standard versions of the Bible the use of 'an' rather than 'a' in front of a spectrum of 'h'-words from habitation to hypocrite indicates that they too were once sounded without their initial letter ('an abitation', 'an ypocrite').

Pronunciation is perhaps the most sensitive area of English since it involves speaking and listening, while errors of spelling and grammar are mostly confined to the page. There are few adults who would 'correct' another's pronunciation face-to-face, even though the way people say things is unquestionably a large factor in how they are regarded. Surveys show that those who speak with certain varieties of northern accent or Scottish lilt are perceived as being warm or trustworthy. This may make them more employable than others (Birmingham or Glaswegian accents are seen as particularly disadvantageous).

The issue of Received Pronunciation has never taken hold in America. Whereas in Britain, accent and pronunciation can still affect a person's chances in a career, let alone the way he or she is perceived by others, the US has shown a more egalitarian attitude. That's not to say that there is no discrimination, but that it is more likely to be made on the basis of well-used and correct forms of English rather than the accent in which they are uttered. In other words, it is a distinction of education rather than background.

Language is not neutral. Everything that is said or written comes with a purpose which may (or may not) be openly declared by the choice of words, the syntax and the style employed by the user. Language can be a weapon, concealed or on display, blunt or delicate. It may be intended to inform, to seduce, to persuade, to deceive, to inspire, to intimidate … This section looks at some of the many ways in which English can be put to work.

ENGLISH: TAKING SIDES

The plainest and briefest bit of written English is premeditated and carries the stamp of the person or group that composed it. This extends as far as advice which seems utterly impersonal. But even the impersonal is personal. Whether it be the electronic sign which gives a warning on a motorway or the printed notice on a shop counter, the very style of the language sends a message that is extraneous to the actual words. The message is: this is authority speaking, take me seriously. The imperative voice (DRIVE CAREFULLY) and the direct vocabulary (SHOPLIFTERS WILL BE PROSECUTED) leave no room for questions.

Slightly more subtle public statements also carry a freight of assumptions, one of which is that there is a direct link between those making the statement and the individual reading it. The popular formulation THANK YOU (FOR DRIVING SAFELY/ FOR NOT SMOKING) appeals to the good nature/sense of obligation/potential for guilt and gratitude in the onlooker. The SORRY FOR ANY DELAY notices that routinely accompany roadworks in Britain sound attractively casual and personal, although it would be impossible to pin the apology to any individual.

The message of these short English sentences is plain, although the thinking behind them may be quite complex. How much more is there to unravel when English is not plain but weighted with hidden meanings and purposes which may be hidden, perhaps from the users themselves. A principal method of hiding things is to employ euphemistic language.

Short, sharp and to the point: a sign in a park admonishes
cyclists against taking a particular route.

An Orthodox Jewish protestor signals his opposition to abortion during the annual March for Life in New York City. Activists on both sides of this debate are keen to annex the positive buzz-word 'right' for their cause: advocates of abortion on demand cite women's 'right to choose'.

EUPHEMISMS

Euphemism is an inescapable part of daily language use. The term defines ways of softening or obscuring facts or ideas which might, if expressed plainly, be considered unattractive or offensive. Euphemisms tend to cluster round those aspects of life that are embarrassing or threatening, areas such as death or sex or bodily functions. Phrases like 'sleep with' or 'go to bed with' or the question to a visitor 'Do you want to wash your hands?' are euphemistic, or at best only part of the story. These daily euphemistic usages, designed to shield people from the embarrassment of plain speaking, are harmless for the most part, since everyone knows what is actually meant.

But there are more contentious areas of politics, religion and social policy involving euphemisms that may be intended to obscure the issue or even to deliberately mislead. The term 'climate change' is preferred by many to 'global warming' because the first expression sounds less alarming. Similarly 'regime change' could describe a gradual non-violent process, although in practice it does not. The debate about abortion, particularly as it is conducted in the United States, arouses deep passions on both sides. From the early 1970s anti-abortion campaigners regularly referred to their campaign as being one for the 'right to life', avoiding the negative associations of being perceived as 'anti-'. Those in favour of making abortion legally available then termed themselves 'pro-choice'. This prompted the other side to call itself 'pro-life'. Each act of renaming was intended to cast an unfavourable light on the opposition by turning them into the negative party.

Another very contentious issue concerns what children should be taught in schools about the origins of life. Here, the 'creationists' who believe in the literal truth of the divine creation of the Earth, now prefer to talk euphemistically about 'intelligent design' or ID. This hints at divine intervention rather than making direct reference to it, and has a respectable, pseudo-scientific air to it.

It is in the field of warfare that euphemisms really thrive. Unintentionally killing someone on one's own side is an instance of 'friendly fire', as opposed to hostile fire, but the result is the same. An unprovoked attack becomes a 'pre-emptive strike', undertaken supposedly to stop the enemy attacking first but giving the aggressor the veneer of self-defence. Bombing raids can be referred to as 'surgical strikes', an ingenious phrase since it conjures up ideas of a necessary medical intervention as well as suggesting something precise and almost humane in its effect. When people are killed other than those who were intended to be killed, then that is described as 'collateral damage'. Genocide can be redefined as 'ethnic cleansing', a very necessary change because signatories to the United Nations Charter are required to act on genocide but not on ethnic cleansing. And if that latter expression is too harsh then it can be replaced by the 'humane transfer of populations', an expression used in negotiations between Serb and Croatian leaders in the wars following the break-up of Yugoslavia in the 1990s.

This connection between war or state violence and euphemisms is not new. In his essay 'Politics and the English Language', written in 1946, George Orwell noted euphemisms such as 'pacification' or 'rectification of frontiers' and claimed that the reality of modern warfare could only be defended by: 'arguments which are too brutal for most people to face, and which do not square with the professed aims of political parties.'

Decades of communist rule across a great swathe of the world produced a rich crop of euphemisms, not least the attachment of the word 'democratic' (as in the German Democratic Republic) to describe a society in which the people had little or no say in how they were governed. The Berlin Wall, built to keep the GDR's citizens in, was officially called the Anti-Fascist Protection Rampart. Other terms used in Joseph Stalin's time, such as 'collectivization' (the forced amalgamation of parcels of land previously in individual hands) and 'purging' (killing off one's opponents), may originally have had a clinical, euphemistic sound but arguably became more sinister than plain talking would have been.

POLITICAL CORRECTNESS

If the effect of euphemisms is to draw a veil over some aspect of life which might be uncomfortable or shocking when referred to in plain English, then the debate about political correctness really starts from the opposite point. It's about stripping the veil away.

In 2006, a British newspaper ran a banner headline: 'Now It's Baa Baa Rainbow Sheep.' The story concerned a group of children at a nursery school who were apparently being taught new words to the traditional rhyme, 'Baa Baa Black Sheep'. The black sheep was to be replaced by a multicoloured one, for fear of offending an ethnic minority. The story, which featured in half a dozen papers, is closer to urban legend than reality. Similar tales surfaced 20 years earlier. In fact, if the children were being encouraged to apply different colours to the sheep (blue, pink), it seems to have been for the sake of expanding their vocabulary.

Don't you see that the whole aim of Newspeak is to narrow the range of thought? In the end we shall make thoughtcrime literally impossible, because there will be no words in which to express it.

GEORGE ORWELL, *1984* (1949)

The Jap Snake struck hard because it was helped by dirty inside work -- Don't kid yourself . . . It CAN happen here! Keep your Eyes Open and your Ears Cocked . . . Report ANYTHING that looks queer.

Political correctness goes by the board in wartime, when vilification of the enemy is at a premium. In addition to using a racial stereotype in portraying the Japanese as a slit-eyed snake, this 1942 poster also uses the un-PC term 'Jap', now wholly unacceptable in polite discourse. Fear of a Japanese Fifth Column led to the internment of thousands of innocent Japanese-Americans during the Second World War.

No matter. To some columnists and commentators, examples of political correctness are like truffles to pigs. When a particularly aromatic example is unearthed, the discovery is almost always accompanied by the cliché about 'political correctness gone mad'. The origins of the phrase itself are obscure, with some claiming that it was once a non-ironic Communist expression which the left then applied ironically to a dogmatic outlook. The term is now found almost exclusively and non-ironically on the right.

At its most benign, political correctness could be described as the display of verbal sensitivity towards members of particular groups, one that aims to avoid the in-built tendency in some language to stigmatize. A very careful user of PC language might avoid expressions like 'turn a deaf ear to', 'seeing things in black and white' since they make careless reference to disability or colour. Even a less than sensitive speaker would probably think twice before employing terms like 'looney bin' or 'deformed', unless he or she was very sure of the audience.

To be called 'politically correct' is never a compliment and usually an outright term of abuse. Those who choose their words carefully to avoid giving offence or raising the spectres of sexism, racism, homophobia, etc. are attacked for their misplaced sensitivity, or their liberal softness, or mocked for their willingness to use expressions which sound contorted or absurd. Much fun is had with descriptions like 'horizontally challenged' (for fat) or 'differently abled' (for disabled). But the protesters themselves often protest too much, and use the notion of 'political correctness' as a stick to beat any and all social changes of which they disapprove. To be sure, there are absurdities in political correctness. To change *history* to *herstory* or to float the idea that *menstruation* become *femstruation* betrays a complete ignorance of language, while suggestions such as converting *manhole* to *personhole* (or *personnel access structure*) seem to spring more from mischief or the desire to discredit the whole PC business.

But the impulses behind political correctness – to avoid giving offence, to show an awareness of the power of words – are decent enough. Surely they are worth a more considered response than the reflex jeer or the PC-gone-mad jibe.

POLITICAL SPEECHES

Nothing much is hidden about political speeches, although they will probably be full of examples of euphemism and 'political correctness'. The aim of a political speech is generally obvious, however garbled the words or inept the speaker. That aim is to win friends and influence people, to gain votes and approval, both for the speaker and for his or her cause. Political oratory is therefore an unabashed example of the deployment of language for persuasion and propaganda.

Britain can claim the most effective speech-maker of the 20th century in Winston Churchill, wartime leader and inspirer through words. American journalist Edward R. Murrow, no mean wordsmith himself, said of Churchill that he: 'mobilized the English language and sent it into battle'. In the English-speaking world, the United States has a long and continuing tradition of political oratory and is arguably pre-eminent in this field today, while politicians in Britain and other Anglophone countries struggle to make much of a mark. Philip Collins, who was a speechwriter for Tony Blair, asserts that Britain is 'too nice a country to live in'. There is no great cause to prompt great speaking, he says, as there was with Churchill or Nelson Mandela or Martin Luther King. For Collins, the essentials of a historic speech are 'vivid phrasing, acute analysis, a core question and a sonorous voice'. Above all, though, is the need for a 'moment', a great occasion or crisis evoking the best from the orator.

This was certainly true of Abraham Lincoln's most famous speech, the Gettysburg Address, which commemorated those who had fallen in the battle of that name (see pages 129–30). There is a story that Lincoln wrote it on the back of an envelope while on the way to the ceremony by train. Not true, although such picturesque details might have been designed to underscore Lincoln's brilliance and faith in his own rhetorical powers. Like almost every political speech of note, the Gettysburg Address was the result of forethought and revision on the part of the orator himself. One of the differences between the 19th and the 20th or 21st centuries is that politicians now are much less likely to compose their own material. They might do the final shaping but will rely on others to assemble the pieces in the first place.

But the good speechwriter will be more familiar with his master's or mistress's voice than his own. He will be intimately involved with fashioning the image which, in early days, is so important for the ambitious politician. One of Margaret Thatcher's most memorable remarks came within her first two years as prime minister as she announced her determination not to change policies when circumstances got tough:

To those waiting with bated breath for that favourite media catchphrase, the 'U' turn, I have only one thing to say. You turn if you want to. The lady's not for turning.

'I Have a Dream': one of the most powerful political speeches of the 20th century was delivered by the civil rights leader Martin Luther King from the steps of the Lincoln memorial in Washington DC, on 28 August 1963. Earlier in his speech, Dr King alluded to Lincoln's famous Gettysburg Address.

PORK BARRELS AND DOUGHNUTTING

The leaders of English-speaking countries may very occasionally rise to the heights of oratory, deploying the English language in ways that are striking and inspiring. At a lower level, politics has thrown up many examples of original and quirky phraseology that give a more accurate picture of reality. The origins of the metaphorical US 'pork barrel' are obscure, but ever since the later 19th century the expression has conveyed, cynically, the process by which federal or state money is allocated to local projects in order to encourage voters in the area to back their legislators. To qualify as 'pork-barrel schemes', such projects have to be unnecessary, even useless.

On the other side of the Atlantic, there was for many years considerable opposition to the televising of the British parliament. When the cameras were eventually allowed into the House of Commons in 1989, strict rules were imposed. Only the speaker of the moment should be shown and without cutaway shots of members dozing, reading or sniggering behind their hands. To give the impression that the debates were well attended – and that voters were getting their money's worth from their elected representatives – the practice of 'doughnutting' arose, whereby other members would surround the speaker to give the impression of a full chamber.

Literal references to food give an idea of just how tough is the politician's life as he or she scrabbles up the 'greasy pole' (Disraeli's phrase for political advancement). From America comes the 'rubber-chicken circuit', the round of mediocre dinners that must be endured while voters and donors are being courted. Even less enticing is the 'mashed-potato circuit'. In mid-1990s Britain, when 'New Labour' was campaigning to wrest power from the Conservative Party, up-and-coming figures like Tony Blair embarked on a 'prawn cocktail offensive', a series of receptions designed to win over the traditionally hostile business and City circles. The prawns must have done their stuff since Labour was returned to power in 1997.

The defiant declaration was greeted with rapturous applause at the 1980 Conservative Party Conference. Quite a few in the audience would have recalled the title of the 1948 play by Christopher Fry which Mrs Thatcher was deliberately echoing (*The Lady's Not for Burning*). All of them would have appreciated the play on words – *'U'-turn/You turn* – which lightened a speech sometimes verging on the sombre. The delivery might have been unique but the words were not her own.

Successful political speech-making seems to depend, linguistically, on a mixture of the familiar and the elevated. Sometimes the familiar is realized through domestic detail. In the Margaret Thatcher speech already mentioned, she refers to having no junior ministers in 10 Downing Street but 'just Denis [her husband] and me', giving a homely if misleading picture of a middle-aged couple pottering uncomplainingly about a large mansion. At his victory speech in Chicago in November 2008, President-Elect Barack Obama could play on his audience's heartstrings by telling his daughters Sasha and Malia – note how accomplished politicians always introduce family members by their first names, so making the audience part of the wider 'family' – that they had 'earned the new puppy that's coming with us to the White House'.

When it comes to the more serious part of the oration, key words and phrases are struck again and again. High-sounding abstract nouns are deployed to suggest that better times are around the corner even while almost unimaginable threats can and will be surmounted. It is important to stir the audience, not so much to action as to fine feeling – or perhaps simply to feeling fine about themselves. As already indicated, American politicians are, by and large, much better at this than leaders of other English-speaking countries. The Inauguration Speech of President John F. Kennedy in January 1961 is still remembered for utterances like:

> *And so, my fellow Americans, ask not what your country can do for you; ask what you can do for your country. My fellow citizens of the world, ask not what America will do for you, but what, together, we can do for the freedom of man.*

Kennedy employed familiar rhetorical devices like the inversion of normal word order (*ask not*), repetition with variations, and what is technically known as *chiasmus*, where the order of words is paralleled and reversed (*your country ... do for you; you ... do for your country*). Nearly half a century later the tradition of uplifting rhetoric was still flourishing in the hands of Barack Obama who, in the same 2008 Chicago victory speech cited above, said:

> *And to all those watching tonight from beyond our shores, from parliaments and palaces to those who are huddled around radios in the forgotten corners of our world – our stories are singular, but our destiny is shared, and a new dawn of American leadership is at hand.*

Notice the assumptions behind this single sentence. First, that the election was of overwhelming interest around the world – which it was – from the highest levels of royalty and government (*parliaments and palaces*) to those who have no access to television but must huddle 'around radios in the forgotten corners of our world'. They may be forgotten by everyone else but the president-elect is thinking of them, while the word *huddled* surely recalls the famous lines engraved on the base of the Statue of Liberty (*Give me your tired, your poor,/Your huddled masses yearning to breathe free*). Obama's words make the shift from the individual to the communal (*singular ... shared*), all of it under the banner of new American leadership. The second and more explicit assumption is that this is a new dawn, a new leader, not just for America but for the world.

Presidential candidate Barack Obama speaking at a rally in New Hampshire in September 2008. Obama echoed the slogan on the rostrum when, in a speech on the eve of the election, he told voters: 'Tomorrow, you can give this country the change we need.'

The only British leader who has approached this level of eloquence in recent years is Tony Blair who, at the moment of his election as prime minister in May 1997, also told his cheering supporters: 'A new day has dawned, has it not?' But, just as George W. Bush was something of an anomaly among American presidents in being linguistically clumsy, so Blair was unusual for his fluency, and often distrusted because of it.

TABOO WORDS

The most contentious area of English, the one that raises the most doubt, discomfort and debate is the use of taboo words and expressions. The assumption is that these must relate principally to sex and body parts but forbidden terms shift through the ages, and current verbal taboos are much more likely to relate to racial questions, not sexual ones.

This is not a fresh subject. We can go back to the Middle Ages in the quest for taboo or dangerous expressions. Take, for example, the Wife of Bath. Here is Geoffrey Chaucer's free-living, free-spoken character from *The Canterbury Tales*, lecturing the other pilgrims on the battle of the sexes. She is something of an expert on the subject, having got through five husbands and learned how to manage them all. As if still speaking to one of them, she gives the company of pilgrims a flavour of her browbeating style:

> *For certeyn, old dotard, by your leve,*
> *Ye shul have queynte right ynogh at eve.*
> *He is too great a nygard that wolde werne*
> *A man to lighte a candle at his lanterne;*
> *He shall have never the lasse light, pardee.*

Which lines could be roughly rendered into modern English as: 'For sure, old fool, if you allow it, you'll get enough sex in the evening. That person who refuses to let another man light a candle from his lantern is a real skinflint – after all, he's not going to receive any the less light, is he?'

The reader may notice that 'sex' is a slightly euphemistic translation of the Wife's – or Chaucer's – own term, *queynte*. Was the poet or his creation being particularly provocative or outrageous by using what is now referred to as the 'c-word'? No, because while *queynte* was a frank term in the medieval period, it was just within the bounds of acceptable usage, even if the Wife of Bath takes care to vary it with other descriptions for the genitals, ranging from the scientific-sounding (*membres, instrument*) to the coy or bizarre (*bele chose* = beautiful thing [French]; *quoniam* = since [Latin]). *Queynte* or its modern equivalent did not become an obscene expression until the 18th century.

Indecent or taboo expressions are as capable of changing as any other area of language. What is constant is that something has to be taboo. Human societies seem to require a few risky terms, the deliberate employment of which will cause horror or shock or guilty amusement to the listeners or readers and (most likely) some pleasure to the user.

But these terms vary across the centuries. Expressions related to *shit* or *piss*, which are frequently spoken but beyond the edge of respectable written use even today, seem to have been part of standard English for hundreds of years. ('I do smell all horse-piss', says Trinculo in Shakespeare's *The Tempest*.) The familiar but still faintly impolite *fart*, which a dictionary may ring-fence with the description 'coarse slang', was sufficiently usual in the Elizabethan period to receive the royal pedigree. According to a story from the diarist John Aubrey, the earl of Oxford broke wind while he was making a low obeisance to Queen Eizabeth: 'at which he was so ashamed that he left the country for 7 years. At his return the Queen welcomed him and said, "My lord, I had forgot the fart".'

*Sexual intercourse began
In nineteen sixty-three
(Which was rather late for me)
Between the end of the
Chatterley ban
And the Beatles' first LP.*

PHILIP LARKIN, 'ANNUS MIRABILIS' (1967)

When it comes to *farts* and *pissing* and other terms that occupy a no-man's-land between the standard and the obscene, we may actually be more prudish than our ancestors. On the other hand, though, it is difficult to credit now that playwright George Bernard Shaw caused a real sensation for theatre audiences in 1913 by having Eliza Doolittle in his play *Pygmalion* utter the notorious line, 'Walk! Not bloody likely … ', with the *bloody* intended as a give-away of Eliza's 'common' background. Even the word 'damn' caused problems in the 1939 film version of *Gone With the Wind*. The emphasis in Rhett Butler's famous departing line, which Clark Gable delivers to Vivien Leigh, was changed so that the stress fell not, as it would naturally, on the final *damn* but on the earlier *give*: 'Frankly, my dear, I don't *give* a damn.'

It took the Lady Chatterley case to make *fuck* acceptable – or at least non-prosecutable – on the printed page in the United Kingdom (see feature page 213), although some years after that key 1960 court case the theatre critic Ken Tynan caused banner headlines and protests by deliberately saying the f-word out loud on a late-night BBC satire show. Now, on mainstream British television, it would take a fast finger on the remote-control to avoid hearing swear-words and obscenities across all the mainstream channels after the watershed hour of 9 p.m. American network television is, by British standards, rather prudish or restrained, with films edited to remove objectionable material (visual and verbal) and fines imposed for any infringement. Only US cable drama escapes the same restrictions.

Perhaps more surprising is the slowness of some dictionaries to include four-letter words. According to Bill Bryson, in his language book *Mother Tongue* (1990), the editors of the *Random House Dictionary* decided against their inclusion in the 1966 edition and it took more than 20 years for the contentious terms to make their dictionary debut under the watchful eye of this particular publisher. The *Oxford English Dictionary* was a little earlier, choosing to include obscenities from the early 1970s, but by then there had been more than a decade of freedom in fiction and elsewhere.

This caution is shared by the print media both in Britain and the US. Outlets with a relatively youthful and largely liberal audience, such as *Time Out, New York* or the on-line *Salon.com*, will sparingly employ the f-word and others, as will British newspapers like *The Guardian* or *The Independent*. But in general obscene and indecent terms are avoided altogether or, if they have to be reproduced, are partly blotted out with asterisks. Decorum is preserved, although some object to the mealy-mouthed nature of the practice.

But the English-speaking peoples do not live in an 'anything-goes' linguistic community. If traditional swear-words and obscenities are acceptable in print, then the racial slurs which would once have been commonplace now cause the same sort of shock and outrage. Casual anti-semitism was rife in the early part of the 20th century. Writers as different and respected as the poet T.S. Eliot and John Buchan, author of *The Thirty-Nine Steps* (1915), make disparaging anti-Jewish references, and the context makes plain that these are neither exceptional nor anything to take exception to.

Mark Twain's great novel *The Adventures of Huckleberry Finn* immediately ran into difficulties on its publication in 1884 on account of its perceived 'coarseness'. But it was the attitude towards black people, and in particular the ubiquitous use of the word 'nigger' in the text, that caused problems for US schools and libraries in the second half of the last century, and probably some discomfort in many readers as well.

Sensitivity to racially charged language is now acute. The principal character in Philip Roth's novel *The Human Stain* (2000), a university professor, loses his job because of a careless use of the term *spooks*, referring to a couple of persistent absentees to class. ('Does anyone know these people? Do they exist or are they spooks?') He forgets that *spooks* is an old disparaging term for blacks, which these students happen to be. In the mass media, even a casual racial reference will be inspected and the speaker will find him or herself criticized and run the risk of a dismissal.

D.H. LAWRENCE AND
LADY CHATTERLEY

English words that have long been regarded as obscene or taboo were at the centre of what was, arguably, the most important literary trial of the 20th century. In 1960 Penguin Books were prosecuted for their publication of D.H. Lawrence's novel *Lady Chatterley's Lover*. The failure of the prosecution was a watershed.

D.H. Lawrence (1885–1930) knew that *Lady Chatterley* was unpublishable in his lifetime. The book was originally printed privately in Italy in 1928 and sent to subscribers in Britain. When it was confiscated by customs and postal officials, its cachet as a 'dirty book' inevitably rose. *Lady Chatterley* led an underground existence for many years until in 1959 the New York Court of Appeals upheld a federal judge's decision that the book had literary merit and that Lawrence's sexual explicitness and frequent use of four-letter words were relevant to plot or character development. This encouraged Penguin to publish the book in the UK, even though they knew they would be prosecuted. It was what was called a 'test case by arrangement', intended to clarify the obscenity laws.

The book describes a passionate affair between an upper-class woman and her social inferior, a gamekeeper on her husband's estate. This sexual crossing of class boundaries was part of the book's shock value but the greater part lay in Lawrence's description of 'thirteen episodes of sexual intercourse' and the taboo-breaking use of four-letter terms. The defence lined up a star-studded array of witnesses, including a bishop and many distinguished

Cause célèbre: a London commuter engrossed in Lady Chatterley's Lover *on 3 November 1960, the day the book went on sale to the general public.*

writers and academics, but most of them weren't required. The prosecution called only one witness: a detective inspector who testified that the book had actually been published.

The most famous quotation from the case is not an example of Lawrence's four-lettered prose but some words from the prosecuting counsel, Mervyn Griffiths-Jones. He asked the jury – who included a furniture-maker, a dock worker and a teacher – 'Is it a book that you would wish to have lying around the house? Is it a book you would even wish your wife or servants to read?' The questions showed how remote the authorities were from everyday life. Within a year of its official publication in Britain, *Lady Chatterley's Lover* had sold more than 2 million copies.

GLOSSARY

Parts of speech in English

Almost all words found in the English language can be categorized under seven headings, collectively referred to as 'parts of speech'. They are adjectives, adverbs, conjunctions, nouns, prepositions, pronouns and verbs. A brief explanation of each is given below. An eighth category, much more usual in speech than in writing, is known as interjections or exclamations, and may describe anything from an expression of surprise (*Ah!*) or disappointment (*Oh*), to a greeting (*Hi!*). Although they have an adjectival function, the definite and indefinite articles – *the* and *a(n)* – are sometimes regarded as a separate category.

Many words are versatile enough to operate as different parts of speech, depending on the particular task they are performing in a sentence. For example, *still* may be either a noun (*still of the night*) or a verb (*to still someone's anxieties*), an adjective (*still waters run deep*) or an adverb (*Are they still here?*). *Either* can be an adjective, adverb, conjunction or pronoun. There is sometimes debate about the 'incorrect' use of one part of speech for another, usually nouns being used as verbs and vice versa (see *English: Right and Wrong*).

Adjective
Adjectives provide additional information about a noun or pronoun. They concern attributes such as colour, size, shape, age, frequency, mood, and so on:

> The <u>Roman</u> conquest of Britain was <u>rapid</u> and <u>overwhelming</u>.

Adverb
Like adjectives, adverbs play a supporting role. Among other functions, they convey information about how an action is performed:

> *To travel <u>hopefully</u> is better than to arrive ...*

- they indicate place or time:

> *He's the same when he's <u>here</u> as he <u>ever</u> was.*

- they modify adjectives:

> *On her first long drive she got <u>uncomfortably</u> sunburned.*

Conjunction
Conjunctions are simple link words such as *and*, *but*, *where*, *either*, *or*, *although*. The vital if unobtrusive role they have in speech and writing points to their derivation from Old English or Anglo-Saxon.

Noun
A noun is a name – of a person, a place, an object, a feeling, an idea. Nouns are sometimes categorized under headings such as 'abstract' to describe feelings and qualities (*grief, integrity*), 'collective' when applied to a group (*crowd, herd, orchestra*), 'proper' to signify the name of a person, place or brand and usually capitalized (*Henry, London, Coca Cola*), and 'compound', in which two terms are joined together, with or without a hyphen (*ice-cap, tradecraft*).

Preposition
Like conjunctions, prepositions are linking words that explain the relationship between verbs and nouns, pronouns and nouns, etc. They include *under, with, in, through, behind, above*. As with conjunctions, their roots generally lie in Anglo-Saxon.

Pronoun
Pronouns are substitutes for nouns and are a good example of linguistic economy since their use avoids the need for cumbersome repetition or circumlocution. They are among the oldest English words. They can be subdivided into various types, including the personal (*I, you, she*), possessive (*mine, their*) reflexive (*himself, itself*) and relative (*who, which*).

Verb
A verb <u>describes</u> an action, state or experience, and <u>is</u> sometimes referred to as a 'doing' word. As with other grammatical definitions, this <u>may be</u> easier to <u>understand</u> through example rather than by explanation. Accordingly, the verbs in these three sentences <u>have been underlined</u>. A verb may be regarded as the most essential part of speech since,

in strict terms, a sentence is only a sentence if it comes equipped with a (finite) verb.

Principal periods covered in *The Story of English*

Celtic period (*c.*750 BC–AD 450): Era named after the various Celtic tribes who lived in the British Isles from the Bronze Age onwards. They coexisted with the Romans but were driven to the margins by Anglo-Saxon settlement.

Roman period (AD 43–410): Roman occupation and settlement of England and Wales beginning with Emperor Claudius's invasion and ending with withdrawal of the last legions.

Anglo-Saxon and Viking era (*c.*410–1066): Period dominated by conquest and settlement of England by tribes from northeastern Europe, including Angles, Saxons and Norsemen. Parts of this period are sometimes known as the Dark Ages, on the (generally exaggerated) belief that culture and learning were in crisis. The era may alternatively be characterized as the Early Middle Ages.

Norman era/Middle Ages (1066–late 1400s): The centuries following the Norman Conquest, which saw the establishment of a common language – a fusion of Norman French and Old English.

Renaissance/Elizabethan/Jacobean era (1500s–1630s): Period of consolidation and expansion of English language, culture and commerce. Across Europe, the Renaissance marks revival of learning and transition between the Middle Ages and the modern world.

Age of Reason/Enlightenment (late 17th century–end of 18th century): The era that saw the rise of science and rationalism across Europe, and which culminated in French Revolution and American Independence.

Victorian era (1830s–early 1900s): Highpoint of British power and prestige, and linguistic influence.

American era (1940s onwards): Period following the Second World War that has witnessed US dominance in English language and many other fields.

Principal historical and literary figures referred to in *The Story of English*

Adams, John (1735–1826): Second US president and one of the architects of Independence, Adams foresaw the supremacy of English as a world language because of the growing power and rising population of America.

Alfred the Great (b.849): King of Wessex (871–99), he conquered the Danes and established sovereignty over southern England; he encouraged learning and translation of (religious) works into English.

Augustine (d.*c.*604–609): Missionary sent by Pope Gregory to (re)convert English and the first Archbishop of Canterbury. The return of Christianity to England introduced new religious terminology to English language.

Bede (*c.*673–735): Benedictine monk and historical/religious scholar; his *Ecclesiastical History of the English People* gives an account of the arrival of Christianity in Britain and provides a unique historical chronology.

Caxton, William (1422–91): Brought printing to England from Europe in 1476; also translated and edited the works he published.

Chaucer, Geoffrey (1345–1400): The greatest English writer of the Middle Ages (*The Canterbury Tales, Troilus and Criseyde*), Chaucer used East Midland dialect, which formed the basis of standard English.

Claudius (10 BC–AD 54): Roman emperor (41–54) who invaded Britain in AD 43, leading to occupation and settlement lasting almost four centuries.

Elizabeth I (b.1533; r.1558–1603): Queen of England during period of growing national confidence, reflected in language and culture as much as in conquest and commerce.

James I (b.1566; r.1603–1625): King of England and Scotland (as James VI), and instigator of new and highly influential translation of the Bible after the Hampton Court conference of 1604.

Jefferson, Thomas (1743–1826): Third US president and a principal author of the American Declaration of Independence, Jefferson predicted a new 'American dialect' to suit the expansion of the new country.

Johnson, Samuel (1709–84): Dominant cultural arbiter of mid-18th century British life; poet, critic, playwright, and lexicographer, Dr Johnson produced the authoritative *Dictionary of the English Language*.

Jones, William (1746–94): Jurist and linguist, Jones was among the first scholars to suggest that present-day Asian and European languages might have a common root; in a key speech in 1786, he forged links between Sanskrit, Greek and Latin.

Lawrence, D(avid) H(erbert) (1885–1930): Nottinghamshire-born novelist and poet; caused outrage with his frank treatment of sex, culminating in a ban on his most explicit book, *Lady Chatterley's Lover*, not openly published in UK until 1960, an event that led to the relaxation of linguistic taboos.

Lincoln, Abraham (1809–65): Sixteenth US president who delivered what is still the most famous oration in American history, the Gettysburg Address, during the Civil War; Lincoln's rhetoric here, and elsewhere, was influenced by the *King James Bible*.

Milton, John (1608–74): Poet, political/religious theorist and supporter of Commonwealth under Oliver Cromwell; Milton's epic *Paradise Lost* (1663) introduced a new, elevated style of poetic diction.

Murray, James (1837–1915): Scottish-born principal editor of the *Oxford English Dictionary*, the most far-reaching and meticulous English dictionary yet attempted. The first volume of the first edition appeared in 1884, the last in 1928.

Shakespeare, William (1564–1616): Playwright, born in Stratford-upon-Avon, whose work and words have had profound effect on English language; coiner of new words and fresh phrases, and dazzling exemplar of the power of language.

Shaw, George Bernard (1856–1950): Irish-born dramatist and controversialist, Shaw attempted to create a new alphabet to resolve the inconsistencies and absurdities of English spelling.

Swift, Jonathan (1667–1745): Dublin-born writer and clergyman; poet, pamphleteer and satirist, Swift was one of the first authorities who wanted to correct and regularize English language.

Twain, Mark (Samuel Langhorne Clemens) (1835–1910): US novelist and journalist; humorous and often acerbic satirist, Twain created what some regard as the 'Great American Novel' in *The Adventures of Huckleberry Finn* (1885), which helped to bring black and southerrn dialects into mainstream culture.

Webster, Noah (1758–1843): Connecticut-born, Webster produced the two-volume *American Dictionary of the English Language* (1828) which established distinctive US spellings and usages.

William I (b.1027; r.1066–87): King of England through victory at Hastings, William brought the culture of Norman France to England, including a new language.

Wyclif (or Wycliffe), John (c.1330–84): Radical figure in the medieval English church who questioned the prestige of bishops and supremacy of pope. Translated the Bible into English to make it accessible to ordinary people.

INDEX

G

Gaelic 19, 23, 146–7
  bilingual signs *147*
Galilei, Galileo 95–6, *95*, 96
gangster slang *171*
Garrick, David 122
Gaskell, Elizabeth 153
-*gate* words 164
gender of nouns 52–3
gentilesse 49, **60**
George, Saint 51
George III 117
German 166
Germanic 28
Gettysburg Address 128–30,
  129, *130*, 207
Glastonbury Abbey 33
Globe Theatre 86, *87*
Goldsmith, Oliver 147
Gone with the Wind 211
Gothic 28
grammar 120, 196–8
Greenwich Observatory 96
Gregory, Pope 32
Grendel 40
Gulliver's Travels 123
Gunpowder Plot 92, 94
Gutenberg, Johannes 70–1
Guthrum 36

H

H, pronunciation of **201**
Hadrian's Wall 20, *21*
Hamlet 84
Harald Hardrada 45
Hardy, Thomas 32–3
Harlem Renaissance 133
Harley, Robert, Earl of
  Oxford 114, 115
Harman, Thomas 86–7
Harold, King (Harold
  Godwinson) *44*, 45–6
Harris, Joel Chandler 133
harrying of the north 46
Harvey, William 96, 98
Hastings, Battle of 45–6
haute couture 47
Helmont, J.B. van 98
Henry IV, coronation *53*, 54
Henry VIII 76
Hepster's Dictionary 171
Hereward the Wake 46
Herson, Benjamin 189–90
*Historia ecclesiastica gentis
  Anglorum* 27, 30, 37, 40

History of England
  (Macaulay) 141–2
Holmes, Sherlock *154*
homophones 196
honorificabilitudinitatibus 85
Hopkins, Anthony 25
hubris 7
*Huckleberry Finn, The
  Adventures of* 130–3, *131*,
  212
The Human Stain 212
Humpty Dumpty 192, *193*
Hundred Years War 50
Huygens, Christiaan 98
hyphens, British *v.* American
  175

I

impede/expede 76
India *137*, 140, **141–2**
  expressions from Indian
    languages adopted into
    English 142
  impact on England and
    English language 142
  place names 146
Indian file 104
Indian summer 104
Indo-European languages
  10–12, *10*, *11*
infinitives, split *197*, 198
information technology (IT)
  152–3, *159*
'ink-horn' terms 75
International Civil Aviation
  Organisation (ICAO) 15
internet terms 98
Inuit expressions **109**
Ireland 147
  mapping 147
  place names 147
  writers 147
Italian terms 166
-*ite* words 168
Ivanhoe 48

J

James I 91–4
  Counterblast to Tobacco 92
jargon 168–71
  thieves' jargon 155, 170
  see also slang
Jefferson, Thomas, on the
  spread of American
  English 126

John, King 50
John of Gaunt 61
John of Trevisa 59
Johnson, Dr Samuel 25,
  112–23, *112*, 150, 152
  Rasselas (novel) 123
  visit to royal library **117**
  see also Dictionary of the
    English Language
Jones, Sir William (judge) 8
Jones, William (philologist)
  141
Jonson, Ben 86, 96
Joyce, James 147
Jutes 27

K

kangaroo 144
Kennedy, John F. 209
Kepler, Johannes 96
Keynes, John Maynard
  167–8
Keynesianism 168
King, Dr Martin Luther *207*
King Arthur's Cross **33**, *33*
King James Bible 79, *90*, 92–5
  editing 127
King's Men 80
knife 41
knight 51

L

Lady Chatterley's Lover
  211–12, **213**, *213*
Langland, William 65, 68
language(s)
  most influential 14
  most popular 12–14
  number of countries in
    which used 14
  number of users 12–14
  primary/secondary
    speakers 12–13
  spread of 10–12
  see also individual languages
larrikin 145
Latin 19, 20–1, 166
  classical Latin 60
  inscriptions on money **22**
  place names from 21
Lauder, Afferbeck (Alastair
  Morrison) 145
law courts, use of English in
  54
Lawrence, D.H. **213**

Leicester, Robert Dudley,
  Earl of 89
Let Stalk Strine 144–5
libraries, circulating 153
Licensing Act 121
Lincoln, Abraham,
  Gettysburg Address
  128–30, *129*, *130*, 207
literacy, growth of 120–1
-*lite* words *165*
Livingstone 143
locomotive 155–6
Lollards 67
London 143
  lure of 60–1
  map 55, *55*
  place names 55
Lord's Prayer 31
Lud, King **55**
Lycidas 97

M

Macaulay, Thomas 141–2
Macbeth 82–3, *84*
McCoy, Joseph 132
Macpherson, James **25**, 79
magazines 123
  headlines *159*
Malaya 177–8
Malta 140
Manchester 143
Manx 19
Marconi, Guglielmo 157
Marlowe, Christopher 79, *79*
Martin Chuzzlewit 173, *174*
Mary I 76–7
Maverick, Samuel 132
Mayflower 101, *102*
Mayhew, Henry 155
mead-hall **29**, 40
The Meaning of Everything 150
melancholy 118
The Merchant of Venice 84
The Merchant's Tale 65–6
microscope 98
Miller Lite *165*
Milton, John 96, **97**
minuscule 163
mondegreens **181**
money *22*, **22**
  Viking coins 39
Morrison, Alastair (Afferbek
  Lauder) 145
Morse, Samuel 157
motel *160*

 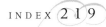

FURTHER REFERENCES

Barrett, Grant (ed.). *The Oxford Dictionary of American Political Slang*. New York: Oxford University Press (2004).

Bate, W. Jackson. *Samuel Johnson*. London: The Hogarth Press Ltd (1984).

Bragg, Melvyn. *The Adventure of English*. New York: Sceptre (2004).

Bryson, Bill. *Mother Tongue*. London: Penguin (1999).

Bryson, Bill. *Made in America*. London: Secker & Warburg (1994).

Burgess, Anthony. *Language Made Plain*. London: Fontana (1975).

Burgess, Anthony. *Shakespeare*. New York: Alfred A. Knopf (1970).

Butterfield, Jeremy. *Damp Squid*. Oxford: Oxford University Press (2008).

Claiborne, Robert. *English: Its Life and Times*. London: Bloomsbury Publishing (1994).

Crystal, David. *The Stories of English*. London: Penguin (2005).

Farb, Peter. *Word Play: What Happens When People Talk*. London: Bantam Books (1975).

Flavell, Linda & R.H. Flavell. *The Chronology of Words & Phrases*. London: Kyle Cathie (1999).

Gooden, Philip. *Faux Pas?: A No-nonsense Guide to Words and Phrases from Other Languages*. London: A & C Black Publishers Ltd (2005).

Green, Jonathan. *Chasing the Sun*. London: Jonathan Cape Ltd (1996).

Hitchings, Henry. *Dr Johnson's Dictionary: The Extraordinary Story of the Book that Defined the World*. London: John Murray Publishers Ltd (2005).

Honan, Park. *Shakespeare: A Life*. Oxford: Clarendon Press (1998).

Keating, Peter. *The Haunted Study: A Social History Of The English Novel 1875-1914*. London: Secker & Warburg (1989).

Macdonald, Peter D. *British Literary Culture and Publishing Practice, 1880-1914*. Cambridge: Cambridge University Press (1997).

McCrum, Robert, William Cran & Robert MacNeil. *The Story of English*. London: Faber and Faber (1987).

Nicolson, Adam. *Power and Glory: Jacobean England and the Making of the King James Bible*. London: HarperCollins Publishers Ltd (2003).

Pinker, Stephen. *The Language Instinct*. London: Penguin (2003).

Poole, Steven. *Unspeak*. New York: Little Brown (2006).

Rosten, Leo. *The New Joys of Yiddish*. London: Arrow Books (2003).

Savan, Leslie. *Slam Dunks and No-Brainers*. New York: Alfred A. Knopf (2005).

Winchester, Simon. *The Meaning of Everything: The Story of the Oxford English Dictionary*. Oxford: Oxford University Press (2003).

PICTURE ACKNOWLEDGEMENTS

2 Photos.com; 4 Photos.com; 5t Photos.com; 5b Shutterstock; 6 akg-images/Electra; 13 Corbis/Swim Ink 2; 15 Shutterstock/Carlos E. Santa Maria; 17 Photos.com; 18 Photos.com; 21 Shutterstock/Ian McDonald; 22 Shutterstock/ Andresr; 23 Shutterstock/John Sones; 24 Photos.com; 26 Corbis/The Gallery Collection; 30 Photos.com; 31 Corbis/Angelo Hornak; 34 Corbis/Ted Spiegel; 37 Corbis/Geoffrey Taunton; Cordaiy Picture Lirary Ltd.; 39 Corbis/Ted Spiegel; 40 Corbis/Werner Forman; 43 Photos.com; 44 Photos.com; 46 Shutterstock/Amra Pasic; 48 Topfoto/The Granger Collection; 51 Corbis/The Gallery Collection; 53 Photos.com; 55 Wikipedia Commons; 56 Photos.com; 61 Corbis/Bettmann; 63 Corbis/Fine Art Photographic Library; 64 Photos.com; 65 Photos.com; 67 Photos.com; 69 Corbis/Blue Lantern Studio; 70 Photos.com; 73 Photos.com; 74 Corbis/ The Gallery Collecton; 77 Topfoto/ Woodmansterne; 79 Topfoto; 80 Corbis/Hulton-Deutsch Collection; 84 Photos.com; 85 Photos.com; 87 Photos.com; 89 Topfoto/ Topham/Fotomas; 90 Topfoto/The Granger Collection; 92 Topfoto/Fotomas; 95 Corbis/The Art Archive; 96 Photos.com; 99 Topfoto/The Granger Collection; 100 Corbis/ Bettmann; 103 Corbis/ Bettmann; 106 Corbis/Peter Finger; 107 Corbis/ Gianni Dagli Orti; 109 Corbis/Historical Picture Archive; 111 Photos.com; 112 Topfoto/The Granger Collection; 115 Photos.com; 116 Photos.com; 117 Topfoto/The Granger Collection; 121 Topfoto/The Granger Collection; 122 Topfoto/The Granger Collection; 123 Topfoto/The Granger Collection; 124 Photos.com; 127 Topfoto/The Granger Collection; 129 Corbis/Bettmann; 130 Corbis; 131 Topfoto/The Granger Collection; 133 Corbis/ Bettmann; 135 Photos.com; 137 Corbis/Hulton-Deutsch Collection; 138 Corbis/Christie's Images; 141 Photos.com; 143 Corbis/Corbis; 144 Corbis/Stapleon Collection; 147 Photos.com; 148 Photos.com; 150 Topfoto/World History Archive; 152 Topfoto/The Granger Collection; 154 Topfoto; 156 Photos.com; 157 Shutterstock/Foto Sergio; 159 Photos.com; 160 Shutterstock/Konstantin Sutyagin; 163 Photos.com; 165 Corbis/George Tiedemann/GT Images; 167 Corbis/Steve Raymer; 168 Corbis/Bettmann; 171 Corbis/Bettmann/Corbis; 172 Corbis/Murray Andrews/Corbis Sygma; 174 Corbis/Lebrecht Music & Arts; 176 Shutterstock/ Perov Stanislav; 178 Corbis/Dave Bartruff; 180 Photos.com; 183 Shutterstock/smilewithme; 185 Corbis/Gideon Mendel; 187 Shutterrstock/Michael Fuery; 188 Chicago Tribune/Abel Uribe; 191 Corbis/Sean Sexton Collection; 193 Topfoto/The Granger Collection; 194 Corbis/Karen Hunt; 197 Corbis/Sunset Boulevard/ Sygma; 198 Corbis/Barry Lewis; 200 Corbis/ Bettmann; 202 Shutterstock/ rorem; 204 Corbis/Ron Sachs/CNP; 206 Topfoto/The Granger Collection; 207 Corbis/Bob Adelman; 210 Corbis/Rick Froedman; 213 Corbis/Hulton-Deutsch Collection

Quercus Publishing has made every effort to trace copyright holders of the pictures used in this book. Anyone having claims to ownership not identified above is invited to contact Quercus Publishing.

I am very grateful to Richard Milbank of Quercus for his editorial support and advice while I was writing *The Story of English*, and to Olivia Marsden for her help and suggestions for illustrations.

Philip Gooden

Quercus Publishing Plc
21 Bloomsbury Square
London
WC1A 2NS

First published in 2009

A CIP catalogue record for this book is available from the British Library

Printed case edition: ISBN–978-1-84724-272-3

Printed and bound in China

1 3 5 7 9 10 8 6 4 2

Designed and edited by BCS Publishing Limited, Oxford.